Prolegomena to the Study of Yeats's Poems

Prolegomena to the Study of Yeats's Poems

by

George Brandon Saul

Philadelphia
University of Pennsylvania Press

Printed in the United States of America
American Book–Stratford Press, Inc., New York

A Note to Which Attention Is Solicited

This book, intended for both students and miscellaneous Yeats enthusiasts, purports to give an accurate commentary on the divisions of the relatively definitive and most readily available *Collected Poems* (London: Macmillan, 1950; N.Y.: Macmillan, 1951); and for individual poems (1) a full record of publication and of title changes (where any occurred), (2) a statement of recorded dates and other significant facts of composition, and (3) an attempted resolution of elsewhere unclarified obscurities (including identification of misprints in the final text of the poems), as well as indication of parallel or closely related passages and recording of available important references and glosses. In the latter instance, the point of reference or gloss is by intention suggested whenever brief indication seemed possible; but no effort is made to list every slight article on Yeats's poetry, though some references are necessarily made for the sake of purely isolated or occasional virtues contained in them. Original explicative notes are added only where they appeared unavoidable. Incidentally, book titles are in the body of the text clipped where intelligibility is not outraged: thus, *The Wanderings of Oisin and Other Poems* appears as *Oisin; The Countess Kathleen and Various Legends and Lyrics,* as *Countess Kathleen;* etc. Indeed, all citations in the text proper are as brief as possible and imply reference to the bibliographical apparatus of the present note.

Unless otherwise specified, all general data are keyed to the following editions of Yeats's work, some of the titles of which are abbreviated as parenthetically indicated:

Collected Poems. N.Y.: Macmillan, 1951 (though labeled "Second Edition, with later poems added, 1950"): first printing.—Individual poems are listed according to the ordering of this volume. (*C. P.*)

Plays and Controversies. N.Y.: Macmillan, 1924. (*P. & C.*)

Plays in Prose and Verse, N.Y.: Macmillan, 1924. (*P. P. V.*)

Early Poems and Stories. N.Y.: Macmillan, 1925. (*E. P. S.*)

Last Poems and Plays. N.Y.: Macmillan, 1940. (*L. P. P.*)

The King of the Great Clock Tower. Dublin: Cuala Press, 1934. (*K. G. C. T.*)

Collected Plays. N.Y.: Macmillan, 1935. (*C. Pl.*)

Wheels and Butterflies. N.Y.: Macmillan, 1935. (*W. & B.*)

The Herne's Egg and Other Plays. N.Y.: Macmillan, 1938. (*H. E.*)

Essays. N.Y.: Macmillan, 1924.

Essays, 1931 to 1936. Dublin: Cuala Press, 1937.

Autobiographies. N.Y.: Macmillan, 1927. (*Auto.*)

Estrangement. Dublin: Cuala Press, 1926.

Dramatis Personae, 1896–1902. N.Y.: Macmillan, 1936. (*D. P.*)

On the Boiler. Dublin: Cuala Press, 1939.

If I Were Four-and-Twenty. Dublin: Cuala Press, 1940. (*If I Were. . . .*)

Pages from a Diary Written in Nineteen Hundred and Thirty. Dublin: Cuala Press, 1944. (*1930 Diary*)

A Vision. N.Y.: Macmillan, 1938.

N.B.: See also, below, C. Bax, Bridge, McHugh, Reynolds, Wade, and Wellesley.

The publication record follows, by permission of The Macmillan Co., the numbering used in the bibliography of the Allt-Alspach variorum edition of Yeats's poems, with added "E" indicating English, "A" American, editions; and *the first printing to reflect either fully or approximately the final reading of a given poem is asterisked* (unless otherwise clearly indicated). An adaptation follows of the Allt-Alspach bibliography, with indication of known months of issue of editions found especially important in the dating of individual poems, dates after the original for any given item being those of reprintings and all revised editions being identified as such.

1: *Poems and Ballads of Young Ireland.* Dublin, 1888, 1889, 1890; 1903.
2: *Fairy and Folk Tales of the Irish Peasantry.* London & N.Y., 1888. Frequently rptd.
Irish Fairy and Folk Tales. London, 1893; N.Y., 1895. Frequently rptd.
3: *The Wanderings of Oisin and Other Poems.* London, Jan. 1889; May 1892.
4: *Representative Irish Tales.* N.Y. & London, 1891; rptd. N.Y. & Dublin, n.d.
5: *The Book of the Rhymers' Club.* London, Feb. 1892.
6: *The Countess Kathleen and Various Legends and Lyrics.* London (Sept.), 1892; Boston & London, 1892.
7: *The Celtic Twilight.* London, Dec. 1893; N.Y., 1894.

8: *The Second Book of the Rhymers' Club.* London
& N.Y., June 1894.

9: *Poems.* London, Oct. 1895; London & Boston, 1895.

10: *The Secret Rose.* London, Apr. 1897; N.Y. & London, 1897; Dublin, 1905.

11: *The Wind among the Reeds.* London, Apr. 1899,
1899, 1900, 1903, 1907, 1911; N.Y., 1899, 1902,
1905.

12: *Poems* (1895). Rev., London, 1899.

13: *The Shadowy Waters.* London, Dec. 1900, 1901;
N.Y., 1901, 1901, 1905.

14: *Poems* (1895). Rev., London, 1901.

15: *The Celtic Twilight.* Rev., London, July 1902; rpt.,
Dublin, 1905, & London and Stratford-upon-
Avon, 1911; N.Y., 1902.

16: *In the Seven Woods.* Dundrum (*Dun Emer*), Aug.
1903 (though completed 16 July).

17: *In the Seven Woods.* N.Y. & London, 1903.

18: *Poems* (1895). Rev., London, 1904.

19: *Stories of Red Hanrahan.* Dundrum (*Dun Emer*),
1904 (So dated because completed in Aug. 1904;
actually pub. 16 May 1905).

20: *Poems 1899–1905.* London & Dublin, 1906.

21: *The Poetical Works of William B. Yeats,* Vol. I,
Lyrical Poems. N.Y. & London, 27 Nov. 1906
("Preface" dated July), 1908, 1911, 1913, 1914,
1915, 1916, 1917, 1920, 1922.

22: *The Poetical Works of William B. Yeats,* Vol. II,
Dramatical Poems. N.Y. & London, 8 July 1907
("Preface" dated Dec. 1906), 1909, 1911.

23: *Poems* (1895). Rev., London, 1908.

24(1)—24(8): *The Collected Works in Verse and
Prose of William Butler Yeats* [8 vols.]. Stratford-

on-Avon, 1908. (Sometimes referred to in the text as *Bullen, 1908.*)

25: *Poems: Second Series.* London & Stratford-on-Avon, Mar. 1910, 1913.

26: *The Green Helmet and Other Poems.* Dundrum (*Cuala*), Dec. 1910 (though completed 30 Sept.).

27: *The Green Helmet and Other Poems.* N.Y., 1911.

28: *Plays for an Irish Theatre.* London & Stratford-upon-Avon, Dec. 1911, 1913.

29: *The Poetical Works of William B. Yeats,* Vol. II, Dramatic Poems. Rev., N.Y. & London, 1912; rpt., N.Y. & London, 1914, 1916, 1917, 1919, 1921.

30: *Poems* (1895). Rev., London, 1912.

31: *The Green Helmet and Other Poems.* N.Y. & London, 23 Oct. 1912.

32: *Poems* (1895). Rev., London, 1913.

33: *A Selection from the Poetry of W. B. Yeats.* Leipzig (*Tauchnitz*), (? Jan.) 1913 ("Preface" dated Oct. 1912), 1922.

34: *Stories of Red Hanrahan: The Secret Rose: Rosa Alchemica.* London & Stratford-upon-Avon, Mar. 1913; N.Y., 1914.

35: *A Selection from the Love Poetry of William Butler Yeats.* Dundrum (*Cuala*), 25 July 1913 (though completed late in May).

36: *Poems Written in Discouragement.* Dundrum (*Cuala*), Oct. 1913.

37: *Nine Poems.* N.Y., 1 Apr. 1914.

38: *Responsibilities: Poems and a Play.* Dundrum (*Cuala*), 25 May 1914 (though completed May Eve).

39. *Eight Poems.* London, Apr. 1916. (There were

probably also advance copies: *v.* Wade *Biblio.*)

40: *Responsibilities and Other Poems.* London, 10 Oct. 1916, 1917; N.Y., 1916.

41: *Easter, 1916.* London, 1916 (Dated 25 Sept.).

42: *The Wild Swans at Coole.* Dundrum (*Cuala*), 17 Nov. 1917 (though completed 10 Oct.).

43: *Per Amica Silentia Lunae.* London & N.Y., 18 Jan. 1918 ("Prologue" and "Epilogue" dated 11 May 1917).

44: *Nine Poems.* London, Oct. 1918.

45: *Poems* (1895). Rev., London, 1919.

46: *The Wild Swans at Coole.* London & N.Y., 11 Mar. 1919 ("Preface" dated Sept. 1918).

47: *Poems* (1895). Rev., London, 1920.

48: *The Wild Swans at Coole.* Rev., London, 1920.

49: *Michael Robartes and the Dancer.* Dundrum (*Cuala*), Feb. 1921 (though completed All Souls' Day 1920).

50: *Selected Poems.* N.Y., 28 June 1921.

51: *Poems* (1895). Rev., London, 1922.

52: *Poems* (1895). Rev., London, 1922.

53: *Seven Poems and a Fragment.* Dundrum (*Cuala*), June 1922 (though completed in Apr.).

54: *Later Poems.* London, 3 Nov. 1922, 1922.

54a: *Plays in Prose and Verse.* London, 1922 (in "Coll. Ed." & "Cardinal Series"), 1922, 1926, 1930; N.Y., 1924; ltd. N.Y. ed., 1924.

54b: *The Player Queen.* London, 1922.

55: *Poems* (1895). Rev., London, 1923.

56: *Poems* (1895). Rev., London, 1924.

57: *Later Poems.* Rev., London, 1924.

58: *Later Poems.* N.Y., 1924, 1928.

59: *Essays.* London (6 May; dedication dated 26 Nov. 1923) & N.Y., 1924.

60: *The Cat and the Moon and Certain Poems*. Dublin (*Cuala*), July 1924 (though completed 1 May).

61: *Early Poems and Stories*. London, 22 Sept. 1925 (Dedication dated May); N.Y., 17 Nov. 1925.

62: *A Vision*. London, 15 Jan. 1926 [Dated 1925].

63: *Later Poems*. Rev., London, 1926.

64: *Poems* (1895). Rev., London, 1927.

65: *Augustan Books of English Poetry/Second Series Number Four/W. B. Yeats*. London, Apr. 1927, 1928, 1931, 1935, 1939.

66: *October Blast*. Dublin (*Cuala*), Aug. 1927 (though completed early in June).

67: *Stories of Red Hanrahan and The Secret Rose*. London, 11 Nov. 1927.

68: *The Tower*. London, 14 Feb. 1928, 1928; N.Y., 1928, 1929.

69: *Poems* (1895). Rev., London, 1929.

70: *The Tower*. Rev., London, 1929.

71: *A Packet for Ezra Pound*. Dublin (*Cuala*), Aug. 1929 (though completed early in June).

72: *The Winding Stair*. N.Y., 1 Oct. 1929.

73: *Selected Poems*. London, 8 Oct. 1929 ("Preface" dated May), 1930, 1932.

74: *Three Things*. London, 9 Oct. 1929, 1929.

75: *Later Poems*. Rev., London, 1931.

76: *Stories of Michael Robartes and His Friends*. Dublin (*Cuala*), Mar. 1932 (Dated, since completed Allhallows Eve, 1931).

77: *Words for Music Perhaps and Other Poems*. Dublin (*Cuala*), 14 Nov. 1932 (though completed late in Sept.).

78: *The Winding Stair and Other Poems*. London, 19 Sept. 1933, 1934; N.Y., 1933, 1933.

79: *The Collected Poems of W. B. Yeats.* N.Y., 14 Nov. 1933 + 15 reprintings through 1949.

80: *The Collected Poems of W. B. Yeats.* London, 1933, 1934, 1935, 1937, 1939.

81: *The Words upon the Window Pane.* Dublin (*Cuala*), Apr. 1934 (though completed late in Jan.).

82: *Wheels and Butterflies.* London, 13 Nov. 1934 ("Preface" dated 4 Aug.); N.Y., 1935.

83: *The Collected Plays of W. B. Yeats.* London, 30 Nov. 1934; N.Y., 1935.

84: *The King of the Great Clock Tower.* Dublin (*Cuala*), 14 Dec. 1934 (though completed late in Oct.).

85: *The King of the Great Clock Tower.* N.Y., 1935.

86: *A Full Moon in March.* London, 22 Nov. 1935.

87: *Poems.* Dublin (*Cuala*), 1935.

87a: *Nine One-Act Plays.* London, 1937.

88: *Selected Poems* (1929). Rev., London, 1936; rep., 1938. [In "Golden Treasury" series, 1951 & 1952.]

89: *The Oxford Book of Modern Verse.* Oxford, 19 Nov. 1936 + 8 reprintings to 1949; N.Y., 1936, 1937, 1947.

90: *A Vision.* London, 7 Oct. 1937; N.Y., 1938.

91: *A Speech and Two Poems.* Dublin, Dec. 1937.

92: *Essays, 1931 to 1936.* Dublin (*Cuala*), 14 Dec. 1937 (though completed late in Oct.).

93: *The Herne's Egg and Other Plays.* N.Y., 12 Apr. 1938.

94: *New Poems.* Dublin (*Cuala*), 18 May 1938 (though completed 9 Apr.).

95: *Last Poems and Two Plays.* Dublin (*Cuala*), 10 July 1939 (though completed in June).

96: *On the Boiler.* Dublin (*Cuala*), 1939 ("Preface" dated Oct. 1938), 1939.

97: *Last Poems and Plays.* London (Jan.) & N.Y., 1940; N.Y., 1940.

98: *The Poems of W. B. Yeats* (2 vols.). London, 25 Nov. 1949.

99: *The Collected Poems of W. B. Yeats.* London, 4 July 1950, 1952, 1954; N.Y., 1951, 1951 (with several corrections), 1951, 1952, 1953, 1954, 1955, 1956 (with further revisions, designed to bring correspondence with 98).

100: *The Collected Plays of W. B. Yeats.* London, 1952; N.Y., 1953.

101: *A Vision* [embodying Yeats's final revisions]. N.Y., 1956.

Except for asterisked items, reference by surname and page only is used in the following cases, among which Professor d'Arbois de Jubainville's work is for economy in later reference listed under its translator's name:

*Æ (G. W. Russell). *Some Irish Essays.* Dublin: Maunsel, & London: Johnson and Ince, 1906.

*————. *Song and Its Fountains.* London: Macmillan, 1932.

Archer, W. *Poets of the Younger Generation.* London & N.Y.: Lane, 1902.

Baring-Gould, S. *Curious Myths of the Middle Ages.* London & N.Y.: Longmans, Green, 1894.

*Bax, A. *Farewell, My Youth.* London: Longmans, Green, 1943.

* Bax, C., ed. *Florence Farr/Bernard Shaw/W. B. Yeats/Letters.* London: Home & Van Thal, 1946.

Beach, J. W. *The Concept of Nature in Nineteenth-Century British Poetry.* N.Y.: Macmillan, 1936.

Best, R. I., tr. *The Irish Mythological Cycle and Celtic Mythology*, by H. d'Arbois de Jubainville. Dublin: Hodges, Figgis, & London: Simpkin, Marshall, 1903.

Bjersby, B. *The Interpretation of the Cuchulain Legend in the Works of W. B. Yeats*. Upsala: Lundequistska Bokhandeln, Copenhagen: Monksgaard, & Dublin: Hodges, Figgis, 1950.

* Bodkin, M. *Studies in Type Images in Poetry, Religion and Philosophy*. London & N.Y.: Oxford Univ. Press, 1951.

Bodkin, T. *Hugh Lane and His Pictures*. Dublin: Browne and Nolan, 1934. (A Pegasus Press ed. appeared in 1932.)

Bowra, C. M. *The Heritage of Symbolism*. London: Macmillan, 1943.

Bridge, U., ed. *W. B. Yeats and T. Sturge Moore/Their Correspondence/1901–1937*. London: Routledge & Kegan Paul, Ltd., 1953.

Bronowski, J. *The Poet's Defence*. Cambridge (England): Cambridge Univ. Press, 1939.

* Brooks, C. *Modern Poetry and the Tradition*. Chapel Hill: Univ. of N. Carolina Press, 1939. (*M. P. T.*)

* ———. *The Well-Wrought Urn*. N.Y.: Reynal and Hitchcock, 1947. (*W. U.*)

———, and Warren, R. P. *Understanding Poetry*. N.Y.: Holt, 1938.

Brown, M. J., ed. *Historical Ballad Poetry of Ireland*. Dublin & Belfast: Educ. Co. of Ireland Ltd., 1912.

Colum, Mary. *Life and the Dream*. Garden City: Doubleday, 1947.

Daiches, D. *Poetry and the Modern World*. Chicago: Univ. of Chicago Press, 1940.

Deutsch, B. *This Modern Poetry*. N.Y.: Norton, 1935.

* Dillon, M. *Early Irish Literature*. Chicago: Univ. of Chicago Press, 1948. (*E. I. L.*)

* ———. *The Cycles of the Kings*. N.Y.: Oxford Univ. Press, 1946. (*C. K.*)

Drew, E., and Sweeney, J. L. *Directions in Modern Poetry*. N.Y.: Norton, 1940.

Dume, T. L. *William Butler Yeats: A Survey of His Reading*. Unpub. Temple Univ. Diss., 1950.

"Eglinton, J." (W. K. Magee) *A Memoir of A E/George William Russell*. London: Macmillan, 1937.

Ellis-Fermor, U. *The Irish Dramatic Movement*. London: Methuen, 1939.

Ellmann, R. *Yeats/The Man and the Masks*. N.Y.: Macmillan, 1948.

* ———. *The Identity of Yeats*. London: Macmillan, 1954. (*Iden.*)

Empson, W. *Seven Types of Ambiguity*. N.Y.: New Directions, rev. ed., 1947.

Fraser, G. S. *W. B. Yeats*. London: Longmans, Green, for Brit. Council & Nat'l Book League, 1954.

Frazer, J. G. *The Golden Bough*. 3d ed. London: Macmillan, 1914.

Gogarty, O. St. J. *It Isn't This Time of Year at All!* Garden City: Doubleday, 1954.

* Gregory, Lady I. A. *Gods and Fighting Men*. London: Murray, 1910; orig. 1904. (*G. F. M.*)

* ———. *Hugh Lane's Life and Achievement*. N.Y.: Dutton, 1921. (*H. L.*)

* ———. *Journals*, ed. L. Robinson. N.Y.: Macmillan, 1947. (*Jour.*)

Griffin, G. *The Wild Geese*. London: Jarrolds, 1938.

Gurd, P. *The Early Poetry of William Butler Yeats*. Lancaster, Pa.: New Era Printing Co., 1916.

Gwynn, S. L., ed. *Scattering Branches*. N.Y.: Macmillan, 1940.

Hall, J., and Steinmann, M., eds. *The Permanence of Yeats*. N.Y.: Macmillan, 1950.

Henn, T. R. *The Lonely Tower*. London: Methuen, 1950.

Hoare, D. M. *The Works of Morris and of Yeats in Relation to Early Saga Literature*. Cambridge (England): Cambridge Univ. Press, 1937.

Hone, J. *W. B. Yeats/1865–1939*. N.Y.: Macmillan, 1943.

* ————. *William Butler Yeats/The Poet in Contemporary Ireland*. Dublin & London: Maunsel, n.d. (Hone *Poet*)

* ————, ed. *J. B. Yeats/Letters to His Son W. B. Yeats and Others*. London: Faber and Faber, 1944; N.Y.: Dutton, 1946. (Hone *Letters*)

Hull, E. *A Text-Book of Irish Literature*. 2 vols. Dublin: Gill, 1906–8.

* Hyde, D. *A Literary History of Ireland*. London: Unwin; N.Y.: Scribner's, 1899.

————. *The Story of Early Gaelic Literature*. London: Unwin, 1894, and later.

Jackson, K. *Studies in Early Celtic Nature Poetry*. Cambridge (England): Cambridge Univ. Press, 1935.

Jeffares, A. N. *W. B. Yeats/Man and Poet*. New Haven: Yale Univ. Press, 1949.

Joyce, P. W. *A Social History of Ancient Ireland*. 2 vols. 3d ed. Dublin & London: Longmans, Green, 1920.

* ————, tr. *Old Celtic Romances*. Dublin & London: Longmans, Green, ed. 1920. (*O. C. R.*)

Keating, G. *Foras Feasa ar Éirinn* ("History of Ireland"). Vol. I ed. & tr. D. Comyn: Irish Texts Soc'y (London: Nutt), Vol. IV, 1901 [1902]; Vols. II & III ed. & tr. P. S. Dinneen: *Idem,* Vols. VIII, 1905 [1908], & IX, 1906 [1908].

Kennedy, P. *Legendary Fictions of the Irish Celts.* London: Macmillan, 1866.

Knight, G. W. *The Starlit Dome.* London & N.Y.: Oxford Univ. Press, 1941.

Koch, V. *W. B. Yeats/The Tragic Phase/A Study of the Last Poems.* London: Routledge and Kegan Paul Ltd., 1951.

Krans, H. S. *William Butler Yeats and the Irish Literary Revival.* N.Y.: McClure, Phillips, 1904.

Lewis, C., ed. *Self-Portrait . . . of Charles Ricketts, R. A.* London: Davies, 1939.

MacBride, Maud Gonne. *A Servant of the Queen.* London: Gollancz, 1938.

McHugh, R., ed. *W. B. Yeats/Letters to Katharine Tynan.* N.Y.: McMullen Books, Inc., 1953.

MacKenna, S., tr. *Plotinus . . . ,* Vol. I. London & Boston: Medici Soc'y, 1917; rpt. of 1926.

Mackimmie, M. G. *A Study of Yeats's "The Two Kings."* Unpub. Univ. of Conn. Diss., 1951.

MacManus, S. *The Story of the Irish Race.* N.Y.: Devin-Adair, ed. 1945.

MacNeice, L. *The Poetry of W. B. Yeats.* London & N.Y.: Oxford Univ. Press, 1941.

Markievicz, Countess. Prison Letters of—. London: Longmans, 1934.

Mégroz, R. L. *Modern English Poetry.* London: Ivor Nicholson & Watson, 1933.

Menon, V. K. N. *The Development of William Butler Yeats.* Edinburgh & London: Oliver and Boyd, 1942.

Mercier, V., and Greene, D. H., eds. *1000 Years of Irish Prose, Pt. I.* N.Y.: Devin-Adair, 1952.

Meyer, K., and Nutt, A. *The Voyage of Bran*. . . . 2 vols. London: Nutt, 1895–97.

Millett, F. B. *The Rebirth of Liberal Education*. N.Y.: Harcourt, Brace, 1945.

Moore, V. *The Unicorn*. N.Y.: Macmillan, 1954.

More, P. E. *Shelburne Essays, First Series*. Boston & N.Y.: Houghton Mifflin, 1904.

Murphy, G., ed. *The Modern Poet*. London: Sidgwick & Jackson, 1938.

Murry, J. M. *Aspects of Literature*. London: Cape, ed. 1934.

O'Casey, S. *Drums under the Windows*. N.Y.: Macmillan, 1946.

"O'Connor, Frank" (Michael O'Donovan). *Leinster, Munster and Connaught*. London: Hale, 1950.

O'Curry, E. *Lectures on the Manuscript Materials of Ancient Irish History*. Dublin: J. Duffy, 1861.

* ———. *On the Manners and Customs of the Ancient Irish*. Ed. with intro. vol. by W. K. Sullivan. 3 vols. London: Williams and Norgate, 1873.

O'Donnell, J. P. *Sailing to Byzantium*. Cambridge: Harvard Univ. Press, 1939.

O'Grady, S. *Finn and His Companions*. Dublin: Talbot Press; London: Unwin, ed. 1921. Orig. London: Unwin, 1892.

* ———. *The Coming of Cuculain*. London: Methuen, 1894. (*C. C.*)

O'Rahilly, T. F. *Early Irish History and Mythology*. Dublin Institute for Advanced Studies, 1946.

Palmer, H. *Post-Victorian Poetry*. London: Dent, 1938.

Parkinson, T. *W. B. Yeats, Self-Critic*. Berkeley: Univ. of California Press, 1951.

Pollock, J. H. *William Butler Yeats*. London: Duckworth; Dublin: Talbot Press, 1935.

Read, H. *A Coat of Many Colours.* London: Routledge, 1945.

Reid, F. *W. B. Yeats/A Critical Study.* London: Secker, 1915.

Reynolds, H., ed. *Letters to the New Island* (Yeats). Cambridge: Harvard Univ. Press, 1934.

Rhys, J. *Lectures on the Origin and Growth of Religion as Illustrated by Celtic Heathendom.* 2d ed. London: Williams and Norgate, 1892.

Richards, I. A. *Coleridge on Imagination.* N.Y.: Harcourt, Brace, 1935.

Robinson, L., ed. *Excerpts from Further Letters of J. B. Yeats.* Churchtown, Dundrum: Cuala Press, 1920.

* ———— and T., and Dorman, Nora [Robinson]. *Three Homes.* London: Michael Joseph Ltd., 1938. (Robinson, *T. H.*)

* Rolleston, C. H. *Portrait of an Irishman.* London: Methuen, 1939.

* Rolleston, T. W. *Myths and Legends of the Celtic Race.* N.Y.: Crowell, n.d. [1913]

* Rothenstein, W. *Men and Memories.* 2 vols. London: Faber and Faber, 1931–32. (*M. & M.*)

* ————. *Since Fifty.* London: Faber and Faber, 1939.

Rudd, M. *Divided Image.* London: Routledge & Kegan Paul Ltd., 1953.

Saul, G. B. *The Shadow of the Three Queens.* Harrisburg: Stackpole, 1953.

* ————. *Stephens, Yeats, and Other Irish Concerns.* N.Y.: N.Y. Public Library, 1954. (*S. Y. O. I.*)

Savage, D. S. *The Personal Principle.* London: Routledge, 1944.

Spence, L. *A Dictionary of Medieval Romance and Romance Writers.* London: Routledge; N.Y.: Dutton, 1913.

Spender, S. *The Destructive Element*. Boston & N.Y.: Houghton Mifflin, 1936.

Stauffer, D. A. *The Golden Nightingale*. N.Y.: Macmillan, 1949.

*———. *The Nature of Poetry*. N.Y.: Norton, 1946. (*N. P.*)

Strong, L. A. G. *A Letter to W. B. Yeats*. London: Hogarth Press, 1932.

*———. *Personal Remarks*. N.Y.: Liveright, 1953. (*P. R.*)

Thurneysen, R. *Die Irische Helden- und Königsage*. Halle: M. Niemeyer, 1921.

Tindall, W. Y. *Forces in Modern British Literature*. N.Y.: Knopf, 1947.

*———. *James Joyce*. N.Y.: Scribner's, 1950.

* Tynan, K. *The Middle Years*. Boston & N.Y.: Houghton Mifflin, 1917. (*M. Y.*)

———. *Twenty-five Years*. London: Murray, 1913.

Ure, P. *Towards a Mythology*. Liverpool Univ. Press & London: Hodder and Stoughton, 1946.

Ussher, A. *Three Great Irishmen*. London: Gollancz, 1952.

Wade, A. *A Bibliography of the Writings of W. B. Yeats*. London: Hart-Davis, 1951.

*———, ed. *The Letters of W. B. Yeats*. N.Y.: Macmillan, 1955. (Wade, *Letters*)

Wain, J., ed. *Interpretations*. . . . London: Routledge & Kegan Paul, 1955. Pp. 194-210.

Wellesley, D., ed. *Letters on Poetry from W. B. Yeats to Dorothy Wellesley*. London & N.Y.: Oxford Univ. Press, 1940.

Wells, J. E. *A Manual of the Writings in Middle English*. New Haven: Yale Univ. Press, 1916.

Wilder, A. N. *The Spiritual Aspects of the New Poetry.* N.Y.: Harper, 1940.

Williams, C. *Poetry at Present.* Oxford: Clarendon Press, 1930.

Wilson, E. *Axel's Castle.* N.Y.: Scribner's, 1931.

Witt, M. "William Butler Yeats." *English Institute Essays, 1946.* New York: Columbia Univ. Press, 1947.

Wrenn, C. L. *W. B. Yeats/A Literary Study.* London: Murby, 1920. (Rpt. from *Durham Univ. Jour.*)

Yeats, J. B. *Early Memories.* Churchtown, Dundrum: Cuala Press, 1923.

The following articles and shorter items (exclusive of Yeats's own) will be found cited:

Adams, H. "Yeats's *Country of the Young.*" *PMLA,* LXXII, 510-19.

Adams, R. M. "Now That My Ladder's Gone—Yeats without Myth." *Accent,* XIII, 140-52.

Allt, P. "Yeats and the Revision of His Early Verse." *Hermathena,* No. 64, 90-101.

———. "Yeats, Religion, and History." *Sewanee Rev.,* LX, 624-58.

Alspach, R. K. "Some Sources of Yeats's *The Wanderings of Oisin.*" *PMLA,* LVIII, 849-66.

———. "The Use by Yeats . . . of the Folklore of Patrick Kennedy." *Jour. of Amer. Folklore,* LIX, 404-12.

———. "Two Songs of Yeats." *Mod. Lang. Notes,* LXI, 395-400.

———. "Yeats's First Two Published Poems." *Mod. Lang. Notes,* LVIII, 555-57.

———. "Yeats's 'Maid Quiet.'" *Mod. Lang. Notes,* LXV, 252-53.

————. "Yeats's 'The Grey Rock.'" *Jour. of Amer. Folklore,* LXIII, 57-71.

Anon. "John O'Leary." *Sinn Féin,* 23 Mar. 1907.

————. Rev. of Apr. 1913 no. of *Poetry. Irish Rev.,* May 1913.

————. "Willie Yeats and John O'Leary." *Irish Book Lover,* Nov. 1940.

Auty, R. A. Letter. London *Times Lit. Supp.,* 11 Aug. 1950.

Baker, H. "Domes of Byzantium." *South. Rev.,* VII, 639-52.

Benson, C. "Yeats's 'The Cat and the Moon.'" *Mod. Lang. Notes,* LXVIII, 220-23.

Blackmur, R. P. "Between Myth and Philosophy. . . ." *South. Rev.,* VII, 407-25.

————. "The Later Poetry of W. B. Yeats." *South. Rev.,* II, 339-62.

Bloom, E. A. "Yeats's 'Second Coming' . . ." *Univ. Kansas City Rev.,* XXI, 103-10.

Bradford, C. S. "Journeys to Byzantium." *Va. Qu. Rev.,* XXV, 205-25.

Brooks, Jr., C. "Yeats: The Poet as Myth-Maker." *South. Rev.,* IV, 116-42.

Burke, K. "On Motivation in Yeats." *South. Rev.,* VII, 547-61.

C., R. J. "Yeats' *The Wild Swans at Coole.*" *Explicator,* II, No. 4, Q. 20.

Campbell, H. M. "Yeats's 'Sailing to Byzantium.'" *Mod. Lang. Notes,* LXX, 585-89.

Christopherson, J. Letter. London *Times Lit. Supp.,* 15 Sept. 1950.

Condry, W. "A Hundred Years of *Walden.*" *Dublin Mag.,* N.S. XXXI (Jan.-Mar. 1955), 42-46.

Craig, M. Letter. London *Times Lit. Supp.*, 1 Sept. 1950.

Davenport, A. "W. B. Yeats and the Upanishads." *Rev. of Eng. Studies*, III, 9, 55-62.

Dobrée, B. Letter. London *Times Lit. Supp.*, 22 Sept. 1950.

Dume, T. L. "Yeats' Golden Tree and Birds in the Byzantine Poems." *Mod. Lang. Notes*, LXVII, 404-7.

Edwards, O. "Yeats's 'The Fisherman.'" *Wales*, VII, 222-23.

Ellmann, R. "The Art of Yeats: Affirmative Capability." *Kenyon Rev.*, XV, 357-85.

Flanders, P. "Padraic Pearse and 'The Splendid Years.'" *Envoy*, V, 20, 58-63.

Freyer, G. "W. B. Yeats." London *Times Lit. Supp.*, 20 Apr. 1946.

Frye, N. "Yeats and the Language of Symbolism." *Univ. of Toronto Qu.*, XVII, 1-17.

Gibbon, M. "Æ and the Early Days of Theosophy in Dublin." *Dublin Mag.*, N.S. XXXII, No. 3, 25 ff.

Gleckner, R. F. "Blake and Yeats." *Notes & Queries*, n.s. II, 38.

Goldgar, H. "*Axël* de Villiers de l'Isle-Adam et *The Shadowy Waters* de W. B. Yeats." *Revue de Litt. Comparée*, XXIV, 563-74.

————. "Yeats and the Black Centaur in France." *West. Rev.*, XV, 111-22.

Greene, D. J. "Yeats's Byzantium and Johnson's Lichfield." *Philol. Qu.*, XXXIII, 433-35.

Gregory, H. "W. B. Yeats and the Mask of Jonathan Swift." *South. Rev.*, VII, 492-509.

Grierson, H. "Fairies—from Shakespeare to Mr. Yeats." *Dublin Rev.*, CXLVIII, 297, 271-84.

Guthrie, W. N. "W. B. Yeats." *Sewanee Rev.*, IX, 328-31.

Gwynn, F. L. "Yeats's Byzantium and Its Sources."
Philol. Qu., XXXII, 9-21.

Haydn, H. "The Last of the Romantics. . . ." *Sewanee
Rev.*, LV, 297-323.

Henn, T. R. "W. B. Yeats and the Irish Background."
Yale Rev., XLII, 35-64.

———. "The Accent of Yeats' *Last Poems.*" *Essays and
Studies by Members of the Eng. Ass'n.*, IX, 56-72.

Higgins, F. R. "As Irish Poet." *The Arrow*, Summer
1939, 6-8.

Hone, J. M. "Yeats as Political Philosopher." *London
Merc.*, XXXIX, 492-96.

Houghton, W. E. "Yeats and Crazy Jane. . . ." *Mod.
Philol.*, XL, 316-29.

Jeffares, A. N. "Notes on Yeats's 'Fragments.' " *Notes &
Queries*, CXCIV, 13, 279-80.

———. "Notes on Yeats's 'Lapis Lazuli.' " *Mod. Lang.
Notes*, LXV, 488-91.

———. "Poet's Tower." *Envoy*, V, 20, 45-55.

———. "The Byzantine Poems of W. B. Yeats." *Rev. of
Eng. Studies*, XXII, 44-52.

———. " 'The New Faces': A New Explanation." *Rev.
of Eng. Studies*, XXIII, 349-53.

———. "The Source of Yeats's 'A Meditation in Time
of War.' " *Notes & Queries*, CXCIII, 522.

———. "Thoor Ballylee." *Eng. Studies*, XXVIII, 161-68.

———. " 'Two Songs of a Fool' and Their Explanation."
Eng. Studies, XXVI, 169-71.

———. "W. B. Yeats and His Methods of Writing
Verse." *Nineteenth Cent. and After*, CXXXIX, 123-28.

———. "Yeats's 'The Gyres': Sources and Symbolism."
Huntington Lib. Qu., XV, 89-97.

Killen, A. M. "Some French Influences in . . . W. B.
Yeats. . . ." *Comp. Lit. Studies*, VIII, 1-8.

Knights, L. C. "W. B. Yeats: The Assertion of Values." *South. Rev.*, VII, 426-41.

Mabbott, T. O. "Yeats' *The Wild Swans at Coole*." *Explicator*, III, No. 1, It. 5.

Mackey, W. F. "Yeats's Debt to Ronsard on a *Carpe Diem* Theme." *Compar. Lit. Studies*, XIX, 4-7.

"Macleod, Fiona" (William Sharp). "The Later Work of Mr. Yeats." *No. Amer. Rev.*, CLXXV, 473-85.

MacLiammóir, M. "Maud Gonne." *Harper's Bazaar*, No. 2908, 124.

Masson, D. I. "The 'Musical Form' of Yeats's 'Byzantium.'" *Notes & Queries*, CXCVIII, 9, 400-1.

————. "Word and Sound in Yeats's 'Byzantium.'" *Jour. Eng. Lit. Hist.*, XX, 136-60.

Matthiessen, F. O. "The Crooked Road." *South. Rev.*, VII, 455-70.

Mercier, V. "'Speech after Long Silence.'" *Irish Writing*, No. 6.

Minton, A. "Yeats' *When You Are Old*." *Explicator*, V, It. 49.

Moult, T. "The Bard of Houlihan." *The Apple*, I, 3.

Murphy, G. Letter. London *Times Lit. Supp.*, 15 Sept. 1950.

Murphy, R. Letter. London *Times Lit. Supp.*, 1 Sept. 1950.

Notopoulos, J. A. "'Sailing to Byzantium.'" *Classical Jour.*, XLI, 78-79.

"O'Connor, F." (M. O'Donovan) "A Lyric Voice in the Irish Theatre." N.Y. *Times Book Rev.*, 31 May 1953, pp. 1, 16.

Olson, E. "*Sailing to Byzantium:* Prolegomena to a Poetics of the Lyric." *Univ. Rev.*, VIII, 209-19.

Palmer, A. "Delacroix." *London Merc.*, XXXVII, 547-48.

Parkinson, T. "The Sun and the Moon in Yeats's Early Poetry." *Mod. Philol.*, L, 50-58.

―――. "The World of Yeats' 'Nineteen Hundred and Nineteen.'" *Univ. of Calif. Pubs., Eng. Stud.*, 11 (1955), 211-27.

Pearce, D. "Yeats's 'The Delphic Oracle upon Plotinus.'" *Notes & Queries*, n.s. I, 175-76.

Quinn, K. "Blake and the New Age." *Va. Qu. Rev.*, XIII, 271-85.

Ransom, J. C. "The Irish, the Gaelic, the Byzantine." *South. Rev.*, VII, 517-46.

Reid, J. D. "Leda, Twice Assaulted." *Jour. of Aesthetics & Art Crit.*, XI, 378-89.

Reinhard, J. H., and Hull, V. E. "Bran and Sceolang." *Speculum*, XI, 42-58.

Robson, W. W. Rev. of Koch. *Dublin Rev.*, No. 453, 83-86.

Rubenstein, J. S. "Three Misprints in Yeats's *Collected Poems*." *Mod. Lang. Notes*, LXX, 184-87.

Rutherford, A. "Yeats' *Who Goes with Fergus?*" *Explicator*, XIII, No. 7, It. 41.

Saul, G. B. "The Winged Image: A Note on Birds in Yeats's Poems." *Bull. of the N.Y. Public Library*, LVIII, 267-73.

―――. "Yeats and His Poems." London *Times Lit. Supp.*, 31 Mar. 1950.

―――. "Yeatsian Brevities." *Notes & Queries*, n.s. I, 535-36.

―――. "Yeats's Hare." London *Times Lit. Supp.*, 11 Jan. 1947.

Savage, D. S. "Two Prophetic Poems." *Adelphi*, XXII, 25-32.

Schneider, E. "Yeats' *When You Are Old*." *Explicator*, VI, It. 50.

Seiden, M. I. "A Psycho-Analytical Essay on William Butler Yeats." *Accent,* VI, 178-90.

Sickels, Eleanor M. "Yeats' 'I Am of Ireland.'" *Explicator,* XV, It. 10.

Smith, G. "Yeats's 'Cat and the Moon.'" *Notes & Queries,* CXCV, 35.

Spender, S. "La Crise des Symboles." *France Libre,* VII, 206-10.

————. "W. B. Yeats as a Realist." *Criterion,* XIV, 17-26.

Spitzer, L. "On Yeats's Poem 'Leda and the Swan.'" *Mod. Philol.,* LI, 271-76.

Stageberg, N. C. "Yeats' *Sailing to Byzantium.*" *Explicator,* VI, It. 14.

Stamm, R. "The Sorrow of Love." *Eng. Studies,* XXIX, 79-87.

Stauffer, D. A. "The Reading of a Lyric Poem." *Kenyon Rev.,* XI, 426-40.

Stein, A. "Yeats: A Study in Recklessness." *Sewanee Rev.,* LVII, 603-26.

Thompson, F. J. "Poetry and Politics: W. B. Yeats." *Hopkins Rev.,* III, 3-17.

Tindall, W. Y. "The Symbolism of W. B. Yeats." *Accent,* V, 203-12.

Trowbridge, H. "'Leda and the Swan': A Longinian Analysis." *Mod. Philol.,* LI, 118-29.

Ure, P. "'The Statues': A Note on the Meaning." *Rev. of Eng. Studies,* XXV, 254-57.

————. "Yeats's Supernatural Songs." *Rev. of Eng. Studies,* n.s., Vol. II, No. 25, 38-51.

Wade, A. "Some Letters from W. B. Yeats to John O'Leary and His Sister." *Bull. of the N.Y. Public Library,* Jan.-Feb. 1953.

Walcutt, C. C. "Yeats' *Among School Children* and *Sailing to Byzantium.*" *Explicator*, VIII, It. 42.

Wasserman, E. E. Rev. of Koch. *Mod. Lang. Notes*, LXVIII, 185-90.

Watkins, V. Letter. London *Times Lit. Supp.*, 22 Sept. 1950.

Weeks, D. "Image and Idea in Yeats' *The Second Coming.*" *PMLA*, LXIII, 281-92.

Whalley, G. "Yeats' Quarrel with Old Age." *Queen's Qu.*, LVIII, 497-507.

Witt, M. "A Competition for Eternity: Yeats's Revision of His Later Poems." *PMLA*, LXIV, 40-58.

———. "The Making of an Elegy." *Mod. Philol.*, XLVIII, 112-21.

———. "Yeats' *A Dialogue of Self and Soul.*" *Explicator*, V, It. 48.

———. "Yeats' Hare." London *Times Lit. Supp.*, 18 Oct. 1947.

———. "Yeats' *Mohini Chatterjee.*" *Explicator*, IV, It. 60.

———. "Yeats' *The Collar-Bone of a Hare.*" *Explicator*, VII, It. 21.

———. "Yeats' *The Moods.*" *Explicator*, VI, It. 15.

———. "Yeats's 'The Song of the Happy Shepherd.'" *Philol. Qu.*, XXXII, 1-8.

———. "Yeats' *The Wild Swans at Coole.*" *Explicator*, III, No. 2, It. 17.

———. "Yeats' *To His Heart, Bidding It Have No Fear.*" *Explicator*, IX, It. 32.

———. "Yeats' *When You Are Old.*" *Explicator*, VI, It. 6.

It may be remarked, finally, that figures out of modern Irish history (for which standard works such as E. Curtis'

History of Ireland are available) and figures out of classical myth and legend (for which the uninitiated may find Blakeney's "Everyman's Library" revision of Smith's *Smaller Classical Dictionary* convenient) have not been defined unless special reason existed; and that corrections or important amplifications of this book would be gratefully received.

ACKNOWLEDGMENTS

Special indebtedness to the poet's widow and to Professors Marion Witt and John V. Kelleher is most gratefully acknowledged; and it is a further pleasure to remark that the late Allan Wade's admirable *Bibliography* was particularly useful in checking and supplementing personal notes, as it is to thank my geneticist friend Dr. Walter Landauer for pinning down the memory-tantalizing Spartan boy in Plutarch. But personal obligation is especially heavy to my friends T. R. Henn, Fellow and Tutor of St. Catharine's College, Cambridge, and Col. R. K. Alspach, Professor of English in the U.S. Military Academy. The former of these has furnished several analyses of individual poems on which I have drawn heavily; the latter has not only examined the manuscript critically and provided important corrections, but has most generously permitted me to use the bibliography and study the typescript of the Allt-Alspach variorum. The convenience of working from this typescript to determine the point at which each poem took essentially final shape and the value of the illumination of the poet's apparent intentions thus acquired were incalculable.

June 1957.

Contents

I

DIVISIONS OF *COLLECTED POEMS* (1951)

"Crossways (1889)": Though dated here, never the title of a volume. In 1895 *Poems*, "Crossways" was a section title for short poems reprinted, sometimes with change of title, from *Oisin* (1889), with which were grouped "The Ballad of Father O'Hart" and "The Ballad of the Foxhunter," from *Countess Kathleen* (1892). In his preface to the 1895 volume, Yeats says that in these poems he "tried many pathways"; in the later *Rosa Alchemica*, he has Michael Robartes remark, "I have been with many and many dreamers at the same crossways" (*E. P. S.*, 473). Stauffer (112) thinks "Crossways" "suggests well enough his vacillation."—For Yeats on the *Oisin* volume, *v.* Tynan, *M.Y.*, Chs. IV and V. (The section motto in *C. P.* is misquoted from Blake's *Vala. . . .*)

"The Rose (1893)": Properly to be dated 1892, though never the title of a volume. In 1895 *Poems*, "The Rose" was a section title for a group of short pieces reprinted, again sometimes with change of title, from *Countess Kathleen* (1892), though "Who Goes with Fergus?" (*v.* II, *inf.*) was first included in the sixth edition (1912) and "To some I have talked with by the fire," first published in 1895, followed the "Preface." In this preface Yeats explains that in "The Rose" poems "he has found, he believes, the only pathway

35

whereon he can hope to see with his own eyes the
Eternal Rose of Beauty and of Peace." Later (*Auto.*,
315), admitting the "rhythm . . . still echoed Morris,"
he identified the "Red Rose" as "Intellectual Beauty"
(cp. "Out of the Rose," *E. P. S.*, 334 ff.), but also as
a symbol of love. (Jeffares, 75: "The Rose poems are
. . . a mixture of intellectual beauty and Maud's
beauty.")—On these and the poems of *The Wind
among the Reeds,* cp. Yeats's comments on Rossetti
in § I of "The Happiest of the Poets" (*Essays,* 64-65).

N.B.: On Maud Gonne at this time, *v.* Yeats's "The
New 'Speranza.' (Miss Maud Gonne.)," *United Ire-
land,* 16 Jan. 1892, and (dated 9 July) Boston *Pilot,* 30
July 1892 (*v.* "Maud Gonne," Reynolds).—Bernard
Shaw is reported by Hone (163, fn.) conversationally
to have called Miss Gonne "outrageously beautiful."
V. also Witt, 84-87; MacLiammóir, "Maud Gonne";
Colum, Chap. 13; Yeats's *Auto.,* espec. Bk. V of "The
Trembling of the Veil."

"The Wind among the Reeds (1899)": Title same as that
of a lyric by Nora Hopper in her earlier published
Ballads in Prose; individual poems now much changed
as to title, less frequently as to text: *v.* II, *inf.* In his
notes (p. 73) to the original edition, Yeats says this
of the characters there named in the titles ("shadowy
projections of various aspects of his personality":
Jeffares, 112): "These are personages in 'The Secret
Rose' but, with the exception of some of Hanrahan's
and one of Aedh's poems, the poems are not of that
book. I have used them in this book as principles of
the mind rather than as actual personages. It is probable that only students of the magical tradition will
understand me when I say that 'Michael Robartes'
is fire reflected in water, and that Hanrahan is fire

blown by the wind, and that Aedh, whose name is not merely the Irish form of Hugh, but the Irish for fire, is fire burning by itself. To put it in a different way Hanrahan is the simplicity of an imagination too changeable to gather permanent possessions, or the adoration of the Shepherd; and Michael Robartes is the pride of the imagination brooding upon the greatness of the possessions, or the adoration of Magi; while Aedh is the myrrh and frankincense that the imagination offers continually before all that it loves." —For speculation on the source of some of the esoteric imagery in this volume, v. Moore, 179-80.

In an attempt to tie them into the "system" of *A Vision*, Yeats was eventually (*1930 Diary*, 19) to call "*The Hosting of the Sidhe*, 'O sweet everlasting voices,' and those lines about 'The lonely, majestical multitude'" efforts to "sing that approach" of a historical cycle "where all shall (be) as particular and concrete as human intensity permits."—As products of the 90's, these poems must have reflected unconscious efforts!—*V.* Menon, 21-35, on this volume; also, *Auto.*, 395-96, and Jeffares, 79.—On the rhythms, cp. *Essays*, 201, ll. 15-20.

"In the Seven Woods (1904)": Properly to be dated 1903, since the original edition (which included "The Old Age of Queen Maeve," "Baile and Aillinn," and "On Baile's Strand") was then published by the Dun Emer Press; this had ten lyrics. *Poems, 1899–1905* (1906) increased the lyric group by three, adding "Old Memory," "Never Give All the Heart," and "The Entrance of Deirdre" (partially printed as " Queen Edaine," *McClure's Magazine*, Sept. 1905; and wholly, as "The Praise of Deirdre," *The Shanachie*, Spring 1906).

Poetical Works, I (1906) has thirteen in the group, but alters "The Entrance of Deirdre" to "Chorus for a Play." (This song next appears in *Deirdre/Being Volume Five of Plays for an Irish Theatre:* 1907.)

Bullen, 1908 adds "The Hollow Wood" (now "The Ragged Wood") and "O Do Not Love Too Long," omitting "Chorus. . . ."—*Poems: Second Series* (1910) also has fourteen titles in the group.

"*From* The Green Helmet and Other Poems (1910)": Properly to be dated 1910 *and* 1912.—In the Cuala *The Green Helmet and Other Poems* (1910), the first eight lyrics are grouped ("Words" being here entitled "The Consolation") under "Raymond Lully and his wife Pernella," though an erratum slip indicates Lully is an accidental substitution for "the later Alchemist Nicolas Flamel" (cp. "Rosa Alchemica," *E. P. S.*, 484); the other lyrics are grouped as "Momentary Thoughts." This volume concludes with "The Green Helmet. An Heroic Farce"; its contents were reprinted in the Paget (N.Y., 1911) edition.

The Macmillan edition of 1912 adds "On Hearing . . . ," "At the Abbey Theatre," "On Those . . ." (though as "The Attack on the 'Play Boy'"), "Friends," "The Cold Heaven," and "That the Night Come"; of these additions, the last four were reprinted (the first as "The Attack on 'The Playboy of the Western World,' 1907") in the Cuala *Responsibilities* (1914).

"Responsibilities (1914)": Except for certain differences in title (noted in II, *inf.*), as in the original Cuala edition, just remarked, which included the five poems originally issued (Cuala, 1913) as *Poems Written in Discouragement*. The Cuala edition also included "The Two Kings" and a revised version of "The Hour-Glass," both now dissociated from the original contents. The 1916 Macmillan *Responsibilities and Other Poems* reprinted the contents of the Cuala edition, added "The Well and the Tree" (*v.* "At the Hawk's Well," *P. & C.*, 355-56), and included a section, "From the Green Helmet and Other Poems," reprinting the nineteen lyrics from the Cuala *Green Helmet* plus "On Hearing . . ." and "At the Abbey Theatre" from the Macmillan *Green Helmet.*—Stauffer (not alone) discounts everything antedating this volume. Ure (and cp. Hone, 317) feels the "discovery of the personality" (32) evident here marks the break with the earlier Yeats and nourishes all the later work. But the "break" had already been plainly suggested in some lyrics of *In the Seven Woods* and was clearly evident in the *Green Helmet.*—Readers seeking adverse comment on this volume can find it in Wrenn. [In the 8th printing of 99A, "Contents" substitutes "Pardon, old Fathers" for "Introductory Rhymes."]

"The Wild Swans at Coole (1919)": Properly to be dated 1917 *and* 1919.—The Cuala *The Wild Swans at Coole, Other Verses and a Play in Verse* (1917) included the material of *Eight Poems* (1916); the play is "At the Hawk's Well." The Macmillan *The Wild Swans at Coole* (1919) adds the lyrics of *Nine Poems* (1918) plus "In Memory of Major Robert Gregory," "An Irish Airman Foresees His Death," "The Sad Shepherd" (now "Shepherd and Goatherd"—not to be confused with the original "The Sad Shepherd" of *Oisin*), "The Phases of the Moon," "The Saint and the Hunchback," "Two Songs of a Fool," "Another Song of a Fool," and "The Double Vision of Michael Robartes."—This volume, which emphasizes Yeats's growing concern with the effects of slightly imperfect rhyme, was pronounced the author's "Swan Song" by J. Middleton Murry (53-59)!

"Michael Robartes and the Dancer (1921)": Contents as in the Cuala edition, which is dated 1920, though not "published" until February 1921, and which includes "Easter 1916," a lyric privately printed by Clement Shorter in 1916.

"The Tower (1928)": Accurately dated as to title-volume, though confusing as to historical implication. The original Macmillan *Tower* included "The Gift of Harun Al-Rashid" (from *The Cat and the Moon and Certain Poems*, 1924), but did not include "Fragments," first inserted in the 1933 edition of *Collected Poems* (*v.* II, *inf.*); of course, the present ordering of the poems and some of the present titles are the result of revisions (*v.*, again, II). The original *Tower* drew its material from three Cuala Press volumes: *Seven Poems and a Fragment* (1922) contained the poems now (and in the majority of cases then) entitled "Nineteen Hundred and Nineteen," "The Wheel," "The New Faces," "A Prayer for My Son," "On a Picture. . . ," "The Fool by the Roadside," and "All Souls' Night"; *The Cat and the Moon . . .* (*cit. sup.*), "Meditations in Time of Civil War," "Youth and Age," "Leda and the Swan," "Owen Aherne and His Dancers"; and *October Blast* (1927) had all the other lyrics except "Fragments" and "Colonus' Praise."—In a letter to Mrs. Olivia Shakespear (25 Apr. 1928: Hone, 424, or Wade, *Letters*, 742), Yeats wrote: "*The Tower* is a great success, two thousand copies in the first month, much the largest sale I have ever had. . . . Re-reading *The Tower* I was astonished at its bitterness. . . . Yet that bitterness gave the book its power and it is the best book I have written. . . ."

"The Winding Stair and Other Poems [*including* "Words

for Music Perhaps" *and* "A Woman Young and Old"]
(1933)": An accurate reflection of the 1933 Macmillan
volume, even as to ordering of poems.—The original
Fountain Press *The Winding Stair* (N.Y., 1929) contained only the first five titles of the present sequence
plus "A Woman Young and Old." All the others except "Crazy Jane Talks with the Bishop" (first printed
in the 1933 volume) had appeared, though in different
order and in some cases under different title, in the
Cuala *Words for Music Perhaps and Other Poems*
(1932). ("Three Things" had in 1929 had even earlier publication as No. 18 of *Ariel Poems;* in *Words*
. . . , "The Choice" is nonexistent as a separate poem,
its text being a part of "Coole Park and Ballylee 1932,"
now ". . . Ballylee, 1931," while "Vacillation" is organized in seven sections.)—The phrase "winding
stair" may be from W. G. Holmes, *The Age of Jus-
tinian and Theodora* . . . (London, 1912): cp. F. L.
Gwynn, "Yeats's Byzantium and Its Sources." Yeats
himself wrote to Sturge Moore, 26 Sept. 1930 (Bridge,
163): "The Winding Stair . . . is the winding stone
stair of Ballylee enlarged in a symbol. . . ."

"*From* A Full Moon in March (1935)": Lyrics follow the
ordering of the "Parnell's Funeral and other Poems"
section of the Macmillan *A Full Moon* . . . , which
contains also the title playlet and a verse version of
The King of the Great Clock Tower. Except for "Two
Songs Rewritten for the Tune's Sake" and Nos. 3, 4,
7, and 8 of "Supernatural Songs," these lyrics had (not
always with title or same title: *v.* II, *inf.*) previously
appeared in the Cuala *The King of the Great Clock
Tower* (1934).

"Last Poems (1936–1939)": Properly to be dated 1940 if
date of first complete assembling, in the Macmillan
Last Poems and Plays, is to be observed. Actually the

first thirty-five in the series come from the Cuala *New Poems* (1938), where "To Dorothy Wellesley" is entitled "To a Friend"; of these thirty-five, "The Three Bushes" had appeared in *A Broadside* (Mar. 1937: Cuala), "The Municipal Gallery Revisited" in *A Speech and Two Poems* (1937), "A Crazed Girl" (as "At Barcelona") in Margot Ruddock's *The Lemon Tree* (1937), and "Come Gather Round . . ." and "Parnell" in the Cuala *Essays, 1931 to 1936* (1937). Of the remainder, "Why Should Not Old Men Be Mad?" "The Statesman's Holiday," and "Crazy Jane on the Mountain" had appeared untitled in the Cuala *On the Boiler* (1939); rest were first collected in the Cuala *Last Poems and Two Plays* (1939).—These verses underscore Yeats's remark in his 17 June 1935 letter to Dorothy Wellesley: "A ferment has come upon my imagination. If I write more poetry it will be unlike anything I have done"; and the Wellesley *Letters* are indispensable for their study.—V. Henn, Chs. 16-17 and "The Accent of Yeats' *Last Poems*," and Rothenstein, *Since Fifty*, 328-29. Vivienne Koch, in *W. B. Yeats/The Tragic Phase* . . . (cp. W. W. Robson, *Dublin Rev.*), attempts to interpret thirteen of these poems in the manner of the "new criticism," though occasionally impelled to bolster her arguments in convential fashion.

"NARRATIVE AND DRAMATIC"

Poems given separate listing in II, *inf.*—The date of the first edition of "The Shadowy Waters" was 1900; Yeats reprints in *C. P.* the revised version of 1906. "The Gift of Harun Al-Rashid" is properly to be dated 1924, since it appeared in *The Cat and the Moon and Certain Poems.*

II

THE INDIVIDUAL POEMS

Crossways

"The Song of the Happy Shepherd": Originally "An Epilogue. / To 'The Island of Statues' and 'The Seeker.' /
Spoken by a Satyr, carrying a sea-shell."—*Dublin Univ.
Rev.*, Oct. 1885. "Song of the Last Arcadian / (*He car-
ries a sea-shell.*)", *Oisin*, 1889; present title since
Poems, 1895; also rptd. in 12, 14, 18, 21, 23, 24(1), 30,
32, 45, 47, 51, 52, 55, 56, 61, *64, 69, 79, 80, 98, 99.—
Perhaps wr. 1884 (cp. Ellmann, 36), though dated 1885
in 1895 *Poems*, as Ellmann (*Iden.*, 287) later recalls in
consonant redating; possessed of no formal title in MS.:
v. Witt, *Philol. Qu.*, XXXII.—One notices the introduction into l. 18 of the Shelleyan epithet "wandering,"
abused by Yeats in his early verse. Miss Gurd (17) relates l. 10 to Wilde and Mohini Chatterjee; and sees
Blake in ll. 18-21, and (18) *Prometheus Unbound*, III.
iii. 170-80, in the references to a sea-shell in this and
the next poem. On St. 2, and the antiscientific bias, *v.*
Beach, 535-36.

"The Sad Shepherd": Originally "Miserrimus," *Dublin
Univ. Rev.*, Oct. 1886; do., *Oisin*, 1889; present title
since *Poems*, 1895; rptd. 12, 14, 18, 21, 23, 24(1), 30,
32, 45, 47, 51, 52, 55, 56, 61, 64, 69, 79, 80, 98, 99.—Wr.
1885 (Ellmann, *Iden.*, 287).—With "The Indian upon
God" and "The Indian to His Love," considered a di-

rect result of Yeats's initial concern with Theosophy.—
Cp. Gurd, *sup.*

"The Cloak, the Boat, and the Shoes": Originally "Voices,"
one of Yeats's first two published lyrics (other: "Song
of a Faery"), *Dublin Univ. Rev.*, Mar. 1885; incorpo-
rated untitled into *The Island of Statues*, Act II, Sc.
iii, *idem*, July 1885; this *scene* reprinted as "Island of
Statues," *Oisin*, 1889; lyric revised and retitled, **Poems*,
1895; rptd. 12, 14, 18, 21, 23, 24(1), 30, 32, 45, 47,
51, 52, 55, 56, 61, 64, 69, 79, 80, 98, 99. (In the second
and third printings the queries and answers are assigned to "Voices"; many printings have quotation
marks at the beginning of each line.) *V. Alspach,
Mod. Lang. Notes*, LVIII.

"Anashuya and Vijaya": Originally "Jealousy" (with variant description of "Scene"), *Oisin*, 1889; present
title since *Poems*, 1895; rptd. 12, 14, 18, 21, 23, 24(1),
30, 32, 45, 47, 51, 52, 55, 56, 61, 64, 69, 79, 80, 98, 99.
Ellmann (*Iden.*, 287) suggests 1887 as possible date
of writing.—Cp. Yeats, *C. P.*, 447; Stauffer (113 and
163 fn. 5) strains to link this with "The Three Bushes"
(*New Poems*, 1938). On the "Indian" poems in general, *v.* Menon's just comment, 12-13.—The original
printing had a footnote identifying Kama as "The
Indian Cupid."—The 8th printing of 99A correctly
deletes the comma from l. 2.

"The Indian upon God": Originally, unsigned, "From
The Book Of Kauri The Indian—/Section V. On The
Nature Of God," *Dublin Univ. Rev.*, Oct. 1886; rptd.
as "Kanva, The Indian, On God," *Oisin*, 1889; present
title since **Poems*, 1895; also rptd. 12, 14, 18, 21, 23,
24(1), 30, 32, 45, 47, 50, 51, 52, 55, 56, 61, 64, 65, 69,
73, 79, 80, 88, 98, 99.—The first two printings used

quotation marks to set off the portions now italicized.
—Wr. 1886 (Ellmann, *Iden.*, 287).

"The Indian to His Love": Originally "An Indian Song,"
Dublin Univ. Rev., Dec. 1886; do., *Oisin*, 1889; present title since *Poems*, 1895, where it is dated 1886;
rptd. 12, 14, 18, 21, 23, 24(1), 30, 32, 45, 47, 51, 52,
55, 56, 61, 64, 65, 69, *79, 80, 98, 99. The first two
printings had an extra stanza between the present first
and second: this merely underscored the "Lotos-
Eaters" quality of the poem.—Cp. Tynan, *M. Y.*, 36;
McHugh, 41.

"The Falling of the Leaves": Originally without initial
article, in *Oisin*, 1889; as now, *Poems*, 1895; rptd.
12, 14, 18, 21, 23, 24(1), 30, 32, 45, 47, 51, 52, 55, 56,
61, 64, 69, 79, 80, 98, 99.—In "Ideas of Good and
Evil" (*Essays*, 25), Yeats says in "Speaking to the
Psaltery" that this was written "to some traditional
air."

"Ephemera": First in *Oisin*, 1889, where alone it is subtitled "An Autumn Idyl"; rptd. *9, 12, 14, 18, 21, 23,
24(1), 30, 32, 45, 47, 51, 52, 55, 56, 61, 64, 69, 79, 80,
98, 99. The first printing had 13 additional and sentimental lines—10 at the end.—Wr. 1884 (Ellmann,
Iden., 287).—Tindall (249) feels this "resembles
Verlaine's '*Colloque sentimental.*'" Miss Gurd (32)
had earlier noted but minimized this resemblance, as
well as the suggestion of Wilde's *Her Voice;* she finds
a more real link "with Maeterlinck's *Trésor des Hum-
bles.*" The 8th printing of 99A properly indicates a
break between ll. 9 and 10.

"The Madness of King Goll": Originally "King Goll./An
Irish Legend" (illustrated by J. B. Yeats), in *The
Leisure Hour* ("the first English magazine to publish"
Yeats: Hone, 60), Sept. 1887; as "King Goll./(*Third*

Century)," in *Poems and Ballads of Young Ireland,*
1888; as "King Goll. (Third Century.)," in *Oisin,* 1889;
present title since *Poems,* 1895; rptd. *12, 14, 18, 21,
23, 24(1), 30, 32, 45, 47, 51, 52, 55, 56, 61, 64, 69, 79,
80, 98, 99.—Wr. 1884 (Ellmann, *Iden.,* 287).—Irish
goll = "one-eyed," and Goll as a name appears promi-
nently in both the Fenian (*e.g.,* Goll Mac Morna) and
the Mythological Cycles of traditional stories (*v.
Echtrae Laegairi,* Dillon, 116-18).—According to
Yeats (*Poems,* 1895), the poem is based on the legend
of a king who "hid himself in a valley near Cork,
where it is said all the madmen in Ireland would
gather were they free, so mighty a spell did he cast
over that valley." One recalls Glenn Bolcáin, in the
twelfth-century MS. of *Buile Shuibni* ("Suibne's
Frenzy") and the "King of France" and the "Valley
of Wild Men" in *The Battle of the White Strand* (*v.*
Lady Gregory, *G. F. M.,* Bk. III, Ch. VII).—Ll. 2-4:
"Ith" = ? Ancient Magh Iotha ("Plain of Ith": so.
Raphoe, Co. Donegal): cp. Rolleston, 130 ff., and
Rhys, 605. "Emain" (the two earliest printings have
"Eman"; all others except for the last four listed edi-
tions, "Emen") = Emain Macha, capital of ancient
Uladh (e. Ulster): cp. Hull, I, 102. "Inver Amergin"
(the spelling prior to that of the last two listed editions was "Invar Amargin") = ? Inber Scene (River
Kenmare, Kerry), named after Amergin's dead wife.
Amergin was the poet of the Milesian invaders of Ireland: are these "the world-troubling seamen"? One
can only speculate, since the involved line in an earlier form ran: "Many a landsman, many a seaman."
Perhaps the reference is now logically to the Norse invaders of St. 2, by implication clearly identified as
such in the earliest version, though this would seem to

confuse the chronological order of events. Yet again, is it unreasonable to interpret the line "He drives away the Northern cold" as meaning "He secures our peace and prosperity by driving away the Norse" in view of the original reading of this line: "He brings the peaceful age of gold"?—"Ollave" (1. 9) = *ollamh:* a member of the highest grade of the ancient Irish order of poet-scholars known as *filid.*—"Orchil" (St. 6): "The queen of the infernal regions" (O'Grady, *C. C.,* Ch. VIII, fn.). Yeats calls her a "Fomorian sorceress" in his notes to *Poems,* 1895, but in the revised editions of this book issued in 1899 and 1901 admits, "I forget whatever I may have once known about her." For "Orchill" as one of the damned, cp. *Countess Cathleen* (*v. P. & C.* version, 278), Sc. V. —*N.B.:* "Goll" was vastly reworked before its fifth, and essentially final, version was reached in the 1899 revision of the 1895 *Poems.* It is now smoother, and in general more artistic and charming; but the initial three versions were perhaps a bit clearer in conveying the story. Thus, the fourth line of St. 3 was originally "A fever and a whirling fire," followed by a clearer description of going mad, breaking the kingly staff, and rushing away singing. The instrument in St. 5 was originally (and more logically for the Old Irish) a *harp;* now it is a *tympan,* or kettledrum, to which the final stanza assigns "kind wires"! Further, the three earliest versions have no reference to Orchil, but tell how Goll's singing attracted "toads and every outlawed thing"; and they make perhaps clearer the fact that his madness was cured by this singing, but that, the harp-strings broken, he was left to wander in grief or "fling" his "laughter to the sun" because his "remembering hour" was "done."

[handwritten marginal note: Wrong! Also means Celtic stringed instrument.]

"The Stolen Child": *The Irish Monthly,* Dec. 1886; rptd.
   1, 2, 3, *9, 12, 14, 18, 21, 23, 24(1), 30, 32, 45, 47,
   51, 52, 55, 56, 61, 64, 69, 73, 79, 80, 88, 98, 99.—Cp.
   Allingham's "The Fairies." Yeats admitted to Katharine Tynan (*v.* her *M. Y.,* 39, but cp. McHugh, 47)
   that this was "not the poetry of insight and knowledge but of longing and complaint—the cry of the
   heart against necessity." His note on p. 345 of the
   Modern Library edition (as in other editions) of *Irish
   Fairy and Folk Tales* says: "The places mentioned are
   round about Sligo. Further Rosses is a very noted
   fairy locality. There is here a little point of rocks
   where, if anyone falls asleep, there is danger of their
   waking silly, the fairies having carried off their souls."
   —"Sleuth," l. 2, is spelled "Slewth" in several early
   printings.

"To an Isle in the Water": First in *Oisin, 1889; rptd. 9,
   12, 14, 18, 21, 23, 24(1), 30, 32, 33, 45, 47, 50, 51, 52,
   55, 56, 61, 64, 65, 69, 73, 79, 80, 88, 98, 99. Included
   in *Irish Love Songs. Selected by Katharine Tynan*
   (London: Unwin, 1892; p. 104).

"Down by the Salley Gardens": Originally "An Old Song
   Re-Sung," *Oisin, 1889; present title since *Poems,*
   1895; rptd. 12, 14, 18, 21, 23, 24(1), 30, 32, 33, 45, 47,
   50, 51, 52, 55, 56, 61, 64, 65, 69, 73, 79, 80, 88, 98, 99.
   Also included, p. 103, in Miss Tynan's *Irish Love
   Songs* (*cit. sup.*). In an *Oisin* footnote, Yeats said:
   "This is an attempt to reconstruct an old song from
   three lines imperfectly remembered by an old peasant
   woman in the village of Ballysodare, Sligo, who often
   sings them to herself"; in his "Notes" to *Bullen, 1908*
   (I, 244), he said the poem was gotten "by adding a
   few lines to a couple of lines I heard sung at Balliso-

dare" (MacNeice, 61, calls it "a trimmed version of an Irish folk-song"). V. Palmer, p. 101, for the first stanza of a South Leinster version; cp. McHugh, p. 66, fn. 1, and Yeats's 25 Sept. 1935 letter in Wellesley (32), as well as his explanation in § VIII of "Magic" (1901), *Essays* (61), of a position similar to the lover's. (Irish linguistic conservatism has probably helped preserve the term *salley* for "willow," or "sallow"; one recalls the "salwes" of l. 655 of the *Wife of Bath's Prologue*.)

"The Meditation of the Old Fisherman": *Irish Monthly*, Oct. 1886; rptd. 1, 3, *9, 12, 14, 18, 21, 23, 24(1), 30, 32, 33, 45, 47, 50, 51, 52, 55, 56, 61, 64, 69, 79, 80, 98, 99. In his notes to 12, Yeats says he got the refrain by rearranging slightly the words of an old fisherman— "a not very old fisherman at Rosses Point," according to his notes (244) in 24(1).—Wr. June 1886.

"The Ballad of Father O'Hart": Originally "The Priest of Coloony" in London 1888 edition of H. H. Sparling's *Irish Minstrelsy;* do. in 2, where the poem is given a prose note; rptd. as "Father O'Hart" in * *Countess Kathleen*, 1892; present title since *Poems*, 1895; later rptd. 12, 14, 18, 21, 23, 24(1), 30, 32, 45, 47, 51, 52, 55, 56, 61, 64, 69, 79, 80, 98, 99.—The present form is revised from the original; the present penultimate stanza is an addition. The source (*Fairy and Folk Tales*, 324; *Countess Kathleen*, 140; Jeffares, 309 fn. 89) is in the Rev. T. F. O'Rorke's *History, Antiquities, and Present State of the Parishes of Ballysadare and Kilvarnet in the County of Sligo* (1878), pp. 198, 206. —Yeats tells us that a *shoneen* (l. 3) is an "upstart" and a *sleiveen* (l. 6) is a "mean fellow" (*Modern Library* ed., *Irish Fairy and Folk Tales*, 236 fn.); and that "Coloony is a few miles south of the town of Sligo.

Father O'Hart lived there in the last century, and was greatly beloved. These lines accurately record the tradition. No one who has held the stolen land has prospered. It has changed owners many times" (*Idem,* 237 fn.). He also says (*Idem,* 349) O'Hart was a friend of Carolan's and died in 1739.—"Inishmurray" is spelled "Innismurry" in the first three printings.

"The Ballad of Moll Magee": Perhaps first published in *The Gael,* 1887: *v.* Wade, 20.—Included in *Oisin,* 1889; rptd. *9, 12, 14, 18, 21, 23, 24(1), 30, 32, 45, 47, 51, 52, 55, 56, 61, 64, 69, 79, 80, 98, 99.—According to Hone (38), Yeats said the original draft was composed when he was seventeen; a note in 24(1), p. 244, says it derived "from a sermon preached in a chapel at Howth."—A *boreen* (l. 32) is a tree-lined lane.— In § IV of *Estrangement* (written in 1909), Yeats remarks: "Years ago Dr. Sigerson said of the last verse of my 'Moll Magee,' 'Why candles? Surely tapers?' "— The "she" of the penultimate stanza presumably refers to the dead child.

"The Ballad of the Foxhunter": Originally "The Ballad of the Old Fox hunter," *East and West,* Nov. 1889; parenthetically subtitled "An incident from Kickham's 'Knocknagow'" when rptd. in *United Ireland,* 28 May 1892; "The Ballad of the Old Fox hunter," *Countess Kathleen,* 1892; present title since *Poems,* 1895; also rptd. 12, 14, 18, 21, 23, 24(1), 30, 32, 45, 47, 51, 52, 55, 56, 61, *64, 69, 79, 80, 98, 99.—Wr. ? July–Oct. 1889 (cp. implications, Wade, *Letters,* 128, 132, 139). —The *Countess Kathleen* version also has a reference in a note to C. J. Kickham's *Knocknagow* (Dublin, 1879 and later: 482-86): cp. Alspach, *PMLA,* LVIII, 857-59.

The Rose

"To the Rose upon the Rood of Time": First in * *Countess Kathleen,* 1892; rptd. 9, 12, 14, 18, 21, 23, 24(1), 30, 32, 45, 47, 51, 52, 55, 56, 61, 64, 69, 79, 80, 98, 99.—Wr. "about 1891" (Ellmann, 137).—On Cuchulain and Fergus, *v.* next two titles. "Eire" (originally the name of a queen of the *Tuatha Dé Danann*) = "Ireland." In *Auto.* (315) Yeats says of the mid-portion of l. 20: "I do not remember what I meant by 'the bright hearts.' . . ." Cp. notes on "The Rose," *sup.;* Wade, *Letters,* 592 & fn. 2; and Haydn, *Sewanee Rev.,* LV, 308-11.

"Fergus and the Druid": *National Observer,* 21 May 1892; *Countess Kathleen,* 1892; rptd. 9, 12, 14, 18, 21, 23, 24(1), 30, 32, 45, 47, 51, 52, 55, 56, 61, 64, 69, *79, 80, 98, 99.—Jeffares' reference (73) to Fergus as a legendary "king who gave up his kingdom for poetry" perhaps implies some oral tradition; certainly the poem is unfaithful to the recorded story in the *Book of Leinster* of how Ness tricked the crown from Fergus as a bride-gift in order to make her son Concobar king of Uladh (modern Ulster). *V.* the Whitley Stokes translation of *Scéla Conchobair maic Nessa,* in *Ériu,* IV, 22. Miss Gurd (68) is reminded by the Druid's fourth speech of Yeats's *The Wisdom of the King;* by Fergus' last, of "Welsh legend and especially . . . Taliesin." *N.B.:* Ll. 27-28 originally read: "A wild and foolish labourer is a king/To do and do and do and never dream." The "knowing all" of l. 38 was originally "being all," and was followed by five lines now deleted. The 8th printing of 99A inserts a comma at the end of l. 21.

"Cuchulain's Fight with the Sea": Originally "The Death

of Cuchullin," *United Ireland,* 11 June 1892; do., *Countess Kathleen,* 1892; ". . . of Cuhoollin," *Poems,* 1895, and 12 and 14; ". . . of Cuchulain," 18, 21, 23, 24(1), 30, 32, 45, 47, 51, 52, 55, 56; present title since *Early Poems and Stories,* 1925; also rptd. 64, 69, *79, 80, 98, 99.—Cuchulain ("Hound of Culann") is the great demigod and hero of the Ulster tales (cp. Saul); the unnamed girl referred to as "sweet-throated" (pp. 33 and 35) and "young sweetheart" is presumably Eithne Inguba (Ethne Ingubai), his concubine: cp. *The Only Jealousy of Emer* and *The Death of Cuchulain* (Yeats) and the legendary *Sickbed of Cuchulainn.*—According to Miss Hoare (116), this much-revised poem is based on oral tradition (and Yeats—*Countess Kathleen,* 140—acknowledged Curtin's *Myths and Folk-Lore of Ireland* as his source, though his version is far from that of Curtin's "Cucúlin"); assuredly it is also far from the MS account in the Ulster Cycle's *Aided Oenḟir Aife,* a ninth century relic in the *Yellow Book of Lecan,* where the boy is Cú's son by Aife, not—as implied here—by his wife Emer.—L. 7 makes it clear that Yeats meant by "raddling raiment" (l. 2), not weaving, but dyeing with red ocher; and indeed, the earliest version has the line "And found her dyeing cloth with subtle care." (Cp. AS *rud,* Ger. *rot,* and recall Hardy's "reddle-man" in *The Return of the Native;* the raiment of ancient Irish aristocrats was often colorful.)—In many of the earlier versions the swineherd is called "Aileel" or "Aleel"; Cú's son, "Finmole."—Ll. 11-13: Cp. "Whether I live or die is in the gods' hands" and "His head is like a woman's head/I had a fancy for," *On Baile's Strand.*

"The Rose of the World": Originally "Rosa Mundi,"

National Observer, 2 Jan. 1892; present title since *Countess Kathleen,* 1892; rptd. *9, 12, 14, 18, 21, 23, 24(1), 30, 32, 33, 35, 45, 47, 51, 52, 55, 56, 61, 64, 65, 69, 73, 79, 80, 88, 98, 99.—Cp. *Auto.,* 315, and Hone, 99 ("As Yeats himself noted . . . the quality symbolised in such poems . . . differs from the intellectual beauty of Shelley and of Spenser in that it is imagined as suffering with man and not as something pursued from afar"); also Haydn, *Sewanee Rev.,* LV, 308.— L. 5: "Usna's children": Naoise, Ainnle, Ardan; *v.* Deirdre story, Saul, 74 ff.

"The Rose of Peace": Originally "The Peace of the Rose," *National Observer,* 13 Feb. 1892; do., 6; present title since *Poems,* 1895; also rptd. 9, *12, 14, 18, 21, 23, 24(1), 30, 32, 33, 45, 47, 51, 52, 55, 56, 61, 64, 69, 79, 80, 98, 99.—Cp. Haydn, *Sewanee Rev.,* LV, 312.

"The Rose of Battle": Originally "They went forth to the Battle,/but they always fell," *Countess Kathleen,* 1892; present title since *Poems,* 1895; rptd. 12, 14, 18, 21, 23, 24(1), 30, 32, 33, 35, 45, 47, 50, 51, 52, 55, 56, 61, 64, 65, 69, 79, 80, 98, 99.—Cp. Haydn, *Sewanee Rev.,* LV, 308. The 8th printing of 99A deletes the comma from the end of l. 16.

"A Faery Song": As "A Fairy Song," *National Observer,* 12 Sept. 1891; do., 5 & 6; present spelling, *Poems,* 1895; also rptd. 12, 14, 18, 21, 23, 24(1), 30, 32, 45, 47, 51, 52, 55, 56, 61, 64, 69, 73, 79, 80, 87, 88, 98, 99.— Five earliest printings, as also 87, indicate the song was sung "over the outlaw Michael Dwyer and his bride, who had escaped into the mountains." [One recalls the outlaw-patriot Michael Dwyer, of '98 fame, to whom the Wicklow Mountains were stronghold: cp. T. D. Sullivan's "Michael Dwyer," *Historical Ballad Poetry of Ireland* (ed. Brown), 229-30.]—For

Diarmuid and Grania, tragic lovers in the Fenian
Cycle of Irish tales, *v.* Saul, 102-3.

"The Lake Isle of Innisfree": *National Observer,* 13 Dec.
1890; *Book of the Rhymers' Club,* 1892; *Countess
Kathleen,* 1892; also rptd. 9, 12, 14, 18, 21, 23, 24(1),
30, 32, 33, 45, 47, 50, 51, 52, 55, 56, 61, 64, 65, 69, 73,
79, 80, 87, 88, 98, 99.—Reid (41) quotes the first two
stanzas as originally written and sent in a letter,
dated 21 Dec. 1888 by Wade (*Letters,* 96), to Katharine Tynan, who published them in her *Twenty-five
Years* (ed. 1913, p. 263); cp. McHugh, 77.—Drew letter
of praise from Stevenson following initial publication.
For inception, cp. the passage in Yeats's *John Sherman*
beginning "Delayed by a crush in the Strand . . ."
and *Auto.,* 189-90. It appears that Yeats's father's
reading of *Walden* had made the poet wish to live on
Innisfree ["Isle of Heather": really "Cat Island," according to O'Connor (256), though Reid (12) calls
it "Rat Island"], Lough Gill; then (*Auto., cit.*)—"when
walking through Fleet Street very homesick I heard
a little tinkle of water and saw a fountain in a shop-
window which balanced a little ball upon its jet, and
began to remember lake water. From the sudden re-
membrance came my poem *Innisfree,* my first lyric
with anything in its rhythm of my own music. I had
begun to loosen rhythm as an escape from rhetoric
and from that emotion of the crowd that rhetoric
brings. . . ." Yeats came later to dislike the "arise and
go" and inversion of the last stanza.—Ellmann (*Iden.,*
22) glosses *New Testament* on opening five words;
Condry (*Dublin Mag., cit.,* 43) finds the seed for the
"nine bean-rows" of l. 3 in *Walden.* First half of l. 7
implies reference to the aurora borealis.—Cp. Mac-
Neice, 53.—In his humorous "On 'And'" (*On,* 1923)

Belloc claims the "and" in this poem "gives the rhythm as well as the mystery"!

"A Cradle Song": *Scots Observer*, 19 Apr. 1890; *Countess Kathleen*, 1892; rptd. 9, 12, 14, 18, 21, 23, 24(1), 30, 32, 45, 47, 51, 52, 55, 56, *61, 64, 69, 73, 79, 80, 88, 98, 99.—In its original printing, this was, like some of Yeats's other lyrics, the residue of Henley's revision. Yeats acknowledged (*v.* Tynan, *M. Y.*, 50) that "The last two lines are suggested by a Gaelic song quoted in Griffin's 'Collegians'": *v.* McHugh, 109, fn. 1; the title is followed by two quoted lines in numerous early versions. A copy of the first MS may be found in Yeats's 13 Jan. 1890 letter to Katharine Tynan (by her misdated—cp. McHugh, 175: *v. Twenty-five Years*, 270, and *M. Y.*, Ch. V); Yeats also sent Miss Tynan an early revised version on 16 Jan. 1890 (McHugh, 142). Reid (42, 50-54) may be consulted on various early versions. As preserved, the poem is *based* on the printing in the 1901 edn. of 1895 *Poems*.—"The Sailing Seven" (l. 7): the line originally ran, "And the old planets seven." In most of the earlier printings, l. 3, st. 3, runs: "Ah, how I shall miss you."

"The Pity of Love": *Countess Kathleen*, 1892; rptd. *9, 12, 14, 18, 21, 23, 24(1), 30, 32, 35, 45, 47, 51, 52, 55, 56, 61, 64, 69, 79, 80, 87, 98, 99.—Allt (*Hermathena*, No. 64, 97) says that this is dated "Dublin—October 1891" in the MS book "begun 'Oct. 20 1891' for Maud Gonne, but never finished, nor, apparently, presented." —Cp. "Proud Costello . . ." (*E. P. S.*, 383): ". . . there came over them. . . ."

"The Sorrow of Love": *Countess Kathleen*, 1892; rptd. 9, 12, 14, 18, 21, 23, 24(1), 30, 32, 45, 47, 51, 52, 55, 56, *61, 64, 65, 69, 73, 79, 80, 88, 98, 99.—Written Oct. 1891 (Ellmann, *Iden.*, 287); much revised since earliest publication. The poem now seems to suggest that to a man formerly of recluse type the sorrow of a "doomed," "proud" woman became emblematic of universal suffering echoed in nature and natural beauty.—The versions of this poem for Maud Gonne preceding that of *E. P. S.* (1925) were inherently more logical and less pretentious, and hence more charming. Incidentally, "that famous harmony of leaves" (l. 3) seems readable merely as a deliberate phrase, without esoteric reference: the original draft (Ellmann, *Iden.*, 317) read, "The song of the ever-singing leaves."—Cp. Stamm's article and, in disapproval of Yeats's rewriting, Read (208-12) and Mac-Neice (69-71).

M "When You Are Old": *Countess Kathleen*, 1892; rptd. 9, *12, 14, 18, 21, 23, 24(1), 30, 32, 35, 45, 47, 50, 51, 52, 55, 56, 61, 64, 65, 69, 73, 79, 80, 87, 88, 98, 99.—According to Allt (*Hermathena*, No. 64, 100), dated 20 Oct. 1891 in one MS (Ellmann, *Iden.*, 287, dates composition 21 Oct.); early draft in 2 Mar. 1892 letter to Miss Tynan (*M. Y.*, 69; McHugh, 136). Final version a considerable improvement on first.—For Maud Gonne, on whom *v.* Witt, 84-87, and MacLiammóir (*Harper's Bazaar*).—Cp. query and discussions in *Explicator* by Minton, Witt, and Schneider; Mackey's art. in *Compar. Lit. Studies*. Though based on Ronsard's *Quand Vous serez Bien Vieille* (*Sonnets pour Hélène*, ii: 1578), the poem is not a translation. (Cp. the W. Thorley translation quoted by Moult in "The Bard of Houlihan," *The Apple*, I, 3.) Cp. Act II, early versions of *Countess Cathleen*—e.g., 24(3): "... growing old and full of sleep."

M "The White Birds": *National Observer*, 7 May 1892; *Countess Kathleen*, 1892; rptd. *9, 12, 14, 18, 21, 23,

24(1), 30, 32, 33, 45, 47, 51, 52, 55, 56, 61, 64, 69, 79, 80, 98, 99.—According to an unpublished MS excerpted by Jeffares (68), the result of a day spent, in the summer of 1891, with Maud Gonne "upon the cliffs at Howth"; Ellmann (*Iden.*, 69) dates it "a year later" than *Oisin.*—Original printing has note following title: "The birds of fairyland are said to be white as snow. The Danaan Islands are the islands of the fairies." (Hence the faery's calling Mary Bruin a "white bird" in *The Land of Heart's Desire.*)—V. MacBride, 17-19 (Maud Gonne loved the cliffs in question, having lived for a while at Howth during childhood). On "Danaan" (*Danann*), st. 3, v. Saul.

M "A Dream of Death": Originally "An Epitaph," *National Observer*, 12 Dec. 1891; do., 5 & 6; present title since *Poems*, 1895. Also rptd. 12, 14, 18, 21, 23, 24(1), 30, *32, 45, 47, 51, 52, 55, 56, 61, 64, 69, 79, 80, 98, 99.— Allt (*Hermathena*, No. 64, 100) says this is dated "'November 22nd' (1891)" in MS.—Concerns Maud Gonne, recuperating at the time of its composition at St. Raphael after overtaxing herself aiding the Donegal poor (cp. *Countess Kathleen*). Yeats sent Miss Gonne a copy in a letter (Hone, 100-1); in *A Servant of the Queen* (147), she professes herself much amused.

"The Countess Cathleen in Paradise": Originally "Kathleen" in *National Observer*, 31 Oct. 1891; reprinted, 1892, as "Song," p. 86, *Countess Kathleen;* appears as "A Dream of a Blessed Spirit" in *Poems*, 1895, as also in 12, 14, 18, 21, 23, 24(1), 30, 32, 45, 47, 51, 52, 55, 56, 61. Rewritten and given present title in 1926: *v.* revised *1927 edition of 1895 *Poems,* a circumstance involving problems of reconciliation in view of the fact that in his 27 Oct. 1927 letter to Olivia Shake-

spear Yeats says he rewrote and retitled the poem
"yesterday" and gives a version almost as in 1933—and
later—*Collected Poems*, remarking also, "I like the
last verse, the dancer Cathleen has become heaven
itself." The revised form also appears in 69, 79, 80,
98, 99.—Griffin (152) quotes Stopford Brooke as having said of this Rossetti-tinged lyric: "If Mr. Yeats
never wrote another line, those verses alone would be
sufficient to stamp him as the greatest poet of the
century."

"Who Goes with Fergus?"—Originally untitled and sung
by Oona in Act II, Sc. II of *Countess Kathleen*
(1892) before Aleel's "Impetuous heart . . . ," in what
is now Sc. IV, was substituted (cp. Gwynn, 82): thus
also in reprintings of the play in 9, 12, 14, 18, 23, and
24(3); printed as "Lyric in Second Act of *Countess
Cathleen*" in *Beltaine*, May 1899. First published as
separate lyric under present title in the revised sixth
edition (1912) of 1895 *Poems;* and rptd. in 32, 45, 47,
51, 52, 55, 56, 61, 64, 69, 79, 80, 98, 99.—Tindall
(*James Joyce*, 47) claims curiously that the "theme
. . . is escape from adult responsibility by retreat to
childhood and the womb." Empson (187-90) discusses
the poem; he is healthily contradicted by Rutherford
(*Explicator*), who sees Fergus here as "an Irish
Dionysos." L. 10: Cp. the Pan of "Island of Statues"
(*Oisin*, 155): "Doth he still dwell within the woody
shade,/And rule the shadows of the eve and dawn?"—
The "fear" of l. 6 is, sensibly, "fears" in all printings
except the last four.

"The Man Who Dreamed of Faeryland": Originally "A
Man . . . Fairyland," *National Observer*, 7 Feb. 1891;
do., 5; as "The Man . . . ," *Countess Kathleen*, 1892;
as "The Man . . . Faeryland," *Poems*, 1895, and 12,

14, 18, 21, 23, 24(1), 30, 32, 33, 45, 47, 50, 51, 52, 55, 56, 61, 64, 69, *73, 79, 80, 88, 98, 99.—"Dromahair" (l. 1) = Dromohair, Co. Leitrim.—"He wandered by the sands of Lissadell" (l. 13) (the Gore-Booth home) suggests the impoverished Yeats during Sligo summers (Jeffares, 76). With next-to-last line, cp. ". . . until God shall burn up the world with a kiss" (*E. P. S.*, 233).—Cp. Daiches, 144-46.

"The Dedication to a Book of Stories Selected from the Irish Novelists": Originally "Dedication," pp. iii-iv, Vol. I, *Representative Irish Tales* (1891); as "Dedication of 'Irish Tales,' " 5; do., but without the single quotation marks in *Contents* listing, 6; present title since *Poems,* 1895 (except for revision in *Irish Statesman,* 8 Nov. 1924, where it is entitled "An Old Poem Re-Written," but referred to by Yeats as "a sheaf of wild oats"): thus in 12, 14, 18, 21, 23, 24(1), 30, 32, 45, 47, 51, 52, 55, 56, 61, 64, 69, 79, 80, 98, 99. The poem is much changed from its sentimental original form, the re-writing for the *Irish Statesman* having been substituted by Yeats in all subsequent printings.—The "green branch" (l. 1) is Manannan's bell-branch in the ancient *Cormac's Adventures in the Land of Promise,* the *Echtrae Cormaic* of the *Yellow Book of Lecan,* the *Book of Ballymote,* and the *Book of Fermoy.* Cp. Alspach, *PMLA,* LVIII, 863-65.

The Lamentation of the Old Pensioner": Originally "The Old Pensioner," *Scots Observer,* 15 Nov. 1890; present title since *Countess Kathleen,* 1892. V. also 9, 12, 14, 18, 21, 23, 24(1), 30, 32, 45, 47, 51, 52, 55, 56, 61, 64, 69, *79, 80, 98, 99. The body of the poem has been markedly different from the somewhat sentimental affair it originally was (*v.* Jeffares, 77, for convenient reprint) since its rewriting for *E. P. S.* (1925).—In the *Countess Kathleen* (128), Yeats called this lyric "little more than a translation into verse of the very words of an old Wicklow peasant"; in Notes (244) to 24(1) he linked it with "words spoken by a man on The Two Rock Mountain to a friend of mine." There is a more elaborate account in *The Celtic Twilight* (p. 23 of the 1893 edition), where "X" is Æ, or George Russell. The 8th printing of 99A deletes the comma from l. 2 (thus confirming Yeats's own mispunctuation).

"The Ballad of Father Gilligan": Originally "Father Gilligan./A Legend told by the People of Castleisland, Kerry." in *Scots Observer,* 5 July 1890; do., but with subtitle italicized and in parentheses, 5; as "Father Gilligan," 6; present title since *Poems,* 1895; also rptd. 12, *14, 18, 21, 23, 24(1), 30, 32, 45, 47, 50, 51, 52, 55, 56, 61, 64, 69, 79, 80, 98, 99.—In "Speaking to the Psaltery" (*Essays,* 25), Yeats says this was written "to a modification of the air *A Fine Old English Gentleman";* cp. also his letter, "Father Gilligan," *Academy,* 19 Mar. 1892 (Wade, *Letters,* 206-7).

M   "The Two Trees": Originally in *Countess Kathleen,* 1892; rptd., 9, 12, 14, 18, 21, 23, 24(1), 30, 32, 33, 45, 47, 50, 51, 52, 55, 56, 61, 64, 69, *73, 79, 80, 88, 98, 99.— Written to Maud Gonne, and according to Miss Moore (425) her "favorite poem"; by confession to Olivia Shakespear (Wade, *Letters,* 256), a favorite of Yeats's.—Tindall (255) calls "the holy tree" (l. 2) "the Sephirotic tree of the cabbala and the tree of knowledge." Presumably Yeats refers to the "Trees of Knowledge and of Life" ("By the Roadside," *E. P. S.,* 313); cp. Blake's so-titled fragment, *Mod. Lib.* ed., *Poems of William Blake* (ed. Yeats), 255-56. In 24(1), 230, Yeats speaks of imagining the Rose, "the western

Flower of Life . . . growing upon the Tree of Life."—
Poem considerably revised; *e.g.*, in all but the last six
printings ll. 14-18 read:

> Winged loves borne on in gentle strife,
> Tossing and tossing to and fro
> The flaming circle of our life.
> When looking on their shaken hair,
> And dreaming how they dance and dart,

—*V. Parkinson*, 13 ff.; Frye (*Univ. of Toronto Qu.*,
§ IV).

"To Some I Have Talked With by the Fire": *Bookman*,
May 1895; *Poems*, 1895; rptd. *12, 14, 18, 21, 23,
24(1), 30, 32, 45, 47, 51, 52, 55, 56, 64, 69, 79, 80,
98, 99.—In the *Bookman* printing, the title runs:
"To . . . Fire/(*The Dedication of a New Book of
Verse.*)"; in 21 and 24(1): "To . . . Fire. A Dedica-
tion to a Volume of Early Poems."—Cp. Ellmann,
Iden., "Notes," 304.

"To Ireland in the Coming Times": Originally "Apologia
Addressed to Ireland in the coming days," *Countess
Kathleen*, 1892; present title since *Poems*, 1895, though
body of poem much changed; rptd. 12, 14, 18, 21,
23, 24(1), 30, 32, 33, 45, 47, 50, 51, 52, 55, 56, *61,
64, 69, 73, 79, 80, 88, 98, 99.—Ll. 6-8: Cp. "The
Crucifixion of the Outcast," *E. P. S.*, 332, l. 13 ff.;
"her" = Beauty?—"Davis, Mangan, Ferguson," of the
second stanza, are Thomas Osborne Davis, one of the
founders of *The Nation*, which aimed at spurring nationalism by denouncing the sectarian and encourag-
ing independent thinking; "Clarence"—really James—
Mangan, author of "The Dark Rosaleen," etc.; and
Sir Samuel Ferguson, Belfast-born lawyer and poet
who helped revive interest in Irish legendary mate-

rial.—St. 2, "elemental creatures . . .": Wrenn (5) recalls the fairy dictating "prophetic mysteries" to Blake
from a table.

The Wind among the Reeds (Cp. in general Reid, 64 ff.)

"The Hosting of the Sidhe": Originally (without italics)
"The Faery Host," *National Observer*, 7 Oct. 1893;
"The Host," entirely italicized, *The Celtic Twilight*,
1893; present title since *The Wind . . .* , 1899, with
body of poem altered. Also rptd. 15 (entirely itali-
cized), 21, 24(1), 25, 33, 50, 54, 57, 58, 63, 65, 73, 75,
79, 80, 88, 98, 99.—Wr. 29 Aug. 1893 (Ellmann,
Iden., 287).—Yeats has a note on the "sidhe" (Ir.
síde: pron. "shee"), *C. P.*, 448. Cp. the section on
The Wind . . . , Pt. I, *sup.*, and "The Untiring Ones,"
E. P. S., 234-35; the opening of "Kidnappers," *idem*,
223-24; and "Drumcliff and Rosses," *idem*, 250.—
"Knocknarea" (Sligo; l. 1) = Ir. *Cnoc-na-righ*:
"Mountain of the King." Technically, Caoilte (Cailte
Mac Ronain: a leading warrior of Finn's host in the
Fenian Cycle of tales: *v.* Saul) should scarcely be
numbered among the *síde* as ordinarily conceived;
and Niamh (pron. "Neeave": Oisin's beloved) might
also seem questionably classifiable, though a mythological figure.

"The Everlasting Voices": Originally without the article,
New Review, Jan. 1896; as now since *The Wind . . .* ,
1899; also rptd., 21, 24(1), 25, 33, 50, 54, 57, 58, 63,
65, 73, 75, 79, 80, 88, 98, 99.—Wr. 29 Aug. 1895 (Ellmann, *Iden.*, 287).—Cp. "The Death of Hanrahan,"
E. P. S., 457-58; and "The Golden Age," *idem*, 269.

"The Moods": *Bookman*, Aug. 1893; untitled, *United
Ireland*, 11 Nov. 1893, and *The Celtic Twilight*, Dec.
1893, as also in 15 and 24(5). (*N.B.*: *The Celtic Twi-*

light readings vary textually from that of *United Ireland,* which, except for punctuation, is nevertheless the final text.) Retitled, *The Wind* . . . , 1899, and rptd. 21, 24(1), 25, 33, 50, 54, 57, 58, 63, 65, 75, 79, 80, 98, 99.—Cp. "The Moods," *Ideas of Good and Evil;* "The Death of Hanrahan," *E. P. S.,* 450; § III, *Rosa Alchemica;* § X, "Anima Mundi" (*Essays,* 523-25).—V. Witt, *Explicator,* VI, It. 15.

"The Lover Tells of the Rose in His Heart": Originally "The Rose in My Heart," *National Observer,* 12 Nov. 1892; do., 8; "Aedh Tells . . . ," *The Wind* . . . , 1899; present title since *Poetical Works,* I, 1906; rptd. 24(1), 25, 33, 35, 50, 54, 57, 58, 63, 65, 75, 79, 80, 87, 98, 99. The 8th printing of 99A deletes the hyphen from "re-made." Cp. (*The Land of Heart's Desire*) "And nothing marred or old to do you wrong."

"The Host of the Air": Originally "The Stolen Bride," *Bookman,* Nov. 1893, with this preliminary "Note": "I heard the story on which this ballad is founded from an old woman at Balesodare, Sligo. She repeated me a Gaelic poem on the subject, and then translated it to me. I have always regretted not having taken down her words, and as some amends for not having done so, have made this ballad. Any one who tastes fairy food or drink is glamoured and stolen by the fairies. This is why Bridget sets O'Driscoll to play cards. 'The folk of the air' is a Gaelic name for the fairies." (*N.B.:* Yeats here dated the poem 1 Oct. 1893.) The second printing, in 8, was entitled "The Folk of the Air"; both of the first two printings had an extra stanza between what are now the last two quatrains, making clear that Bridget had died. The present title dates from *The Wind* . . . , 1899. Also rptd., 21, 24(1), 25, 54, 57, 58, 63, 75, 79, 80, 98, 99.—Cp. Yeats's note, *C. P.,*

448; *If I Were* . . . , 60-1; orig. edn. of *The Wind* . . . , 105. The version in 8 is closer than the final one to the original story on which the ballad is based: *v.* "Kidnappers," *E. P. S.*, 227-28.—On the fairies of the early poems and drama, who "have lost their own joys, and not gained ours," *v.* Grierson's art. in the *Dublin Rev.*

M "The Fish": Originally "Bressel the Fisherman," *Cornish Magazine,* Dec. 1898; "Breasal the Fisherman," **The Wind* . . . , 1899; "The Fisherman," *Poetical Works,* I, 1906; do., 24(1), 25, 54, 57, 58, 63, 65, 75; present title since *Coll. Poems* of 1933—probably because of the later "Fisherman" (*C. P.*, 145); later rptd., 80, 98, 99.—Name "Bressel" has presumably no special implication, though *The Wooing of Emer* (the longer of whose two major redactions may be found in *The Book of the Dun Cow*) has "Bresal," a druid of the *síde,* and "Bresel Brec," a king of Leinster.—Miss Witt (87: a bit whimsically?) seems to equate the fish with Maud Gonne.—There is a reference to "Bresal the Fisherman" in the original *Hour-Glass: v. No. Amer. Rev.,* Sept. 1903, p. 446.

"The Unappeasable Host": Originally "A Cradle Song" (and printed as the first of "Two Poems Concerning Peasant Visionaries"), *Savoy,* Apr. 1896; without title, in "The Cradles of Gold," *Senate,* Nov. 1896; as "A Cradle Song," *The Wind* . . . , 1899; do., *21, 24(1), 25, 54, 57, 58, 63, 75; present title, *Selected Poems,* 1929, and 79, 80, 88, 98, 99.—L. 1, "Danaan children": fairy children.

"Into the Twilight": Originally "The Celtic Twilight," *National Observer,* 29 July 1893; present title since *The Celtic Twilight,* Dec. 1893, in which the poem stands as a sort of epilogue; rptd. *11, 15, 21, 24(1),

24(5), 25, 33, 50, 54, 57, 58, 61, 63, 73, 75, 79, 80, 87, 88, 98, 99. Allt (*Hermathena*, No. 64, 100) says this is dated " '30th of June' (presumably 1893)" in MS.— St. 2, "Eire": Ireland, so named after a queen of the ancient *Tuatha Dé Danann.*

"The Song of Wandering Aengus": Originally "A Mad Song," *The Sketch,* 4 Aug. 1897; present title since **The Wind . . . ,* 1899.—Alspach (*Mod. Lang. Notes,* LXI) notes the poem was inserted untitled in the story of "Hanrahan's Vision" for two appearances only (*v. Stories of Red Hanrahan,* 1904, and *McClure's Magazine,* Mar. 1905, where the story was called "Red Hanrahan's Vision").—Also rptd., 21, 24(1), 25, 33, 37, 50, 54, 57, 58, 63, 73, 75, 79, 80, 87, 88, 98, 99.— Wr. 31 Jan. 189(3?) (Ellmann, *Iden.,* 287).—Recalling Yeats's speaking of merrows in his notes to *The Wind . . .* but saying: "The poem was suggested to me by a Greek folk song . . . ," Alspach suggests "The Three Fishes" (in which there are three transformations) of Lucy Garnett's *Greek Folk Poesy* (1896), reviewed by Yeats in the Oct. 1896 *Bookman* (all of which suggests that Ellmann's dating may well be four years too early). But Alspach also points to Samuel Lover's "The White Trout," included by Yeats in *Irish Fairy and Folk Tales* (1888).—Ellmann (*Iden.,* 298) cps. the second line with Symons' "That day a fire was in my blood" (*The Broken Tryst*). Cp. Miss Gurd's gloss (67) from J. Bonwick's *Irish Druids and Old Irish Religion* (London, 1894), 243; on ll. 5-6, she glosses *Lamia,* l. 220; on "hollow lands," William Morris. Some will accept Tindall (*Accent*) on the concluding metaphor, however unimaginative and pedestrian the interpretation; the metaphor itself is echoed in *Baile and Aillinn* (l. 4, p. 398, *C. P.*). (On the *god* Aengus, *v.* the notes, *inf.*, to "Under the Moon.")

"The Song of the Old Mother": *Bookman*, Apr. 1894 (cp. the fairy's lines beginning "From dawn, when you must blow the fire ablaze," *Land of Heart's Desire*, produced 29 Mar. 1894); rptd. in 8 before inclusion in *The Wind . . .* , 1899; also rptd., 21, 24(1), 25, 33, 50, 54, 57, 58, 63, 73, 75, 79, 80, 88, 98, 99.—The *Bookman* printing has this "Note" following the text: "The 'seed of the fire' is the Irish phrase for the little fragment of burning turf and hot ashes which remains in the hearth from the day before."

"The Heart of the Woman": Originally untitled in "Those Who Live in the Storm," *The Speaker*, 21 July 1894; this story, with the poem still untitled, became "The Rose of Shadow": *v.* *The Secret Rose*, 1897 (cp. Reid, 141 ff.). Present title, *The Wind . . .* , 1899; further rptgs: 21, 24(1), 25, 33, 50, 54, 57, 58, 63, 65, 75, 79, 80, 98, 99.—Wr. 1894 (Ellmann, *Iden.*, 287).— L. 7: Cp. "Under a cloudy blossoming of hair," *Land of Heart's Desire* (*P. & C.*, 314). P. E. More (181-82) once counted, with disapproval, twenty-three allusions to women's hair in *The Wind . . .* ! (Jeffares, 102-3, finds "over twenty-three.")

M "The Lover Mourns for the Loss of Love": Originally the second lyric of "Aodh to Dectora/Three Songs," *The Dome*, No. 5 (May 1898); "Aedh Laments the Loss of Love," *The Wind . . .* , 1899; present title since *Poetical Works*, I, 1906; rptd. 24(1), 25, 35, 54, 57, 58, 63, 65, 75, 79, 80, 98, 99.—The "beautiful friend" is Mrs. Olivia Shakespear, Yeats's so-called "Diana Vernon," a cultivated woman who was reputedly his mistress *c* 1896 and with whom he once considered an elopement (*v.* Hone, 131-32); "She" is Maud Gonne. —Cp. Ellmann, 157.

"He Mourns for the Change . . .": Originally "The Desire of Man and of Woman," printed—with a foreword explaining that "the boar without bristles is the ancient Celtic image of the darkness which will at last destroy the world, as it destroys the sun at nightfall in the west"—and dated "Sligo, June 1897" in *The Dome*, No. 2 (June 1897); as "Mongan Laments the Change That Has Come upon Him and His Beloved," *The Wind* . . . , 1899; present title (minus the comma, which appears in the last two printings), *Poetical Works*, I, 1906; rptd. 24(1), 25, 33, 35, 50, 54, 57, 58, 63, 65, 75, 79, 80, 98, 99.—Yeats has a note in *C. P.*, 448-49.—L. 10, "Boar without bristles": On the "porcine representation of darkness," *v.* Rhys, 511 ff.

"He Bids His Beloved Be at Peace": Originally "Two Love Poems/The Shadowy Horses," *Savoy*, Jan. 1896 (MS dated 24 Sept. 1895); as "Michael Robartes Bids . . ." in *The Wind* . . . , 1899; present title since *Poetical Works*, I, 1906; rptd. 24(1), 25, 33, 35, 50, 54, 57, 58, 63, 73, 75, 79, 80, 88, 98, 99.—For "Diana Vernon" (cp. Scott's *Rob Roy*), really Mrs. Olivia Shakespear, cp. Jeffares, 100-1, 103, 324.—L. 3, "The North . . .": In one ancient Celtic tradition, the location of the infernal regions.—Cp. Ellmann's *Iden.*, fn. p. 31, where is recalled this note from *The Wind* . . . : "I follow much Irish and other mythology, and the magical tradition, in associating the North with night and sleep, and the East, the place of sunrise, with hope, and the South, the place of the sun when at its height, with passion and desire, and the West, the place of sunset, with fading and dreaming things."

"He Reproves the Curlew": Originally "Windlestraws/I.

O'Sullivan Rua to the Curlew," *Savoy,* Nov. 1896; as "Hanrahan Reproves . . . ," *The Wind . . . ,* 1899; present title since *Poetical Works,* I, 1906; rptd. 24(1), 25, 33, 35, 50, 54, 57, 58, 63, 65, 73, 75, 79, 80, 88, 98, 99. *N.B.:* The earliest reading differs from the latest only in having "waters" for "water" in l. 2.

"He Remembers Forgotten Beauty": Originally "O'Sullivan Rua to Mary Lavell," *Savoy,* July 1896; as "Michael Robartes Remembers Forgotten Beauty," *The Wind . . . ,* 1899; present title since *Poetical Works,* I, 1906. Rptd. 24(1), 25, 33, 35, 50, 54, 57, 58, 63, 65, *73, 75, 79, 80, 88, 98, 99. (In the original version, the concluding image is that of "seraphs, brooding," "throne on throne," on Beauty's "mysteries.")

"A Poet to His Beloved": Originally second of two poems published in *The Senate,* Mar. 1896, as "O'Sullivan the Red to Mary Lavell." These were reprinted in *United Ireland,* 4 Apr., and again, in a corrected text and under the title "Two Poems by O'Sullivan the Red concerning Mary Lavell," 11 Apr. "A Poet to His Beloved" first appears as a title in *The Wind . . . ,* 1899, where the title of the other poem is "Aedh Tells of the Perfect Beauty." This latter title became "He Tells of the Perfect Beauty" (*q. v.*) in *Poetical Works,* I, 1906. "A Poet to His Beloved" also appears in 21, 24(1), 25, 35, 54, 57, 58, 63, 65, 75, 79, 80, 98, 99.— Wr. 1895 (Ellmann, *Iden.,* 287).

"He Gives His Beloved Certain Rhymes": Originally untitled in the story "The Binding of the Hair," *Savoy,* Jan. 1896, and *The Secret Rose,* 1897; as "Aedh Gives His Beloved Certain Rhymes," *The Wind . . . ,* 1899; present title since *Poetical Works,* I, 1906. Rptd. 24(1), 25, 33, 35, 50, 54, 57, 58, 63, 65, 75, 79, 80, 98, 99. (In the *Savoy* printing, the poem is set in single

quotation marks.)—In his "Commentary," *K. G. C. T.*,
19-20, Yeats recalls that in the prose tale (included
only in pre-1908 issues of *The Secret Rose*) "A certain
man swears to sing the praise of a certain woman, his
head is cut off and the head sings. . . . 'He Gives
His Beloved Certain Rhymes' was the song of the
head."—Hone (131) claims Yeats's authority for saying the poem was written for "Diana Vernon" (i.e.,
Mrs. Olivia Shakespear, on whom *v*. Yeats's 8 Oct.
1938 letter to Dorothy Wellesley).—According to Ellmann (*Iden.*, 287), wr. "before Aug. 1895."—Sharply
attacked by Savage, 67-91; cp., however, Æ, "The
Poet of Shadows," *Some Irish Essays*, 39.

"To His Heart, Bidding It Have No Fear": Originally
"Windlestraws/II. Out of the Old Days," *Savoy*, Nov.
1896; as "To My Heart . . . ," *The Wind* . . . , 1899;
do., 21, 24(1), 25, 33, 50; present title since **Later
Poems*, 1922; do., 57, 58, 63, 65, 73, 75, 79, 80, 88, 98,
99.—V. Ellmann, 142-44, for successive drafts showing evolution from a MS of 1894; and cp. Witt, *Explicator*, IX.—The italicized lines were used by Yeats
to head § II of his "Poetry and Tradition." The phrase
"the flame and the flood" comes from the initiation
ritual, Order of the Golden Dawn: cp. Moore, 136.

"The Cap and Bells": Originally "Cap and Bell," *National
Observer*, 17 Mar. 1894; present title since *Second
Book of the Rhymers' Club*, 1894. Rptd. *11, 21,
24(1), 25, 33, 50, 54, 57, 58, 63, 73, 75, 79, 80, 88, 98,
99.—Yeats has a note, *C. P.*, 449; he used to say of
this poem (Hone, 159) that "it was 'the way to win
a lady,' whereas . . . 'Embroidered Cloths' of the same
period was the way to lose one."—Wr. 1893 (Ellmann,
Iden., 287; reject Hone on date of composition: Saul,
LTLS, 31 Mar. 1950; 208).—Presumably there are

some who would not be nauseated by Seiden's handling of this charming lyric in *Accent*, where the *Oisin* is, with consonant brilliance, also considered.—Yeats's title is the same with that of an unfinished Keats narrative (courtesy Susan Birmingham).

"The Valley of the Black Pig": Originally printed as the second of "Two Poems Concerning Peasant Visionaries" in the *Savoy*, Apr. 1896, with this note following the title: "The Irish peasantry have for generations comforted themselves, in their misfortunes, with visions of a great battle, to be fought in a mysterious valley called, 'The Valley of the Black Pig,' and to break at last the power of their enemies. A few years ago, in the barony of Lisadell, in county Sligo, an old man would fall entranced upon the ground from time to time, and rave out a description of the battle; and I have myself heard said that the girths shall rot from the bellies of the horses, because of the few men that shall come alive out of the valley." Present title since *The Wind . . .* , 1899. Rptd. 21, 24(1), 25, 33, 50, 54, 57, 58, 63, 75, 79, 80, 98, 99. Yeats has notes, pp. 96-97, orig. ed., *The Wind . . .* , and *C. P.*, 449-50. Cp. also his "Rosa Alchemica," *E. P. S.*, 483; "War," *idem*, 276-77; and *Auto.*, 415, 445.—When the Milesian invaders came to Ireland, the *Tuatha Dé Danann*, it is said, cast a spell that made the island look like a huge pig: cp. Lady Gregory, *G. F. M.*, 65.

"The Lover Asks Forgiveness Because of His Many Moods": Originally "The Twilight of Forgiveness," *Saturday Rev.*, 2 Nov. 1895; as "Michael Robartes Asks . . . ," *The Wind . . .* , 1899; present title since *Poetical Works*, I, 1906. Also rptd. 24(1), 25, 33, 35, 50, 54, 57, 58, 63, 75, 79, 80, 98, 99.—On Niamh, *v*.

"The Hosting of the Sidhe" and ". . . Oisin."—Wr. 23 Aug. 1895 (Ellmann, *Iden.*, 287).

"He Tells of a Valley Full of Lovers": Originally "The Valley of Lovers," *Saturday Rev.*, 9 Jan. 1897; "Aedh Tells . . . ," *The Wind . . .* , 1899 (in which the italicized portions are set in quotation marks); present title since *Poetical Works*, I, 1906. Also rptd. 24(1), 25, 35, 54, 57, 58, 63, 75, 79, 80, 98, 99.

"He Tells of the Perfect Beauty": *V.* "A Poet to His Beloved," *sup.* The poem assumes, except for minor punctuation, final form in 11; it was rptd. in 21, 24(1), 25, 33, 35, 50, 54, 57, 58, 63, 65, 75, 79, 80, 98, 99. Ellmann (155) prints an early MS version dated 1 Sept. 1891 and labeled "Dedication of 'John Sherman and Dhoya' "; in *Iden.* (288) he dates the present version Dec. 1895.

"He Hears the Cry of the Sedge": Originally the first of "Aodh to Dectora/Three Songs," *Dome*, No. 5 (May 1898); as "Aedh Hears . . . ," *The Wind . . .* , 1899; present title since *Poetical Works*, I, 1906. Rptd. 24(1), 25, 33, 50, 54, 57, 58, 63, 65, 75, 79, 80, 98, 99.—*V.* Notes, 230-32, 24(1).—Jeffares (118) fancies a debt to *La Belle Dame sans Merci* and quotes from an unpublished MS: "It was a time of great personal strain and sorrow—since my mistress had left me no other woman had come into my life and for nearly seven years none did. I was tortured with sexual desire and disappointed love. Often as I walked in the woods at Coole it would have been a relief to have screamed aloud."—Cp. Deutsch, 201-2.—L. 7 relates to the phraseology of the "Golden Dawn" initiation ceremony (cp. Moore, 139).

"He Thinks of Those Who Have Spoken Evil of His Beloved": Originally the third of "Aodh to Dectora/

Three Songs," *Dome, No. 5 (May 1898)—and set
to music by Thomas F. Dunhill as "Aodh to Dectora,"
Dome, N.S., Vol. V (Jan. 1900). As "Aedh Thinks
. . . ," The Wind . . . , 1899; present title since Poetical
Works, I, 1906. Rptd. 24(1), 25, 54, 57, 58, 63, 75, 79,
80, 98, 99. L. 5: The first of the Musicians' closing
songs in At the Hawk's Well has "a mouthful of sweet
air"—an exact repetition of a phrase Ellmann (Iden.,
325) recalls from Yeats's "Tales from the Twilight"
(Scots Observer, 1 Mar. 1890); and in John Sherman
(1891) an old woman asks, "For what have we in this
life but a mouthful of air?", while the concluding song
of 85 has "O, what is life but a mouthful of air?"

"The Blessed": The Yellow Book, XIII (Apr. 1897); rptd.
*11, 21, 24(1), 25, 54, 57, 58, 63, 75, 79, 80, 98, 99.—
On Cumhal (called "Cumhal the king" in the Y. B.
printing) and Dathi, cp. "The Crucifixion of the Outcast," E. P. S., 321 ff., whence it appears Yeats had
Dathi, son of Fiachraidh, in mind (cp. reference to
death), however inappropriate seem the reading here
of the conqueror's character: v. Keating, II, 413.
("Cumhal" could on no rational grounds be here
equated with the god Camulus or with Finn's father,
Cumall, whose name is the Irish equivalent of the
god's: cp. Rhys, 40, 178.)—On ll. 3-4, st. 8, Miss Gurd
(90-91) glosses Renan (Poetry of the Celtic Races,
9-10) and tales concerning (1) Christ and Peter and
(2) the Friars of Urlaur in Hyde's Religious Songs of
Connaught. In st. 9, Wrenn (5) sees "Blake's doctrine
of the eternal holiness of Passion," with the Rose, in
Yeats's own explanatory note, symbolizing "the highest spiritual ideal."

"The Secret Rose": Originally "O'Sullivan Rua To The
Secret Rose," Savoy, Sept. 1896; next in The Secret

Rose, 1897, as "To the Secret Rose"; do., 24(7), 34, 61, 67; present title, *The Wind . . .* , 1899. Other rptgs: 21, 24(1), 25, 54, 57, 58, 63, 75, 79, 80, 98, 99.— Yeats has an important clarifying note, *C. P.*, 450-51. —Cp. Forgael, in the "Acting Version" of *The Shadowy Waters* (*P. P. V.*, 169): "The red rose where the two . . . ," etc.—Mrs. Yeats (Henn, 239) thinks the image in ll. 7 ff. may owe to Botticelli's "Adoration of the Magi."—L. 9: Read *king* for misprint *kings* in pre-eighth printings of 99A.—L. 15 is more histrionic than accurate in implication if one remembers the ancient Ulster Cycle's amusing *Sickbed of Cuchulainn:* Emer retains her Cuchulainn despite the efforts of Fand, wife of the sea-god Manannan Mac Lir.

"Maid Quiet": Twice-rewritten version, first appearing in *Coll. Works*, Vol. I, 1908, of what was originally an untitled poem in "The Twisting of the Rope," *National Observer*, 24 Dec. 1892, and 10 (*The Secret Rose*). It was reworked as "O'Sullivan the Red upon His Wanderings" in *The New Review*, Aug. 1897. The title became "Hanrahan Laments Because of His Wanderings" in *The Wind . . .* , 1899; "The Lover Mourns Because of His Wanderings" in *Poetical Works*, I, 1906, after which the poem underwent final revision. Rptgs after 24(1): 25, 54, 57, 58, 63, 75, 79, 80, 98, 99.—V. Alspach, *Mod. Lang. Notes*, LXV.

"The Travail of Passion": Originally "Two Love Poems/ The Travail of Passion," *Savoy*, Jan. 1896; rptd. 11, 21, 24(1), 25, 33, 35, 50, *54, 57, 58, 63, 75, 79, 80, 98, 99.—Jeffares (102), differing from Hone (131), names this and "He Bids His Beloved Be at Peace" as written for "Diana Vernon."

"The Lover Pleads with His Friend for Old Friends": Originally "Song," *Saturday Rev.*, 24 July 1897; pres-

ent title since *The Wind . . . , 1899. Rptd. 21, 24(1),
25, 33, 35, 50, 54, 57, 58, 63, 73, 75, 79, 80, 88, 98, 99.

"The Lover Speaks to the Hearers of His Songs in Coming Days": Originally untitled in "The Vision of
O'Sullivan the Red," New Review, Apr. 1896, which
story became "The Vision of Hanrahan the Red" in
The Secret Rose, 1897. Title "Hanrahan Speaks to
the Lovers of His Songs in Coming Days" given the
poem for The Wind . . . , 1899; became "A Lover
Speaks to the Hearers of . . . ," Poetical Works, I,
1906; do., 24(1), 25, *54, 57, 58, 63, 75; present title,
Coll. Poems, 1933, and 80, 98, 99.—Wr. Nov. 1895
(Ellmann, Iden., 288—and cp. 306-07).

"The Poet Pleads with the Elemental Powers": This
much-revised poem developed from "A Mystical
Prayer to the Masters of the Elements, Michael,
Gabriel, and Raphael," Bookman, Oct. 1892, which
appears as "A Mystical Prayer . . . , Finvarra, Feacra,
and Caolte" in The Second Book of the Rhymers'
Club, 1894. Reworked, it became "Aodh Pleads . . . ,"
*Dome, N.S., Vol. I (Oct.–Dec. 1898); "Aodh" be-
came "Aedh," The Wind . . . , 1899, and the present
title appeared in Poetical Works, I, 1906. Rptd. 24(1),
25, 54, 57, 58, 63, 75, 79, 80, 98, 99.—The Dome printing was prefaced by this note: "The Seven Lights are
the seven stars of the Great Bear, and the Dragon is
the constellation of the Dragon, and these, in certain
old mythologies, encircle the Tree of Life, on which
is here imagined the Rose of the Ideal Beauty growing before it was cast into the world. Three or four
lines are taken from a poem of the author's on the
same subject in 'The Second Book of the Rhymers'
Club.'"—Though the earliest version is a poorer
poem, it has clearer internal logic.—V. Notes, pp.

230-32, 24(1); cp. Henn, 240.—Tindall (255) labels the "Powers" "Mme Blavatsky's elemental spirits"; the "Seven Lights" (l. 3), "the seven planets of Theosophy."—With particular reference to st. 2, cp. "The Heart of the Spring," *E. P. S.,* 355-56.—With the dragon, Ellmann (*Iden.,* 313) cps. certain other Yeatsian serpents.

"He Wishes His Beloved Were Dead": Originally "Aodh to Dectora," *The Sketch,* 9 Feb. 1898; as "Aedh Wishes . . . ," *The Wind . . . ,* 1899; as now, *Poetical Works,* I, 1906. Rptd. 24(1), 25, 33, 35, 50, 54, 57, 58, 63, 75, 79, 80, 98, 99.

"He Wishes for the Cloths of Heaven": Originally "Aedh Wishes . . . ," *The Wind . . . ,* 1899; present title since *Poetical Works,* I, 1906. Rptd. 24(1), 25, 33, 35, 50, 54, 57, 58, 63, 65, 73, 75, 79, 80, 87, 88, 98, 99.—V. Ellmann (155) for an early MS version dated 5 July 1891 and called "Your Pathway."—Cp. "The Cap and Bells," *sup.;* Joseph Conrad had a particular fondness for this lyric.—On the "cloths" figure, Miss Gurd (95-6) cps. Porphyry and, less convincingly, *The Witch of Atlas.*

"He Thinks of His Past Greatness . . .": Originally "Song of Mongan," *Dome,* N.S., Vol. I (Oct.–Dec. 1898); as "Mongan Thinks of His Past Greatness," *The Wind . . . ,* 1899; present title since *Poetical Works,* I, 1906. Rptd. 24(1), 25, 54, 57, 58, 63, 75, *79, 80, 98, 99.— The *Dome* printing has a prefatory note identifying Mongan (cp. James Stephens' *Irish Fairy Tales*) as a wizard-king in ancient Celtic verse "who remembers his passed lives," the "Country of the Young" as the Celtic "Country of the gods and of the happy dead," and the "hazel-tree" (l. 3) as the "Irish tree of Life or of Knowledge, and . . . doubtless . . . the tree

of the heavens." It also identifies the Gaelic "Crooked
Plough" as the "Plough" [the Dipper, or the full constellation of *Ursa Major*], the "Pilot" as the Pole Star.
("Pilot Star," l. 4, is "Pole Star" in the *Dome* printing.)—V. Notes, pp. 230-32, 24(1).—*N.B.*: The original form of the two concluding lines may seem preferable to many readers:

> Although the rushes and the fowl of the air
> Cry of his love with their pitiful cries.

"The Fiddler of Dooney": *Bookman,* Dec. 1892; *Second
Book of the Rhymers' Club,* 1894; in the original *The
Wind . . . ,* 1899, printed after "The Song of the Old
Mother." Rptd. 21, 24(1), 25, 33, 50, 54, 57, 58, 63,
65, 73, 75, 79, 80, 87, 88, 98, 99. (Originally, the place-
name in l. 4 was "Rosnaree" and brother and cousin
were transposed; the final assignments and order of
the priests were established in 11, but in seven printings the substituted place-name is spelled "Mohara-
buiee.")—Wr. Nov. 1892 (Ellmann, *Iden.*, 288).—
Henn (288) glosses *A Winter's Tale:* "When you do
dance, I wish you/A wave o' the sea . . ." (Florizel
to Perdita, IV, iv); cp. "The Heart of the Spring,"
E. P. S., 354, and "Dust Hath Closed Helen's Eye,"
idem, 168. *The Countess Cathleen* has (Sc. I) "Wandering and singing like a wave of the sea."

In the Seven Woods

"In the Seven Woods": Printings: *16, 17, 20, 21, 24(1),
25, 54, 57, 58, 63, 65, 75, 79, 80, 98, 99.—Dated Aug.
1902 in *C. P.;* dedicated to Florence Farr in *Poems
1899–1905.*—L. 1, "Seven Woods": A part of Coole,
then Lady Gregory's estate.—L. 6, "Tara": Seat of the
legendary High Kings of Ireland; in Meath (ancient

Mide).—Ll. 6-8: Jeffares (143) calls these lines (which Hone, 238, recalls Miss Horniman, the English benefactor of the Abbey Theatre, disliked) "a veiled and rude allusion to the coronation of Edward VII and Alexandra."—Ll. 10-11: Cp. third st. from the end of "Baile and Aillinn."—L. 12, "Great Archer": Sagittarius.—L. 14: "Pairc-na-lee": one of the Seven Woods: *v.* dedicatory verses to "The Shadowy Waters."

ʍ "The Arrow": Printings: 16, 17, 20, 21, 24(1), 25, *54, 57, 58, 63, 65, 75, 79, 80, 98, 99.—Jeffares (127) dates composition 1901 and glosses the preface to Blake's *Milton* as possibly appropriate; later (314 n. 12) he remarks a parallel description of Maud Gonne in the *Autobiographies* (ed. London, 1926; p. 152).

"The Folly of Being Comforted": *The Speaker*, 11 Jan. 1902; rptd. 16, 17, 20, 21, 24(1), 25, 33, 35, 50, 54, 57, 58, 63, *73, 75, 79, 80, 88, 98, 99.—L. 12: Cp. Decima, in *The Player Queen*: ". . . all summer in a look. . . ." The eighth printing of 99A corrects "seems" (l. 5) to "seem."

"Old Memory": Originally in *Wayfarer's Love* (ed. Duchess of Sutherland), London, 1904; rptd. *20, 21, 24(1), 25, 33, 35, 50, 54, 57, 58, 63, 75, 79, 80, 98, 99. V. note on *In the Seven Woods* in Pt. I, *sup.*—Ellmann (*Iden.*, 288) dates this "Nov. or Dec. 1903"; however, Yeats, in a 21 Jan. 1904 letter to Lady Gregory (Wade, *Letters,* 427), says it was written "in a railway train coming from Canada," a circumstance suggesting composition between 18 and 25 Dec. 1903, and probably close to the latter date, when he was again back in New York. (Cp. Wade, *idem,* 416-17.)

"Never Give All the Heart": *McClure's Magazine*, Dec. 1905; rptd. *20, 21, 24(1), 25, 33, 50, 54, 57, 58, 63, 75, 79, 80, 98, 99. V. *In the Seven Woods*, Pt. I, *sup.*—

Jeffares (127) relates this to Blake's "Love's Secret" ("Never seek to tell thy love").

"The Withering of the Boughs": Originally "Echtge of Streams," *The Speaker,* 25 Aug. 1900; present title since *In the Seven Woods,* 1903; rptd. 17, *20, 21, 24(1), 25, 33, 50, 54, 57, 58, 63, 73, 75, 79, 80, 88, 98, 99.—The "Echtge" in this lyric (a favorite of John Masefield's) is Slieve Aughty, of medieval lyric association (*v.* Jackson, 40, n. 2, iii); cp. Yeats's *Red Hanrahan* and Bk. Nine, Ch. I, of Lady Gregory's *G. F. M.* On the folk belief memorialized in the refrain, cp. *E. P. S.,* 283, and *If I Were . . . ,* 33. Ll. 1 and 2, st. 3, remind one of the silver-chained birds of the *Tuatha Dé Danann* (Best, 110 and fn. 2; Rhys, 174); in a footnote to "Baile and Aillinn" as printed in the *Monthly Review,* July 1902, Yeats remarks that when the lovers of that poem "take the shape of swans linked with a golden chain, they take the shape that other enchanted lovers took before them in the old stories."

M "Adam's Curse": *Monthly Rev.,* Dec. 1902, and *The Gael* (N. Y.), Feb. 1903; rptd. 16, 17, 20, 21, 24(1), 25, 33, 35, 50, *54, 57, 58, 63, 75, 79, 80, 98, 99.—Wr. "before Nov. 20, 1902" (Ellmann, *Iden.,* 288).—Cp. *Essays,* 334; *Auto.,* 248-49, 448; notes to "The Phases of the Moon," *inf.;* and, on the two opening paragraphs of the poem, "1904/The Dramatic Movement," *P. & C.,* 82.—Hone, who fancies (197) an echo of Baudelaire's *Recueillement* in the fifth segment, recalls (164-65) Maud Gonne's account of the inception of this poem in a remark of her sister's to the effect that "it was hard work being beautiful" (MacBride, 328).— Stephen Spender's interpretation of this poem (*Criterion*) may sensibly be rejected.—Perhaps the final line connotes Shelley's "weary moon." *N.B.:* Many will prefer, as more musical, the book versions of this poem prior to 54.—The 8th printing of 99A removes the improper break between ll. 6 and 7 and replaces the commas with colons in ll. 4, 18, and 21.

M "Red Hanrahan's Song about Ireland": Originally an untitled song in "Kathleen-ny-Hoolihan," *National Observer*, 4 Aug. 1894; reworked, still untitled, when the story became "Kathleen the Daughter of Hoolihan and Hanrahan the Red," *The Secret Rose*, 1897; remained untitled when printed alone in *A Broad Sheet*, No. 16 (Apr. 1903); entitled "The Song of Red Hanrahan" in *In the Seven Woods*, 1903, but again untitled in *Stories of Red Hanrahan*, 1904, and subsequent reprints [*i.e.*, in 24(5), 34, 61, 67]; as "The Song . . . ," 20; given present title, *Poetical Works*, I, 1906; rptd. 24(1), 25, 33, 50, 54, 57, 58, 63, 73, 75, 79, 80, 88, 98, 99.—Cp. Yeats's *Cathleen Ni Houlihan* and *E. P. S.*, 424 ff.—Jeffares (138) calls *this* Maud Gonne's favorite (but *v.* "The Two Trees," *sup.*) and says (138-39): "The theme was probably suggested by James Clarence Mangan's 'Kathleen Ny-Houlihan, a Jacobite relic translated from the Irish of William Heffernan, called William Dall, or blind William.'" Jeffares also remarks (315 fn. 31) that Mangan was included in H. H. Sparling's *Irish Minstrelsy*.—L. 2, "the left hand": "the unlucky hand and . . . side according to Irish tradition" (Gurd, 34).—Maeve (*Medb*), supposedly buried on Knocknarea, Sligo, is the wild queen of Connacht (and in popular tradition a queen of the *síde*) counted responsible for the war with Ulster memorialized in the great *Táin Bó Cuálnge* ("Cattle-Raid of Cooley"); *v.* notes on *Wanderings of Oisin*, *inf*. On "Clooth-na-Bare," *v.* "The Hosting of the Sidhe," *sup.*—The "clinging air" of st. 3 is, of course, a reference to the characteristic moistness of the Irish atmosphere. (Cp. Bjersby, 61.)

"The Old Men Admiring Themselves in the Water": *Pall Mall Magazine (where the lines now in quotation marks were in italics), Jan. 1903, and The Gael (N. Y.), Sept. 1903; rptd. 16, 17, 20, 21, 24(1), 25, 33, 50, 54, 57, 58, 63, 65, 73, 75, 79, 80, 88, 98, 99.— Wr. "before Nov. 20, 1902" (Ellmann, Iden., 288).— Ll. 5-6: The Old Man in At the Hawk's Well is "doubled up" like "The old thorn-trees."

"Under the Moon": The Speaker, 15 June 1901; rptd. 16, 17, 20, 21, 24(1), 25, 33, 35, 50, *54, 57, 58, 63, 75, 79, 80, 98, 99.—"Brycelinde" (l. 1): the forest of Brécéliande, Broceliande, or Brécilien (cp. E. E. T. S. Merlin), Brittany, where Viviane enchanted Merlin (cp. Chrétien de Troyes's Yvain); "Avalon" (l. 2) is Arthur's final bourne; "Joyous Isle" (idem) may be found in the "Agravain" portion of the Prose Vulgate Lancelot: Yeats's reference implies a confusion of the story of Lancelot and Pelles' daughter; "Uladh" (l. 4) is modern Ulster; "Land-under-Wave" (l. 6—Ir. Tir-fa-tonn) labels one of the old Irish conceptions of the Otherworld; "Land-of-the-Tower" (l. 8) recalls Yeats's references to Aengus' "tower of glass" (e.g., in "The Harp of Aengus") in Faery. Of the characters referred to, Lancelot will be familiar as the Arthurian knight; Naoise, nephew of Concobar, a king of Uladh in pre-Christian tradition, was the lover of the tragic Deirdre and carried her away to Alba (Scotland); Aengus is the ancient Celtic god of love and beauty, a son of the Dagda Mor, or "Great God": v. notes on "The Shadowy Waters," inf.; Branwen may be located in The Mabinogion as "Branwen, Daughter of Llyr": cp. Rhys, 94-96; Guinevere was Arthur's queen;

Niamh is Oisin's lover in medieval Irish tradition: *v. Wanderings of Oisin, inf.;* "Laban" (though there is a druidess by that name in the Yeats-Moore *Diarmuid and Grania,* and Keating has a druid named "Labhan Draoi") is pretty obviously *Liban,* sister of Manannan Mac Lir's wife Fand, changed to an otter by her magic well: cp. Welsh *Llivon* and *v.* Rhys, 463, and for the story of "Liban the Mermaid," Joyce, *O. C. R.,* 94 ff.— Saul may be consulted, *passim,* on various figures out of Irish story. The "Wood-of-Wonders" (l. 9) and the "wood-woman" (l. 13) have to date escaped identification.

"The Ragged Wood": Originally untitled in "The Twisting of the Rope," *Stories of Red Hanrahan,* 1904; the tale itself was earlier in *The National Observer,* 24 Dec. 1892, and appears as "The Twisting of the Rope and Hanrahan the Red" in *The Secret Rose,* 1897. The lyric found insertion in the present group, under the title "The Hollow Wood," in Vol. I of Bullen's 1908 coll. ed., and was next printed in 25. The present title first appears in 33. Rptgs: *54, 57, 58, 63, 73, 75, 79, 80, 88, 98, 99.

"O Do Not Love Too Long": Without "O" in title, *The Acorn,* Oct. 1905; as now, in 24(1), 25, 54, 57, 58, 63, 75, 79, 80, 98, 99.—Wr. "before Feb. 23, 1905" (Ellmann, *Iden.,* 288).—V. notes on *In the Seven Woods,* Pt. I, *sup.*—The atrocious grammar of the second st. of this triviality is inexplicable.

"The Players Ask for a Blessing on the Psalteries and on Themselves": Without second "on," *16, 17, 20, 21; with second "on" inserted, 24(1), 25, 54, 57, 58, 63, 75, 79, 80, 98, 99.—In a 3 June 1902 letter to Dolmetsch, Yeats says he is working on this, which he calls "Prayer to the Seven Archangels to bless the

Seven Notes," and which is to employ *two* voices only.
—The psaltery was an Arnold Dolmetsch musical de-
vice for the Yeats-Florence Farr experiments: cp.
"Speaking to the Psaltery," *Ideas of Good and Evil.*—
L. 14: Though superficially the Trinity is referred to,
Yeats was making vague reference only; as Allt says
(*Sewanee Rev.*, LX, 631): ". . . in fact the poet has
merely deprived a traditional term of its meaning."

"The Happy Townland": *The Weekly Critical Review*
(Paris), 4 June 1903; as "The Rider from the North"
(and ascribed to "The Country of the Young," a play
extant only in rough typescript) in *In the Seven
Woods,* 1903; original title restored in *Poems, 1899–
1905,* 1906, where (except for italics and minor punctuation) the poem assumes essentially final form.
Rptd. 21, 24(1), 25, 33, 50, 54, 57, 58, 63, 73, 75, 79,
80, 88, 98, 99. [Cp. untitled excerpts in "The Twisting
of the Rope" and "Hanrahan's Vision": 24(5), 34, 61,
67.]—Ll. 7-8: cp. Midir's song to Etain (*v.* refs.,
"The Two Kings," *inf.*) to win her back to the "Great
Land" of the Immortals: "Warm streams flow through
the land, the choicest mead and wine" (Best, 180).—
Krans (106) perhaps rightly complains of "what
seems like wanton obscurity" in the fifth stanza;
nevertheless, cp. Miss Gurd, who (83) points anent
"Gabriel" to Bertrand's *Le Religion des Gaulios,* with
its "figures with human heads and fish tails," and who
(82) speaks of "an old horn/Of hammered silver" in
the Dublin Art Museum.—The poem is most charm-
ingly discussed by Bowra (190), who finds a folklore
source "in the Irish notion that certain men are 'away,'
entirely absorbed in the search for an Earthly Paradise
which is hidden behind the appearances of the visible
world." (Thus "The Happy Townland" is, "naturally,"

" 'the world's bane.' ")—Col. Alspach has queried to me a possible association of this lyric with *The Land of Cockaygne*. V. H. Adams. In Act II of *The Unicorn from the Stars*, Martin calls Paradise "that happy townland."

From *The Green Helmet and Other Poems: V.* Note on this in Pt. I, *sup.*

"His Dream": Originally "A Dream," *Nation* (London), 11 July 1908; present title, 1910 *Green Helmet*; rptd. 27, 31, 33, 35, 40, 50, *54, 57, 58, 63, 75, 79, 80, 98, 99. Dated 3 July, The Seven Woods, in *Nation*, where it has the following prefatory note: "A few days ago I dreamed that I was steering a very gay and elaborate ship upon some narrow water with many people upon its banks, and that there was a figure upon a bed in the middle of the ship. The people were pointing to the figure and questioning, and in my dream I sang verses which faded as I awoke, all but this fragmentary thought, 'We call it, it has such dignity of limb, by the sweet name of Death.' I have made my poem out of my dream and the sentiment of my dream, and can almost say, as Blake did, 'The Authors are in Eternity.' "—This note would seem to invalidate much of the interpretive comment of Daiches (161), Henn, and, most emphatically, Ransom (*South. Rev.*). It is significant that the ninth line originally read: "And fishes, bubbling to the brim." —V. sect. note, I, *sup.*

M "A Woman Homer Sung": 26, 27, *31, 33, 35, 37, 40, 50, 54, 57, 58, 63, 65, 75, 79, 80, 98, 99.—Wr. "April 5-15, 1910" (Ellmann, *Iden.*, 288).—Concerns Maud Gonne. —V. sect. note, I, *sup.*

M "Words": Originally "The Consolation" in 26; do., 27, *31, 35, 40, 54, 57, 58, 63, 75; present title since *Coll.*

Poems, 1933; rptd. 80, 98, 99.—Jeffares (141) says the poem follows this entry in Yeats's diary for 22 Jan. 1909: "To-day the thought came to me that P. I. A. L. (Maud Gonne) never really understands my plans or notions or ideas. Then came the thought—what matter?—how much of the best that I have done and still do is but the attempt to explain myself to her? If she understood I should lack a reason for writing. . . ."—Hone (223-24) recalls that Miss Gonne was constantly reproaching Yeats for not making his art into nationalistic propaganda.—"That," in st. 4, means, of course, "If."—*V.* sect. note, I, *sup.* (*N.B.:* The poem were better punctuated with a period at the end of the third stanza, as in its third, fourth, and fifth printings.)

ℳ "No Second Troy": *26, 27, 31, 33, 35, 40, 50, 54, 57, 58, 63, 65, 75, 79, 80, 98, 99.—Hone (241) says this begins the journal "started after a visit to Maud Gonne in Paris in December 1908."—*V.* sect. note, I, *sup.*

ℳ "Reconciliation": 26, 27, *31, 33, 35, 40, 50, 54, 57, 58, 63, 75, 79, 80, 98, 99.—Hone (243) notes that an earlier version of the opening five lines is recorded in Yeats's journal for 26 Feb. 1909 as composed "about six months ago."—Concerns Maud Gonne.—*V.* sect. note, I, *sup.*

ℳ "King and No King": 26, 27, *31, 33, 35, 40, 50, 54, 57, 58, 63, 75, 79, 80, 98, 99.—Dume (220) locates the title in Beaumont and Fletcher; Ellmann (*Iden.,* 252) explains the opening two lines by reference to Arbaces in these authors' *King and No King.*—L. 11 implies a reference to the fact that Maud Gonne had become a convert to Roman Catholicism.—Wr. 7 Dec. 1909 (Ellmann, *idem,* 288).—*V.* sect. note, I, *sup.*

ℳ "Peace": 26, 27, 31, 35, *40, 54, 57, 58, 63, 75, 79, 80, 98,

99.—Hone (252) says this and the next lyric were written during Yeats's May 1910 visit to Maud Gonne's Normandy house, "Les Mouettes," "above the sea-shore at Colville, near Calvados."—V. sect. note, I, *sup.*

M "Against Unworthy Praise": 26, 27, *31, 33, 35, 37, 40, 50, 54, 57, 58, 63, 75, 79, 80, 98, 99.—Wr. 11 May 1910 (Ellmann, *Iden.*, 288).—Jeffares (140-41) connects lines 15-18 with the hissing of Maud Gonne MacBride at the Abbey by her husband's partisans following her undertaking a separation.—There is properly a break between ll. 10 and 11.—V. sect. note, I, *sup.*

"The Fascination of What's Difficult": 26, 27, 31, 40, *54, 57, 58, 63, 75, 79, 80, 98, 99.—Prose draft, Sept. 1909 diary; complete diary version, Mar. 1910.—Cp. *Auto.*, 435-36, recording Yeats's struggle toward that "Unity of Being" impossible "without a Unity of Culture in class or people."—Jeffares (147-48) gives history and analysis, remarking Sturge Moore's use of the Pegasus image in *Art and Life* and finding a possible "source for a double borrowing" in Heine.—In 26 and 27, this poem is grouped under "Momentary Thoughts."

"A Drinking Song": *26, 27, 31, 37, 40, 54, 57, 58, 63, 75, 79, 80, 98, 99.—Wr. 17 Feb. 1910 (Ellmann, *Iden.*, 288).—In mood, pathos, and perfection of statement, suggestive of Storm's "Heute, nur heute . . ." (*Immensee*).—In 26 and 27, among "Momentary Thoughts."

"The Coming of Wisdom with Time": As "Youth and Age," *McClure's Magazine,* Dec. 1910; present title, 1910 *Green Helmet;* rptd. 27, 31, 40, 54, 57, 58, 63, 75, 79, 80, 98, 99.—Wr. Mar. 1909 (Ellmann, *Iden.*, 288). —In 26 and 27, among "Momentary Thoughts."

"On Hearing That the Students of Our New University

Have Joined the Agitation against Immoral Literature": Originally "On Hearing . . . Joined The Ancient
Order of Hibernians And The Agitation . . . ," 1912
Green Helmet; do., 40; present title, *Later Poems,*
1922; rptd. 57, 58, 63, 75, *79, 80, 98, 99.—Wr. 3 Apr.
1912 (Ellmann, *Iden.,* 288).

"To a Poet, Who Would Have Me Praise Certain Bad
Poets, Imitators of His and Mine": Originally, ". . .
and of Mine," 1910 *Green Helmet;* present title, 27;
rptd. 31, 40, *54, 57, 58, 63, 75, 79, 80, 98, 99.—Wr.
Apr. 1909 (Ellmann, *Iden.,* 288).—In 26 and 27,
among "Momentary Thoughts."—Jeffares (144) identifies the poet addressed as, naturally, George Russell,
and the "imitators" as some of the fledglings of *New
Songs.*—Cp. Arnold Bax, 98.

м "The Mask": Originally "A Lyric from an Unpublished
Play," *1910 *Green Helmet;* do., 27 and 31; present
title since the Cuala *A Selection from the Love Poetry
of William Butler Yeats,* 1913; also rptd. 37, 40, 50,
54 (cp. 54a, 54b, 100), 57, 58, 63, 73, 75, 79, 80, 88,
98, 99.—Wr. Aug. 1910 for *The Player Queen* (*q. v.,*
P. P. V., 398): cp. Ellmann, 171-72.—For an astrolog-
ical explanation of l. 1, *v.* Moore, 215-17.—Henn, im-
plying this is a Yeats-Maud Gonne dialogue, recalls
(56 fn. 1) that "Beatrice in the *Purgatorio* has emer-
ald eyes (xxxi)."—In 26 and 27, among "Momentary
Thoughts."

"Upon a House Shaken by the Land Agitation": Originally, "To a Certain Country House in Time of
Change," *McClure's Magazine,* Dec. 1910; as "Upon
a Threatened House" in 1910 *Green Helmet;* do., 27;
present title since *1912 *Green Helmet;* also rptd. 40,
54, 57, 58, 63, 75, 79, 80, 98, 99.—Wr. 7 Aug. 1909
(Ellmann, *Iden.,* 288).—The "house" is Lady Greg-

ory's, at Coole; *v. Auto.* (ed. N.Y., 1938), 332 ff.—
Hone (242) quotes the following prose draft from
Yeats's journal: "How should the world gain, if this
house failed, even though a hundred little houses were
the better for it; for here power has given poetry or
legend, giving energy, precision, and it gave to a far
people beneficial rule, and still under its roof the
living intellect is sweetened by old memories of its
descent from far off. How should the world be better
if the wren's nest flourish and the eagle's house be
shattered!"—Jeffares (317 fn. 58) shows Blake as the
source of the eagle imagery; cp. "To a Wealthy Man
. . . ," "Friends," and "His Phoenix."—Ll. 10-12 refer
to Sir William, Lady Gregory's dead husband, and to
Lady Gregory's own writing.—*V.* Witt, 87-89; Colum,
Chap. 11.—In 26 and 27, among "Momentary
Thoughts."

"At the Abbey Theatre": With the subtitle notation
merely italicized, in the *1912 *Green Helmet* (23
Oct.) and *The Irish Review,* Dec. 1912; as now, 40,
54, 57, 58, 63, 75, 79, 80, 98, 99.—Wr. May 1911
(Ellmann, *Iden.,* 288).—"Craoibhin Aoibhin" (l. 1)
= "Pleasant Little Branch": pseudonym of Dr. Douglas Hyde; cp. *Auto.,* 266-70. Hyde's "An Answer . . ."
appeared in the Jan. 1913 number of the *Irish Rev.*—
The 8th printing of 99A restores subtitle italics.

"These Are the Clouds": *26, 27, 31, 33, 40, 50, 54, 57,
58, 63, 73, 75, 79, 80, 88, 98, 99.—Wr. May 1910 (Ellmann, *Iden.,* 288).—Henn (30) considers the "friend"
addressed (l. 7) to be Lady Gregory, seriously ill in
1909; cp. Jeffares, *Rev. of Eng. Studies,* XXIII, 353.—
MacNeice (102) regards this piece as a portrayal of
"the decline of Irish nationalism."—In 26 and 27,
among "Momentary Thoughts."

"At Galway Races": Originally "Galway Races," *English Review,* Feb. 1909; present title, 1910 *Green Helmet;* rptd. 27, 31, 33, 40, 50, 54, 57, 58, 63, 75, *79, 80, 98, 99.—Hone (240) assigns the poem to Yeats's 1908 summer at Coole, but Ellmann (*Iden.,* 288) moves the date to 21 October.—In 26 and 27, among "Momentary Thoughts."—Cp. J. B. Yeats's picture of George Pollexfen on horseback, and his comment on the Irish "passion for horses," in *Early Memories,* 18-19. The Irish concern with horse-racing is evident as early as the great pre-Christian "fairs"—perhaps was indulged even in the funeral games out of which these fairs presumably grew.

"A Friend's Illness": *26, 27, 31, 40, 54, 57, 58, 63, 75, 79, 80, 98, 99.—§XXIX of *Estrangement* (wr. 1909) relates this poem specifically to the illness of "A—C—" (= Lady Gregory: cp. notes to *Estrangement*), illness resulting "from overwork" (Henn, 30).—Wr. Feb. 1909 (Ellmann, *Iden.,* 288); Jeffares (*Rev. of Eng. Studies,* XXIII, 352) says the poem is in the 1909 Diary.—In 26 and 27, among "Momentary Thoughts."

"All Things Can Tempt Me": Originally "Distraction," *English Review,* Feb. 1909; present title, 1910 *Green Helmet;* rptd. 27, *31, 40, 54, 57, 58, 63, 65, 75, 79, 80, 98, 99.—Hone (240) suggests composition at Coole, July 1908.—Cp. Thompson, *Hopkins Rev.,* III, 10.

"Brown Penny": Originally "The Young Man's Song" in *1910 *Green Helmet;* do., 27, 31, 37, 40, 54, 57, 58, 63, 75; present title, *Coll. Poems,* 1933; also rptd. 80, 98, 99.—Except in punctuation and the writing of "Oh" for "O," the final version copies the original; however, the logical stanzaic break after l. 8 is not observed in 79 and the first 7 printings of 99A. The 8th printing

of 99A unhappily replaces the comma ending l. 1 with
the illogical period of 98.—In 26 and 27, among "Momentary Thoughts."

Responsibilities

M Untitled Prefatory Poem ("Introductory Rhymes" in *Contents* of 99): 38, 40, 54, 57, 58, 63, *73, 75, 79, 80, 88,
98, 99.—Dated Jan. 1914 by Yeats; assigned to Dec.
1913 by Ellmann (*Iden.*, 288).—Supposedly stimulated by George Moore's nastiness in "Ave," of *Hail
and Farewell.* Hone (294, fn.) says: "By making old
William Pollexfen, trader and ship-owner, the hero of
this poem Yeats thought to turn the tables on George
Moore of Moore Hall." Hone also notes (515) that
lines 9-12 were revised from "Pardon, and you that
did not weigh the cost, / Old Butlers when you took
to horse and stood / Beside the brackish waters of the
Boyne / Till your bad master blenched and all was
lost" when Yeats discovered that the Butler involved
had fought *for* King William at the Boyne! The original version stands in 38-63 and 75.—Cp. Yeats's
Reveries. . . .—The "merchant" (1. 3) was Jervis Yeats:
cp. note, *C. P.*, 451. The "scholar" (1. 5) was John
Yeats, the clergyman, born in 1774, three years before
Emmet; he died in 1847: *v. Auto.*, 23, 25. The "skipper" (1. 13) was William Pollexfen. (*Auto.*, 44; cp.
J. B. Yeats, *Early Memories,* 92: "Inarticulate as the
sea cliffs were the Pollexfen heart and brain, lying
buried under mountains of silence.")—L. 16 originally
ran: "Because you were the spectacle. . . ."—The reference to a "barren" passion (1. 19), of course, has to
do with Yeats's unrequited love for Maud Gonne.—
The 8th printing of 99A deletes "the" from l. 3.
"The Grey Rock": Originally in *British Review* and

Poetry (Chicago), both Apr. 1913; rptd. 38, 40, 54, *57, 58, 63, 73, 75, 79, 80, 88, 98, 99.—Wr. 1913 (Ellmann, *Iden.*, 288).—Took *Poetry's* £50 prize for the year, but Yeats returned £40 to be given a younger writer, retaining the ten in order to procure a bookplate and not to seem snobbish (Hone, 292; Wade, *Letters,* 584-85: Yeats suggested Pound for the £40). —An anonymous review of the Apr. 1913 number of *Poetry* in the May 1913 *Irish Review* calls "The Grey Rock" "somewhat bewildering. . . . The narrative concerns Aoife, the Woman of the Sidhe, who, according to the legend, promised love and immortality to Morrogh, Brian's son. The old story tells us how Morrow made a renunciation and died fighting for his people." In this view, Yeats apparently departed from legend in making his hero "a young man," but not Morrogh: "Murrough" in his spelling, loved by Aoife; but cp. Bk. IV, Ch. VI, of Lady Gregory's *G. F. M.* and Alspach's study (*Jour. Amer. Folk.*, LXIII), which shows Yeats followed recorded tradition.—Ure (32) describes the theme as "the rejection of the inhuman spiritual in favour of that in human life which is heroical and passionate, and which, it is implied, because conditional on death and time, is only to be found in a human context." (*V.* also, *idem,* 33 ff. One might cp. *The Two Kings.*)—"The Grey Rock" itself is *Craig Liath* ("Carrick-lee"), Aoife's here-supposed home near Killaloe.—The "Cheshire Cheese" (l. 2) was the London meeting place of Yeats and his fellows of the Rhymers' Club.—"Goban" (l. 10) = Goibniu, the ancient Celtic god, referred to as "the legendary mason" by Yeats in "Aristotle of the Books" (*The Celtic Twilight*), who was originally a smith but later became famous as an architect and builder: cp. Ella Young's

The Wonder-Smith and His Son and Seumas Mac-Manus' *Heavy Hangs the Golden Grain*. The "wine" of l. 17 were more properly "ale," wine having apparently been unknown in very early Ireland: on Goibniu as brewer, *v.* Best, 174-75.—Florence Farr is (cp. Alspach) probably the "woman" of l. 13, p. 102; "Slievenamon," l. 15 (*Sliabh na m-Ban,* Co. Tipperary), is the reputed site of the god Bodb Derg's palace.—The phrase "the windy light" (l. 11, p. 104) occurs also in "Reveries . . ." (*Auto.*, 91); cp. *Essays,* 360, l. 22.—The last stanza is Yeats's way of saying his ideal for Ireland was not that of the rabblement, and that he was unwilling to make his art the tool of narrow propaganda and provincialism.—Cp., with caution, Bronowski, 233-34.

"To a Wealthy Man . . .": Originally "The Gift . . . ," *Irish Times,* 11 Jan. 1913; as "To a Wealthy Man, Who Promised a Second Subscription If It Were Proved the People Wanted Pictures" in **Poems Written in Discouragement,* 1913; present title since Cuala *Responsibilities,* 1914. Also rptd. 40, 50, 54, 57, 58, 63, 75, 79, 80, 98, 99.—Dated Dec. 1912 in *C. P.;* 8 Jan. 1913 in *Irish Times;* 24 Dec. 1912 by Ellmann (*Iden.*, 288). V. Yeats's letters to Lane and Lady Gregory, Wade, *Letters,* 573-74; and, *idem,* 579-80, 616-23. Yeats has a note, *C. P.,* 451-52.—The "wealthy man" is William Martin Murphy (1844–1919); cp. "September 1913" and "To a Shade."—This verse relates to the offer of Sir Hugh Lane (Lady Gregory's nephew: *v.* Wade, *Letters,* 501 fn. 2) to give his pictures to Dublin. Lane wanted a bridge site provided by the Dublin Corporation and a building designed by the Englishman Sir Edward Lutyens. Opposed by the Nationalists, he finally placed his pictures in the National Gallery, London. Before starting for America on the *Lusitania,* with which he went down, he drew up a codicil to his will, giving the pictures to Dublin and naming Lady Gregory as sole trustee. But since the codicil was not witnessed, the Tate Gallery subsequently refused to give up the pictures. (*V.* Bodkin; Hone *Poet,* Chap. III, § VII; Lady Gregory, *H. L.* and *Jour.:* "V. The Lane Pictures.") Henn (88), writing early in 1948, says the Dublin Municipal Gallery keeps a room, empty except for a bust of Lane, waiting.—On "Lane's last moments," *v.* Lewis, entry for 21 May 1915, pp. 239-40.—Jeffares, who (170) labels the piece "a reproof to Lord Ardilaun's argument," refers (321 fn. 35) to the passage in Castiglione's *Courtier* picturing Duke Ercole I of Ferrara as a patron of the theater who had five plays by Plautus produced in 1502 for his son Alphonso's wedding to Lucrezia Borgia, and also (171) to the segment describing the luxurious palace of Guidobaldo de Montrefeltro, Duke of Urbino.—"Cosimo" is Cosimo de Medici; "Michelozzo" was the architect of the Library of St. Mark's, Florence, built for Cosimo the Elder, with frescoes by Fra Angelico; "Paudeen" and "Biddy" are generic names, used contemptuously for the "common herd."—On the concluding lines, cp. the "eagle" figure of "Upon a House Shaken . . . ," "Friends," and "His Phoenix."—In general connotation, one may cp. Symonds' *The Renaissance in Italy.*

M "September 1913": Originally, with the parenthetical explanation "On reading much of the correspondence against the Art Gallery," "Romance in Ireland," *Irish Times,* 8 Sept. 1913; present title adopted in *Poems Written in Discouragement,* 1913, though a substitute, "Romantic Ireland. / (September, 1913)," appears in *Nine Poems . . . ,* 1914. Poem also rptd. 38, 40, 50, 54, 57,

58, 63, 73, 75, 79, 80, 88, 98, 99.—Except for the alteration of "ha'pence" to "halfpence" in l. 3 and many changes in punctuation, the poem stands as originally published. In the *Irish Times* it is dated 7 Sept. 1913 (Dublin). It relates to the employers' lockout of the strikers led by James Larkin and the consequent suffering. Larkin had "said some words in favour of Lane" (Hone, 286) during the picture-gallery troubles (*v.* note, *sup.*), while the employers were led by William Martin Murphy, proprietor of the *Irish Independent* and Yeats's opponent in the Lane affair. Maud Gonne will have it (*v.* Gwynn, 31) that Yeats wrote the refrain as in the first three stanzas "because he had lost contact with those who were working for Ireland's freedom." Of the "wild geese" (st. 3) Yeats was later to remark, in "A People's Theatre," "since the Wild Geese fled . . . [Ireland] has had but political leaders" (*P. & C.*, 215). On st. 3, cp. Stein, *Sewanee Rev.*, LVII, 616.—O'Leary is, of course, Yeats's friend John O'Leary (ob. 1907: cp. *Auto.*, 117 ff., 257 ff.; also, "Poetry and Tradition," *Essays*, 304 ff.), of whom Jeffares remarks (34-35): "O'Leary, when a medical student at Trinity College, had been inspired by the Young Ireland movement and had become a leader of the Fenian movement which succeeded it. He was condemned to twenty years' penal servitude, but had been set free after five years on condition that he did not return to Ireland for fifteen years. His exile was spent in Paris, and on his return he was highly respected by all parties in Dublin." (His sister, Ellen, wrote verse.)—Cp. "Willie Yeats and John O'Leary," *Irish Book Lover,* Nov. 1940; Thompson, *Hopkins Rev.;* "John O'Leary," *Sinn Féin,* 23 Mar. 1907; Tynan, *Memories;* Hone *Letters,* pref. *et passim;* Ellmann, *passim;* and Witt, 80-81. Rolleston's *Portrait of an Irishman* has one or two brief but charming pictures of O'Leary. *V.* also Hone *Poet,* Chap. II.

"To a Friend Whose Work Has Come to Nothing": Originally in *Poems Written in Discouragement,* 1913; republished in *Poetry* (Chicago), May 1914; also in 38, *40, 50, 54, 57, 58, 63, 73, 75, 79, 80, 88, 89, 98, 99.—Wr. Sept. 1913 (Ellmann, *Iden.,* 289).—For Lady Gregory (*C. P.,* 452); Henn (91) ascribes the indicated attacks to "journalists."

"Paudeen": Originally in *Poems Written in Discouragement,* 1913; later in *Poetry* (Chicago), May 1914, and *The New Statesman,* 9 May 1914; rptd., with only changes in punctuation to differentiate it from the earliest version, in 38, 40, 50, 54, 57, 58, 63, 75, 79, 80, 98, and 99.—Wr. 16 Sept. 1913 (Ellmann, *Iden.,* 289). —Cp. *Auto.,* 465, ll. 25-28, and Cathleen's twelfth speech in *The Countess Cathleen,* Sc. II?

"To a Shade": Originally in *Poems Written in Discouragement,* 1913; later in *Poetry* (Chicago), May 1914, and *The New Statesman,* 9 May 1914; rptd. 38, 40, 50, *54, 57, 58, 63, 73, 75, 79, 80, 88, 98, 99.—Dated 29 Sept. 1913. The "Shade" is Parnell; the "man" of the second paragraph, Hugh Lane: cp. "To a Wealthy Man . . . ," *sup.;* the "old foul mouth," according to Jeffares (173), William Martin Murphy, opponent of both Parnell and Lane. Glasnevin is the cemetery in which Parnell is buried.

"When Helen Lived": *Poetry* (Chicago), May 1914; rptd. 38, 40, 50, 54, 57, 58, 63, 65, 73, 75, 79, 80, 88, 98, 99.—Wr. 20-29 Sept. 1913 (Ellmann, *Iden.,* 289). —The phrase from Marlowe in l. 8 will be obvious to readers.

"On Those That Hated 'The Playboy of the Western World,' 1907": Originally "On Those Who Dislike the

Playboy," *Irish Review,* Dec. 1911; as "The Attack on the 'Play Boy'" in the 1912 *Green Helmet;* as "The Attack on 'The Playboy of the Western World' 1907" in the Cuala *Responsibilties,* 1914; do., 40; present title since **Later Poems,* 1922, except that the N.Y. 1924 ed. of *Later Poems* has "Play-Boy." Other rptgs: 57, 63, 75, 79, 80, 98, 99.—Wade (*Letters,* 525 fn. 2) speaks of Yeats's having recited a version of this poem to him "in June or July 1909"; Ellmann (*Iden.,* 289) also dates composition 1909.—For Yeats's political application of the eunuch image, *v.* §§ XLI-XLII of *Estrangement* (wr. 1909). In a 8 Mar. 1909 letter to Lady Gregory (Wade, *Letters,* 525), the poet compares "Griffith and his like to the Eunuchs in Ricketts's picture watching Don Juan riding through Hell."

"The Three Beggars": Originally without the article, *Harper's Weekly,* 15 Nov. 1913; as now, 1914 *Responsibilities;* rptd. 40, *54, 57, 58, 63, 75, 79, 80, 98, 99. (The magazine printing lacks italics.)—MacNeice (112) calls this "a satirical comment upon everyday avarice; the hero is a crane who . . . shows no competitive spirit. . . ." Henn (91) equates the crane with Yeats.—Jeffares (176 ff.) sees Synge behind this and the next four pieces.—Ll. 5 and 7: "lebeen-lone":? A Lady Gregory—Yeats concoction for "rubbish": *leidhbín* (a small clover straw) *lón* (food) (Speculation of Prof. Kelleher).—L. 8: "King Guaire": Identification problematical, though Keating mentions a King Guaire, as does Miss Hull (I. 221-23), and Yeats's monarch in *The King's Threshold* (1903) is named Guaire. Incidentally, the spelling is "Guari" in all printings prior to 98 except 79 and 80, where it is "Guare."

"The Three Hermits": *The Smart Set,* Sept. 1913; *Nine*

Poems . . . , 1 Apr. 1914; Cuala *Responsibilities,* 25 May 1914; rptd. *40, 54, 57, 58, 63, 75, 79, 80, 98, 99. —Although Jeffares (176) dates composition 15 Mar. 1913, at Stone Cottage, Ellmann's correction of the date (*Iden.,* 289) to 5 Mar. seems warranted: cp. Wade, *Letters,* 577.—N.B.: All but the last three printings have a less ambiguous period in place of l. 7's colon.

"Beggar to Beggar Cried": *Poetry* (Chicago), May 1914; rptd. 38, 40, 54, 57, 58, 63, 75, 79, 80, 98, 99. (*N.B.:* Only the last four use italics.)—Wr. 5 Mar. 1913 (Ellmann, 208).—Hone (321) thinks this one of the suggestions of disillusionment which "may perhaps be traced" to the fact that "When he was about forty-five Yeats had formed a liaison with an unmarried woman past her first youth" whom he now unjustly suspected of "embarrassing designs upon him."—Cp. Ellmann, 208-9; Jeffares (London ed.), 175-76.

"Running to Paradise": *Poetry* (Chicago), May 1914; rptd. 38, *40, 50, 54, 57, 58, 63, 73, 75, 79, 80, 88, 98, 99. (Only the first 7 printings of 99A have the refrain entirely italicized; elsewhere the "is" is in roman.)— Wr. 20 Sept. 1913 (Ellmann, *Iden.,* 289).

"The Hour before Dawn": 1914 *Responsibilities;* rptd. 40, *54 (though l. 118 has the misprint "upon" for "up"), 57, 58, 63, 73, 75, 79, 80, 88, 98, 99.—Wr. 19 Oct. 1913 (Ellmann, *Iden.,* 289).—"Cruachan" (l. 4; spelled "Croghan" in 54-75 and 88): the capital of ancient Connachta, the kingdom of Medb and Oilioll. —"Maeve's nine Maines" (l. 8): One son of Medb named Maine, slain by Concobar, was the husband of Ferbe: cp. Dillon, xv; Thurneysen, 359. One tradition speaks of *seven* outlawed, piratical Maines (or Manés), sons of Oilioll (Ailill) and Medb, who helped

Conaire Mór's evil foster-brothers raid Erin and also joined in Medb's hosting against Uladh (*v.* Rolleston, 169, 204); but there is also authority for speaking of *eight* or *nine: v.* Rhys, 367-70.—"Hell Mouth" (1. 25): Cave of Cruachan, known in antiquity as the "Hell-gate of Ireland" and the supposed home of goblins and monstrous, poison-exhaling birds.—"Goban's mountain-top" (1. 50): *v.* "The Grey Rock," *sup.*— MacNeice (113), who regards this piece as "a defence of the waking life against the man who intends to sleep till the Day of Judgment," sees Synge's *In the Shadow of the Glen* (Dublin: Maunsel, ed. 1915; p. 26) in the next-to-last stanza.—Cp. Henn, 345-46.

"A Song from 'The Player Queen'": Originally "The Player Queen/*Song from an Unfinished Play*," *Poetry* (Chicago), May 1914; thereafter there is some variation in the typography of the subtitle, which in the case of 50 reads "Song from a Play." Title exactly as now since 79.—Printings after initial one: 38, *40, 50, 54 (cp. 54a, 54b, 100), 57, 58, 63, 75, 79, 80, 98, 99.

"The Realists": *Poetry* (Chicago), Dec. 1912; rptd. *38, 40, 54, 57, 58, 63, 75, 79, 80, 98, 99.—Here Yeats seems to be suggesting that imaginative escape alone aborts the desire for death that mere facing of the "realities" of life would induce.

"The Witch": *Poetry* (Chicago), May 1914, *unnumbered;* rptd. 38, 40, 54, 57, 58, 63, 75, 79, 80, 98, 99.—No variants except for the fact that the question mark does not appear before 79.—Wr. 24 May 1912 (Ellmann, *Iden.*, 289).—Cp. Jeffares, 175.

"The Peacock": *Poetry* (Chicago), May 1914, *unnumbered;* rptd. *38, 40, 54, 57, 58, 63, 75, 79, 80, 98, 99.*— Cp. Hone's speculations, 259; 291, fn.

"The Mountain Tomb": Published successively in *Poetry*

(Chicago), Dec. 1912; 33; and *The Quest* (London), Apr. 1913: thereafter in 38, *40, 50, 54, 57, 58, 63, 73, 75, 79, 80, 88, 98, 99.—Wr. on a visit to "the Gonnes [at Colleville] in Normandy in August 1912" (Hone, 281).—Cp. "The Body of the Father Christian Rosencrux" (dated 1895), *Essays*, 241.—On Christian Rosenkreuz, *v.* also Ellmann, 96, 189; Moore, 150 ff.

M "I/To a Child Dancing in the Wind" and "II/Two Years Later": What is now "I" appeared as "To a Child Dancing upon the Shore" in *Poetry* (Chicago), Dec. 1912, but was reprinted in 33 as "To a Child Dancing in the Wind" (Wade, 108). Nevertheless, in May 1914 *Poetry* published what is now "II" as "To a Child Dancing in the Wind." Then, in the *1914 *Responsibilities,* I and II became a numbered two-stanza poem (still slightly mispunctuated) entitled "To a Child Dancing in the Wind" (Wade, 115); do., 40 and 50; "Two Years Later" first appears as a title, and the poem precisely in its present form, in *Later Poems*, 1922. Later rptgs: 57, 58, 63, 73, 75, 79, 80, 88, 98, 99. —Ellmann (289) dates "I" 1912; "II," "Dec. 3, 1912 or 1913."—The child is Iseult, the adopted daughter of Maud Gonne; she became eventually the wife of Francis Stuart, the novelist.

"A Memory of Youth": Originally "Love and the Bird," *Poetry* (Chicago), Dec. 1912; present title since *1914 *Responsibilities;* rptd. 40, 54, 57, 58, 63, 75, 79, 80, 98, 99.—Wr. 13 Aug. 1912 (Ellmann, *Iden.*, 289). —Henn (157) recalls a letter to George Russell, perhaps written in 1899, in which Yeats says, "Last night I had a dream about two lovers who were being watched over by a blackbird or a raven, who warned them against malice and the slander of the world. Was this bird a transformation of Ængus or one of his

birds?"—L. 6: "cut-throat North": because the North
was the region whence the old Scandinavian invaders
descended upon Ireland?

ℳ "Fallen Majesty": *Poetry* (Chicago), Dec. 1912; next in
the *Tauchnitz *Selection* . . . , 1913; rptd. 38, 40, 50,
54, 57, 58, 63, 65, 75, 79, 80, 98, 99.—Wr. 1912 (Ellmann, *Iden.*, 289).—For Maud Gonne. (Cp. *Auto.*,
especially 447-48.)—On concluding metaphor, cp.
Cuchulain, *On Baile's Strand:* "Have seen the heavens
like a burning cloud."

ℳ "Friends": 31, 33, 38, 40, 50, 54, 57, 58, 63, 73, 75, *79,
80, 88, 98, 99.—Wr. Jan. 1911 (Ellmann, *Iden.*, 289).
—The three women successively referred to have
been identified by Jeffares (175), on Mrs. Yeats's cited
authority, as Lady Gregory, "Diana Vernon" (Olivia
Shakespear), and Maud Gonne, respectively. On the
eagle imagery (l. 25), cp. "Upon a House Shaken
. . . ," "To a Wealthy Man . . . ," and "His Phoenix."

ℳ "The Cold Heaven": 31, 33, 38, *40, 50, 54, 57, 58, 63,
65, 73, 75, 79, 80, 88, 98, 99.—Henn (92) regards this
poem as "the first in which the debt to the metaphysical poets appears to be clearly defined," partly a result of Professor Grierson's having sent Yeats in 1912
his edition of Donne; Whalley (*Queen's Qu.*, LVIII,
502), who sees Yeats here "celebrating Maud Gonne's
disastrous marriage," is in apparent agreement. In
connection with the concluding lines, Henn (94 fn. 1)
also recalls Berkeley's belief that the ghost quickens
only some time after seeming death: cp. Eithne Inguba's remark, "The Only Jealousy of Emer," *P. & C.*,
foot of p. 363.

ℳ "That the Night Come": *31, 33, 37, 38, 40, 50, 54, 57,
58, 63, 65, 73, 75, 79, 80, 88, 98, 99.—Obviously anent
Maud Gonne.

"An Appointment": Originally "On A Recent Government Appointment In Ireland," *English Review*, Feb. 1909; present title since Cuala *Responsibilities*, 1914; rptd. 40, *54, 57, 58, 63, 75, 79, 80, 98, 99.—Hone (240) dates composition at Coole, summer of 1908; Ellmann (*Iden.*, 289) says 1907.—The government, through Lord Aberdeen and Birrell, had refused to make Hugh Lane director of the Dublin National Gallery; Count Plunkett received the appointment. Cp. "To a Wealthy Man . . . ," "To a Shade," and Lady Gregory, *H. L.*, 83 ff.

"The Magi": *Poetry* (Chicago), May 1914, and *New Statesman*, 9 May 1914; rptd. 38, *40, 54, 57, 58, 63, 73, 75, 79, 80, 88, 98, 99. (In 38-63 and 75, the title is "I/The Magi.")—Wr. 20 Sept. 1913 (Ellmann, *Iden.*, 289).—Henn (95) recalls Yeats's vision, "a company of people in blue robes swept by me in a blinding light," recorded in the preface to Horton's *Book of Images* (1898).—Yeats eventually attempted to relate this lyric to his later-developed "system" (cp. *A Vision*, 105).—Cp. *Ideas of Good and Evil*, London: ed. Bullen, 1903; pp. 235-36.

"The Dolls": First in *(essentially) 1914 *Responsibilities*; rptd. 40, 54, 57, 58, 63, 75, 79, 80, 98, 99. (In 38-75, the title is "II/The Dolls.")—According to Ellmann's earlier volume (208), written "late in 1912"; according to his *Iden.* (289), 20 Sept. 1913.—Yeats has a note, *C. P.*, 452; he conceived of this and the preceding as complementary poems. For speculation on these pieces as reflecting "the dialectic between Being and Becoming," one may consult MacNeice (116). Jeffares (178) finds the source of the doll "idea" in Synge's *Aran Islands*.

"A Coat": *Poetry* (Chicago), May 1914, but note misprint: "world's eye," l. 6; rptd. 38, 40, 54, 57, 58, 63, 75, 79, 80, 98, 99.—Wr. 1912 (Ellmann, *Iden.*, 289).—Comment on the original MS version may be found in Jeffares' *Nineteenth Cent. and After* article. Cp. also Gleckner.

Untitled Epilogue ("Closing Rhyme" in *Contents* of 99): Originally "Notoriety/(*Suggested by a recent magazine article.*)," *New Statesman*, 7 Feb. 1914, but only there; rptd. 38, *40, 54, 57, 58, 63, 75, 79, 80, 98, 99.—Wr. 1914 (Ellmann, *Iden.*, 289).—This sonnet is also conceived to be an answer to Moore's *Hail and Farewell.*—One presumes the "reed-throated whisperer" to be the Muse.—L. 5: Dume (257) locates "the dull ass's hoof" in an epilogue to Jonson's *The Poetaster*, in *Underwoods* retitled "An Ode to Himself."—L. 7, "Kyle-na-no": one of the "Seven Woods" of Coole: *v.* notes to *The Shadowy Waters, inf.*—In his *1930 Diary*, Yeats refers to the last line as an adaptation of "a metaphor from Erasmus."

The Wild Swans at Coole

"The Wild Swans at Coole": *The Little Review*, June 1917, where alone what is now the last stanza is printed as the third; *42, 46, 48, 50, 54, 57, 58, 63, 65, 73, 75, 79, 80, 88, 98, 99.—Dated Oct. 1916 in *L. R.*—Coole was Lady Gregory's estate in Co. Galway; cp. Ir. *cúl* or *cúil:* a niche, or set-back place; hence, a spot for retirement.—Cp. Stauffer, 65 ff., or *Kenyon Rev.*—Query, speculation, and comment by R. J. C., Mabbott (discount his pronunciation), and Witt in the *Explicator.*—Yeats counted swans among "the natural symbols of subjectivity" (*P. & C.*, 472; cp. Saul, *Bull., N. Y. Pub. Lib.*).

"In Memory of Major Robert Gregory": Originally "In

Memory of Robert Gregory," *English Review,* Aug. 1918, and *Little Review,* Sept. 1918; present title, *1919 *Wild Swans;* rptd. 48, 50, 54, 57, 58, 63, 73, 75, 79, 80, 88, 98, 99.—All but eighth stanza (wr. in May) wr. 14 June 1918 (Ellmann, *Iden.,* 289).—Anent Lady Gregory's aviator son, killed 23 Jan. 1918 in action over Italy and buried at Padua; *v.* Yeats's "Major Robert Gregory," *Observer,* 17 Feb. 1918, for charming tribute (rptd. *L. R.,* Nov. 1918). *V.* also *1930 Diary,* § XXVI, and Wade, *Letters,* 645-46. A June 1918 letter from Yeats to his father says the poem has just been finished and is one of his best (Hone, 332). On its genesis, *v.* Witt, *Mod. Philol.*—Cp. next poem; and for "Reprisals," a previously unpublished poem on Robert Gregory, *v.* Ellmann, *Kenyon Rev.,* XV, 372-73, or *Rann,* Autumn 1948 no.—St. I, l. 1, "our house": Thoor Ballylee.—St. III, l. 3, "much falling": Jeffares (98) glosses the opening of Lionel Johnson's *Mystic and Cavalier.* (On Johnson, *v. Auto.,* 273 ff., 375 ff.)—St. IV, l. 7, "a race": the Aran Islanders. (On Synge, *v. Auto.,* 423 ff., and "The Cutting of an Agate," *Essays.*)—St. V, "George Pollexfen": Yeats's Sligo astrologer-uncle (cp. *Auto.*); l. 7, "By opposition . . .": as Henn (114 fn. 3) explains, a reference to stars 180°, 90°, and 120° apart, respectively.—St. VII: Hone (332) notes that this marks the introduction of Thoor Ballylee into Yeats's verse, though St. I might better have been named.—St. VIII: Ure (39) notes the "shifting of key" at the end.—St. IX: Cp. Henn, 344.—St. X: Before his marriage, Yeats used to discuss making over Thoor Ballylee with Robert Gregory. *V.* notes on "To Be Carved on a Stone . . . ," *inf.*

"An Irish Airman Foresees His Death": 46, *48, 50, 54, 57, 58, 63, 73, 75, 79, 80, 88, 89, 98, 99.—Wr. 1918

(Ellmann, 230).—Concerns Robert Gregory.—Cp. *1930 Diary*, § XXVI, p. 23; notes to preceding poem.

M "Men Improve with the Years": Dated 19 July 1916 and published in *The Little Review*, June 1917; rptd. *42, 46, 48, 50, 54, 57, 58, 63, 65, 75, 79, 80, 98, 99.—Said by Jeffares (206) to record "the effect of Iseult's [i.e., Iseult Gonne's] beauty."

"The Collar-Bone of a Hare": Dated 5 July 1915 and published in *The Little Review*, June 1917; rptd. *42, 46, 48, 50, 54, 57, 58, 63, 65, 75, 79, 80, 98, 99.—Misdated, Hone *Letters:* 251, fn.; cp. Saul and Witt in *LTLS*.—V. also *E. P. S.*, 246, and Miss Witt's note in *Explicator*, VII.—On l. 7, cp. *P. & C.*, p. 94, ll. 5-8.

"Under the Round Tower": Dated May 1918 and published in *The Little Review*, Oct. 1918; also in *Nine Poems*, Oct. 1918; rptd. *46, 48, 50, 54, 57, 58, 63, 75, 79, 80, 98, 99.—*N.B.:* Ellmann (*Iden.*, 289) dates the poem Mar.—Menon (61), fortified by *A Vision* (270), will have it that "The golden king and the silver lady . . . (who are also the Sun and Moon) symbolise the continual oscillation which represents the horizontal movement of the historical cones (refer section III of 'Dove and the Swan' [*A Vision*])." Ellmann (231) follows this interpretation, but sees a humorous intent. Others may be content to enjoy this wild plum of a poem without reference to any "system."—St. 2: Cp. "Stream and Sun at Glendalough."

"Solomon to Sheba": *Little Review*, Oct. 1918; *Nine Poems*, do.; rptd. 46, 48, 54, 57, 58, 63, 75, *79, 80, 98, 99.—Wr. 1918 at Glendalough, according to Jeffares (207), who calls it "a poem symbolising the pleasant relationship of the poet and his wife"; and (325 fn. 65) remarks that "Solomon and Sheba occur as symbols of perfect love in the 1909–12 diaries." The 8th printing of 99A corrects "Said Solomon" (St. 3) to "Sang Solomon."

M "The Living Beauty": *Little Review*, Oct. 1918; *Nine Poems*, do.; rptd. 46, 48, 54, 57, 58, 63, 75, *79, 80, 98, 99.—Jeffares, relating this to Yeats's proposal of marriage to Iseult Gonne, gives two dates for composition: 1915 (190) and 1917 (206); Ellmann (*Iden.*, 289) says 1917, which seems the more likely date. Cp. Yeats's 12 Aug. 1917 letter to Lady Gregory: Wade, *Letters*, 628-29 and ff.

"A Song": *Little Review*, Oct. 1918; *Nine Poems*, do.; rptd. 46, 48, *54, 57, 58, 63, 65, 75, 79, 80, 98, 99. (Italics first appear in 79.)—Wr. 1915 (Ellmann, *Iden.*, 289).—Hone (290, fn.) refers the opening lines to Ezra Pound's teaching Yeats fencing when digestion was troublesome during the winter of 1912–13. —Cp., on refrain, "Ephemera," *C. P.*, 17.

M "To a Young Beauty": *Nine Poems*, 1918; rptd. 46, 48, 54, 57, 58, *63, 75, 79, 80, 98, 99.—Jeffares (212) dates the poem 1918, says it reflects Yeats's anxiety when Iseult Gonne "came to Dublin and began to mix in its Bohemian circles," and compares the opening of the second stanza with the end of "Michael Robartes and the Dancer" (*C. P.*, 174).—The real point of the reference to Ezekiel's visions seems unclear: cp. Ezekiel, 1. 10, 10. 14, and 41. 18. "Beauvarlet" (also in the second stanza) is presumably Jacques-Firmin Beauvarlet (1731–97): *v. La Grande Encyclopédie* (Paris, 1885–1902), Vol. 5, p. 1076; but prior to the revised London *Later Poems* of 1926, Yeats prints "Beaujolet." —On the concluding line, cp. Williams, 58.

M "To a Young Girl": *Little Review*, Oct. 1918; *Nine Poems*, do.; rptd. 46, 48, 54, 57, 58, 63, 65, 73, 75, 79,

80, 88, 98, 99.—Wr. "1913 or 1915" (Ellmann, *Iden.*, 289).—For Iseult Gonne.

*"The Scholars": Oddly enough, first published in *Catholic Anthology* (London: Mathews), 1915; next in *Poetry* (Chicago), Feb. 1916; rptd. 42, 46, 48, 54, 57, 58, 63, *73, 75, 79, 80, 88, 98, 99.—Jeffares (177) says this "was originally written, under Pound's influence, in 1915," and later toned down; Ellmann (*Iden.*, 289) dates composition "1914 and April 1915."—The toning down was certainly unfortunate: the earlier version (*v.* printings prior to 73) is in every way more cogently and pithily phrased.

"Tom O'Roughley": Dated 16 Feb. 1918 and published in *The Little Review*, Oct. 1918; *Nine Poems*, do.; rptd. *46, 48, 54, 57, 58, 63, 75, 79, 80, 98, 99.—Ure (102-3) compares the fool ("Phase 28") of *A Vision.* —Incidentally, "Roughley" is the name of a "seaboard district" of wild fighters mentioned in § I, "The Thick Skull of the Fortunate," *Celtic Twilight.*—L. 4: In fn. 1 to "Bishop Berkeley" (Cuala *Essays 1931 to 1936*, p. 43), Yeats says Berkeley's "Complacency seems . . . to . . . constitute the essence of volition" is "what I meant when I wrote 'An aimless joy is a pure joy.'"

"Shepherd and Goatherd": Originally "The Sad Shepherd," 1919 *Wild Swans;* next in 48, 54, 57, 58, 63, 75; present title, *79: *C. P.*, 1933; rptd. 80, 98, 99.—Wr. at Glendalough, 1918 (Jeffares, 219): Miss Witt (*Mod. Philol.*, XLVIII, 113) says the MS. is dated 20 Mar.; Ellmann (*Iden.*, 289; and cp. Wade, *Letters*, 647) dates composition 19 Mar.—Concerns Robert Gregory: *v.* notes on "In Memory of Major Robert Gregory," *sup.*; on Lady Gregory, *Auto.* (ed. N.Y., 1938), 334 ff.—In a letter to Lady Gregory (Hone,

330), Yeats calls it "a pastoral similar to what Spenser wrote of Sydney . . ."; *v.* Wade, *Letters,* 646-48.—In Henn's view (115), "Shepherd" and "Goatherd" here represent Yeats himself "in youth" and "in age," respectively.—Ure (40) calls this, with considerable justification, "perhaps the only thoroughly bad poem to be found in Yeats' post-1914 collections."—L. 3, p. 142: " 'the speckled bird' ": title of extract from an unfinished novel by Yeats, published in *The Bell* (Dublin), Mar. 1941, with annotations by Hone.— For a brief Yeatsian explanation of the Goatherd's song, p. 143, *v.* "Note on 'The Dreaming of the Bones,' " *P. & C.,* 467-68, and *Auto.,* 464.—On "pern" (p. 143, l. 5), *v.* Yeats's note, *C. P.,* 453.—The sixth line from the end ("we'll to the woods") recalls A. E. Housman's version of Banville's *Nous n'irons plus au bois,* made in April 1922.

"Lines Written in Dejection": 42, 46, *48, 54, 57, 58, 63, 65, 73, 75, 79, 80, 88, 98, 99.—Wr. "Oct. (?) 1915" (Ellmann, *Iden.,* 290).—Allt, says Henn (240-41), thinks this "may have, in whole or in part, a literary source in Ferguson's translation of 'Deirdre's Lament for the Sons of Usnach.' . . ."—One may cp. Parkinson's art., *Mod. Philol.*—V. Henn, 166.—Miss Moore (217) says Yeats calls the sun "embittered" because he defined it as "objective, unmental, unvisionary."

"The Dawn": *Poetry* (Chicago), Feb. 1916; also in *Form* and *Eight Poems* (pub. by *Form*), Apr. 1916, though *Eight Poems* is labeled "January 1916" (*v.* Wade, 118-20); rptd. 42, 46, 48, 50, 54, 57, 58, *63, 73, 75, 79, 80, 88, 98, 99.—L. 3: Refers to Emain Macha, Armagh (cp. *Annals of Tigernach:* Henn, 249).—Ll. 11 and 12: cp. Phaëthon and the chariot of the sun.

"On Woman": First pub. with "The Dawn"; pub'n details

as for that poem, except that 46 should be asterisked.
—Dated 25 May 1914 by Miss Moore (255); "May
21 or 25, 1914," by Ellmann (*Iden.*, 290).

"The Fisherman": Publication data as for preceding, except that 48 should be asterisked.—Jeffares (*Nineteenth Cent. and After*) reports the present version as
dated 4 June 1914 in Yeats's MS-book, with anticipa-
tory matter recorded "between May 18th and 23rd,
1913." L. 14, "The dead man": probably John Synge.
—On concluding lines, cp. the letter from J. B. Yeats
quoted by Hone (289): "a liberating splendour cold
as the sunrise." *Auto.* (255) has "manner at once cold
and passionate"; cp., *idem*, 339.—In *Early Memories*
(42), Yeats's father writes: "To be fond of fishing ran
in the family. . . ."—Cp. Ure, 19-20; Deutsch, 202-3;
Jeffares, 174; Wilson, 36; Strong (*v.* Gwynn, 200);
and Edwards (*Wales*), who writes of the ambiguity
resulting from Yeats's faulty punctuation and suggests a comma after "race" (l. 11) and a colon after
"reality" (l. 12); and who endorses Jeffares' interpretation, queries Arthur Griffith as the "clever man"
(l. 20), names W. M. Murphy (*v.* "To a Wealthy
Man . . . ," *sup.*) "probably among the persons deroga-
torily referred to," and asserts that the conclusion of
St. 1 "alludes, of course, to Hugh Lane and the great
paintings. . . ."

"The Hawk": *Poetry* and *Form* publication as for preceding; rptd. 42, *46, 48, 54, 57, 58, 63, 75, 79, 80, 98, 99.
—Cp. *Auto.*, 236; Ure, 20.—Yeats includes the hawk
among his "natural symbols of subjectivity": *v.* notes
on "The Wild Swans . . . ," *sup.*

"Memory": *Poetry* and *Form* publication as for preceding, though the *Poetry* version should be asterisked;
do., 42; title as now, 1919 *Wild Swans;* rptd. 48, 54,

57, 58, 63, 65, 73, 75, 79, 80, 88, 98, 99.—Wr. "1915–16" (Ellmann, *Iden.*, 290).—Hone (120) identifies "One" (l. 1) as Olivia Shakespear.

M "Her Praise": Originally "The Thorn Tree," with *Poetry* and *Form* publication as for preceding; title changed, 1917 *Wild Swans;* rptd. *46, 48, 54, 57, 58, 63, 65, 75, 79, 80, 98, 99.—Wr. 27 Jan. 1915 (Ellmann, *Iden.*, 290).—Concerns Maud Gonne.

M "The People": Originally "The Phoenix," with *Poetry* and *Form* publication as for preceding; title changed, 1917 *Wild Swans;* rptd. *46, 48, 54, 57, 58, 63, 75, 79, 80, 98, 99.—Wr. 10 Jan. 1915 (Ellmann, *Iden.*, 290). —Ll. 6 ff.: In the spring of 1907 Yeats had traveled in northern Italy with Lady Gregory and her son, at which time the former had introduced him to Castiglione's *The Courtier,* which excited his admiration (cp. Hone, 233, and "To a Wealthy Man . . ."). V. the supposed letter fragment of perhaps 1901: Wade, *Letters,* 355-56.—Cp. § II of "Poetry and Tradition," in *The Cutting of an Agate.*—L. 10, p. 149, "my phoenix": Maud Gonne. Hone (223) says the passage dependent on this reference recalls Yeats's fury when she was hissed at the Abbey by "partisans" of her husband after her 1905 action (supported by her "French confessor") to gain a separation.—Cp. Ellmann, 178 ff., on Yeats's hatred of the middle class, a hatred reproved by Maud Gonne. Ellmann (177) prints some bitter lines, unpublished by Yeats, bearing on this fact.

M "His Phoenix": Originally "There Is a Queen in China," with *Poetry* and *Form* publication as for preceding; title changed, 1917 *Wild Swans;* rptd. 46, 48, 54, 57, 58, 63, 73, 75, 79, *80, 88, 98, 99.—Wr. Jan. 1915 (Ellmann, *Iden.*, 290).—The "phoenix" is Maud Gonne: cp. the extract from Yeats's 1909 diary excerpted by Miss Moore, 202-3.—The "girl" in l. 4 is Leda; the Gaby of "Gaby's laughing eye," l. 9, is Gaby Deslys; the "player" of l. 12 is Julia Marlowe, whose Juliet Yeats had seen on his 1903-4 lecture tour in America; the eagle figure of the fourth line from the end recalls those of "Upon a House Shaken . . . ," "To a Wealthy Man . . . ," and "Friends."—Jeffares (323 fn. 84) finds "a possible source" in "The Red Man's Wife" (*Irish Street Ballads,* ed. C. O'Lochlain, Dublin: Three Candles Press, 1939; p. 193).

"A Thought from Propertius": *42, 46, 48, 54, 57, 58, 63, 75, 79, 80, 98, 99.—Apparently wr. in 1915 (cp. Jeffares, 183); Ellmann says "by Nov. 1915" (*Iden.,* 290).—Propertius is, of course, the Roman poet Sextus Propertius (?50-?15 B.C.).

"Broken Dreams": Dated Nov. 1915 when first published in *The Little Review,* June 1917 (though Ellmann, *Iden.,* 290, claims composition for 24 Oct.); rptd. 42, 46, 48, 50, 54, 57, 58, 63, 75, 79, *80, 98, 99.—On l. 7, cp. l. 16 of "Adam's Curse."—Anent Maud Gonne.—The 8th printing of 99A properly inserts a break between ll. 36 and 37.

"A Deep-Sworn Vow": Dated 17 Oct. 1915 in *The Little Review,* June 1917; here alone the hyphen is omitted. Rptd. *42, 46, 48, 54, 57, 58, 63, 75, 79, 80, 98, 99.—Presumably anent Maud Gonne.—Characteristically anatomized by Brooks and Warren, 273-77.

"Presences": Dated Nov. 1915 in *The Little Review,* June 1917; rptd. *42, 46, 48, 54, 57, 58, 63, 75, 79, 80, 98, 99.—Jeffares (184 and 190) relates the lyric to Iseult and Maud Gonne.

"The Balloon of the Mind": *New Statesman,* 29 Sept. 1917; rptd. 42, 46, 48, 54, 57, 58, 63, 75, *79, 80, 98, 99.—Image also in *Auto.,* 50.

"To a Squirrel at Kyle-na-no": *New Statesman,* 29 Sept.
1917, where the spelling is "Kyle-no-gno," which becomes "Kyle-na-gno" in the 1917 *Wild Swans* (as it
is in Lady Gregory's *Journals:* Robinson, 39); do., 46,
48, 54, 57, 58, 63, 75; present spelling, *C. P.,* 1933;
rptd. 80, 98, 99.—Wr. Sept. 1912 (Ellmann, *Iden.,*
290).—"Kyle-na-gno": one of the "Seven Woods" of
Coole. V. "The Shadowy Waters," *inf.* (Of course, this
lyric is mispunctuated: the question mark should come
at the end.)

"On Being Asked for a War Poem": Originally "A Reason
for Keeping Silent," in *The Book of the Homeless,* ed.
Edith Wharton (London: Macmillan, 1916); present
title since 1917 *Wild Swans,* whose version seems
more vigorous than the final one; rptd. 46, 48, 54, *57,
58, 63, 75, 79, 80, 98, 99.—Wr. 6 Feb. 1915 (Ellmann,
Iden., 290); *v.* Wade, *Letters,* 599-600, for copy in 20
Aug. 1915 letter to Henry James.

"In Memory of Alfred Pollexfen": Originally "In Memory,"
Little Review, June 1917; do., 42; as now, 1919 *Wild
Swans;* rptd. 48, 54, 57, 58, 63, 75, 79, 80, *98, 99.—
Jeffares dates writing 1915 (181); Ellmann (*Iden.,*
290) says Aug. 1916.—William Pollexfen, l. 2: Yeats's
maternal grandfather; *v. Auto.,* 83.—The "tomb," l. 5,
is in St. John's Churchyard.—George Pollexfen, l. 8,
died 1910; *v.* Hone, 264-65, *Auto.,* 316 ff., and Wade,
Letters, 551-54.—On third line from end, cp. *Auto.,*
12.

"Upon a Dying Lady": Originally "Seven Poems," *Little
Review,* Aug. 1917 (where I is called "Upon a Dying
Lady" and IV, V, and VI lack formal titles); do., *New
Statesman,* 11 Aug. 1917; present title, 1917 *Wild
Swans;* rptd. 46, 48, 50, 54, 57, 58 (where IV is en-
titled "The End of the Day"), 63, 73, 75, *79, 80, 88,

98, 99.—V. Jeffares, 166-67, for a tender unpublished portion of the sequence, which concerns Aubrey Beardsley's sister, Mabel, once an actress (and wife to actor George Bealby Wright), apparently in her early forties at the time of her fatal illness. The individual poems were apparently written at widely separated intervals before her slowly approached death of cancer, which was preceded by a "very black" struggle to live during "the last five months," as recorded in Lewis (256-57) under date of 8 May 1916; but exact dating is a problem. Ellmann (*Iden.*, 290) names the period 1912–14; and dates I Jan. 1913, II Jan. 1912, and VII "about July 14, 1914." But Yeats's 8 Jan. and 11 Feb. 1913 letters to Lady Gregory (Wade, *Letters*, 574-75), which particularly illuminate the portions separately dated by Ellmann, show the sequence in active process of composition; and the earlier suggests that Miss Beardsley was not stricken until June 1912. Cp. Hone, 287; Wellesley, 51. (On Aubrey Beardsley, *v. Auto.*, especially 405 ff.)— "J., New York" has a charming letter about Miss Beardsley, Yeats, and other friends in the *Little Review* for Sept. 1917 (pp. 30-31).—On Petronius Arbiter, the Roman satirist mentioned in I, cp. Septimus, in *The Player Queen:* "like Petronius Arbiter, will tell witty, scandalous tales. . . ."—II implies reference to four dolls made by Charles Ricketts and suggested by Aubrey Beardsley drawings.—For l. 1 of VI, cp. *Oisin* (Bk. I) and "The Fiddler of Dooney." Diarmuid and Grania will be familiar to students of Irish literature as the central figures of *The Pursuit of Diarmuid and Grania,* a romance of the Fenian cycle (one may cp. Saul). "Timor" = Tamerlane (?1333–1405); Babar: founder, Mogul Empire in India (1483–1530); "Barhaim" = ? "Bahrám, that great Hunter" of the *Rubáiyát* (Fitzgerald version). The Venetian painter Giorgione and the Homeric hero Achilles should be familiar figures.

"Ego Dominus Tuus": *Poetry* (Chicago), Oct. 1917; *New Statesman,* 17 Nov. 1917; rptd. 42, 43, 46, 48, 54, 57, 58, 59, 63, 75, *79, 80, 98, 99.—Mrs. Yeats dates the first MS. Oct., the second Dec., 1915; Ellmann (*Iden.,* 290) specifies only 5 Oct.—Ure (62) calls *Per Amica Silentia Lunae* "the key" to this, and Jeffares (194-95) refers to specific parallel passages. Cp. *Essays,* 493, 496; *Auto.,* 337 ff., 385 ff.; Witt, 92-99; Ellmann, 197 ff.; and recall Septimus, *The Player Queen:* "Man is nothing till he is united to an image."—On Robartes, *v.* "The Phases of the Moon," *inf.*—"Lapo" and "Guido" (158) are Lapo Gianni and Guido Cavalcanti: *v.* Dante's sonnet to latter (in *Poems and Translations* by Dante Gabriel Rossetti, *Everyman's Library,* No. 627, p. 326).—Perhaps the *"Hic—Ille"* labeling was suggested by William Morris' *Hapless Love.*

"A Prayer on Going into My House": *Little Review,* Oct. 1918; rptd. 44, 46, 48, 54, 57, 58, *63, 75, 79, 80, 98, 99.—Wr. 1918 (Ellmann, *Iden.,* 290).—Cp. the proposed "Letter to Michael's Schoolmaster" in § XXXIII, *1930 Diary* (p. 37). Anent ll. 3-4, Jeffares (219) says the "Heavy elm furniture" for Thoor Ballylee was "made on the spot by local carpenters."—L. 11, "Loadstone Mountain": Presumably the mountain at whose base Sindbad (*Arabian Nights*) was wrecked on his sixth voyage; cp. Henn, 249-50.

"The Phases of the Moon": 46, 48, 54, 57, 58; as "The Wheel and the Phases . . ." opens Bk. I of the 1925 *Vision;* rptd. under original title also in 63, 75, 79, *80, 90, 98, 99, 101.—Wr. in 1918, it summarizes the doctrine of the central part of *A Vision,* Yeats's "lunar parable." The poet has a note, *C. P.,* 453; cp. also his *Auto.,* 359-64, and "Note on 'The Only Jealousy of Emer,'" *P. & C.,* 440-41. In general, *v.* Henn, Ch. 10. —Aherne and Robartes, Yeats's fictitious mouthpieces, appear frequently: cp. *Rosa Alchemica, The Tables of the Law,* etc.—On "Shelley's visionary prince" (l. 3, p. 161), Henn (14 fn. 1) points *Prince Athanase* (". . . he sate/Apart from men, as in a lonely tower . . ."). —"The lonely light . . . Palmer engraved" (l. 4, p. 161) refers to "The Lonely Tower," in illustration of "Il Penseroso" and reference to Milton's "some high lonely Tower," in the Sealey and Co. edition of *The Minor Poems of Milton* (London, 1889).—"Twenty-and-eight . . . ," Robartes' third speech: Chaucer speaks in the *Franklin's Tale* of the moon's "eighte and twenty mansiouns." In the same speech, "From the first crescent to the half" includes Phases 2 to 8 of *A Vision;* "the full" indicates Phase 15, that of complete subjectivity and perfect beauty.—On the dialogue of mid-162, cp. Hone, 243; the opening song, *The Only Jealousy of Emer;* "A Bronze Head"; *Auto.,* 448; and "The Statues" (*v.* Ure, 21); also Morris' *Well at the World's End,* in which (Bk. II, Ch. II) The Lady of Abundance tells Ralph, "I am both well-knit and light-foot as the Wood-wife and Goddess of yore agone. Many a toil hath gone to that. . . ."—On Robartes' first speech, 163, cp. *Auto.,* 241; *A Vision* (ed. 1937), 83; and The Hebrew's concept of Christ in *The Resurrection* as one who thought himself the Messiah "because of all destinies it seemed the most terrible."—"Hunchback and Saint and Fool" (l. 2, p. 164) belong to Phases 26, 27, and 28, respectively (*A Vision*). On ll. 3-4, p. 164, *v.* Henn, 241.—The 8th printing of 99A deletes the comma (illogically, Yeats to the contrary) from l. 115.

"The Cat and the Moon": 44, 46, 48, 50, 54, 57, 58; *Criterion* and *Dial,* both July 1924; next printed as a song, though broken into three paragraphs and untitled, in the playlet of the same name published in the Cuala *The Cat and the Moon and Certain Poems* (1924), and so printed in subsequent editions of the play; thereafter rptd. in *63, 75, 79, 80, 82, 83, 98, 99, 100.— Wr. 1917 (Ellmann, *Iden.,* 290).—V. Yeats's first note in the Cuala volume and his introduction to the play in *W. & B.,* 124.—L. 15: The referent-lacking "that courtly fashion" is clear in the "her courtly fashion" of the earlier printings.—Smith (*N & Q*), recanting an earlier article in *The Western Review* (XI, 241-44), suggests an analogue to the action of the cat's pupils in Plutarch's *Isis and Osiris* (lxiii).—Benson (*Mod. Lang. Notes*) suggests as possible "ultimate source" Mme. Blavatsky's *The Secret Doctrine* and notes Henn, 178.

"The Saint and the Hunchback": *46, 48, 54, 57, 58, 63, 65, 75, 79, 80, 98, 99.—Dated 1918 by Jeffares (200). —The two characters (*v.* "The Phases of the Moon," *sup.*) are to be understood as speaking of previous incarnations. The saint's "taws" are birch rods: cp. "Among School Children," *inf.* The "honoured" Alcibiades (450-404 B.C.), a debauched friend of Socrates, was a Greek politician and general, eventually assassinated.—V. Henn, 174-77.—On this and the next, cp. Ussher, 102-3.

M "Two Songs of a Fool": 46, 48, 50, 54, 57, 58, 63, *73, 75, 79, 80, 88, 98, 99.—This is the poem that should have been dated *c* 20 Sept. 1918 by Hone (cp. Wade, *Letters,* 653), who confused it with "The Collar-Bone of

a Hare" (*q. v.*). Jeffares (326 fn. 73) says, "The poem
was written between July and September 1918 when
Yeats and his wife were living at Ballinamantane
House, near Gort"; but in his *Eng. Studies* (XXVI)
article (169) he suggests "in September 1918."—The
"speckled cat" and "tame hare" of l. 1 are supposed to
be Mrs. Yeats and Iseult Gonne (for whom Yeats had
found employment in London), respectively (Jeffares,
212: *v.* also his just-cited *Eng. Studies* art., which calls
the poem "a symbolic account of how, in the preoccu-
pations of marriage, Yeats neglected to think of Iseult's
welfare, and feared that for want of advice or atten-
tion she might be tempted or tortured by life . . .").—
V. Ussher, 102-3.

"Another Song of a Fool": *46, 48, 50, 54, 57, 58, 63, 75,
79, 80, 98, 99.—Cp. *Auto.*, 255 and preceding pp.—
Yeats apparently means, in some vague way, to relate
this to his efforts to fight a merely sentimental concept
of Ireland in the days of division "after Parnell."

"The Double Vision of Michael Robartes": 46, 48, 54, 57,
58, 63, 75, *79, 80, 98, 99.—Wr. 1919 (Ellmann, *Iden.*,
290).—V. "The Phases of the Moon," *sup.*—Yeats has
a brief note, *C. P.*, 453.—On this difficult piece, which
in its first two printings had no break between the
first two stanzas of the second part, *v.* Jeffares, 200-1;
Hone, 337; Ure, 63; Henn, 179-80, 237; Bowra (especially), 207; and Ellmann, *Iden.*, 255-56.—The third
line of St. 6 of Pt. II originally ran: "So that she
danced. No thought," and stands thus in the first five
printings.—The last line refers to Cashel, Tipperary,
associated with two Munster kings, Cormac mac Cuil-
leanaín (10th cent.) and Cormac mac Carthy (12th
cent.: restorer of the now-ruined chapel), as Ellmann

recalls.—The 8th printing of 99A corrects "thing" to "things" in l. 2, st. 5, § II.

Michael Robartes and the Dancer

M "Michael Robartes and the Dancer": *Dial*, Nov. 1920; rptd. *49, 54, 57, 58, 63, 75, 79, 80, 98, 99.—Ellmann (*Iden.*, 290) dates this 1918; Jeffares (212) dates it 1919 and relates it to Yeats and Iseult Gonne. Jeffares also calls the opening "a description of Bordone's St. George and the Dragon in the National Gallery, Dublin"; but Henn (236 fn. 2) counts "this altar-piece" (l. 2) a reference to Cosimo Tuva's "St. George and the Dragon," seen by Yeats in 1907 in Ferrara Cathedral.

"Solomon and the Witch": 49, 54, *57, 58, 63, 75, 79, 80, 98, 99.—Wr. 1918 (Jeffares, 207: Jeffares sees the poem as suggestive of the "acceptance and contentment" found in marriage by Yeats).—L. 7, p. 175: cp. Hardy's preface to *Late Lyrics and Earlier*.—Ll. 12 ff.: cp. § VII, *Estrangement;* on "a spider's eye," *v.* Henn, 57.—Cp. Ellis-Fermor, "The Shadowy Waters," *inf.*— Ure (65) finds relationship with the concept of the "Fifteenth Phase" of *A Vision*.

"An Image from a Past Life": *Nation* (London), 6 Nov. 1920; rptd. 49, *54, 57, 58, 63, 75, 79, 80, 98, 99.—Wr. Sept. 1919 (Jeffares, 207); called by Ellmann (*Iden.*, 256) "the first poem to be written" at Thoor Ballylee. —It would seem that interpretation should emphasize literally the title. Yeats gives a long exposition in his notes (dated 1920) in the Cuala *Michael Robartes and the Dancer.*

"Under Saturn": *Dial*, Nov. 1920; 49, *54, 57, 58, 63, 75, 79, 80, 98, 99.—Dated Nov. 1919 by Yeats; Nov. 1918 by Ellmann (*Iden.*, 290).

𝑀 "Easter 1916": First issued in a privately printed edition of 25 copies by Clement Shorter (Biblio., *sup.*, No. 41), and there dated 25 Sept. 1916, though Yeats's 11 May 1916 letter to Lady Gregory (Wade, *Letters*, 613) shows he was then "trying to write" it; later (and in this case undated) in *New Statesman*, 23 Oct. 1920, and *Dial*, Nov. 1920, before inclusion in *Michael Robartes . . .* , 1921; rptd. 54, 57, 58, 63, *73, 75, 79, 80, 88, 98, 99. (Except for *Dial*, printings through 88 have a comma after *Easter;* the MS., together with a letter to Shorter, is in the Berg Collection, N. Y. Public Library.)—Maud Gonne (*v.* Gwynn, 31) says Yeats "had sown with pious exaltation, but left others to water" the seed of this rebellion, at which he "stood amazed and abashed"; she also tells how Yeats worked all of one night on the poem and read it to her the next morning (in Sept. 1916) on a Normandy seashore, though one reflects that the letter to Lady Gregory indicates it was not purely an overnight affair: there had obviously been spadework.—Cp. "The Ghost of Roger Casement," "The O'Rahilly," the third of "Three Songs to the One Burden," "Sixteen Dead Men," "The Rose Tree," "On a Political Prisoner," "Nineteen Hundred and Nineteen," and the play *The Death of Cuchulain.*—Ll. 14-20, p. 178, refer to Constance Gore-Booth Markievicz; ll. 21-22, to Padraic Pearse (cp. A. Bax, 105-6; Flanders, *Envoy;* O'Casey; Colum, Chap. 14); ll. 23-27, to Thomas MacDonagh (MacNeice, 131, recalls Yeats's reflections on meeting MacDonagh in 1909; *v. Estrangement,* § xliv, and *The Death of Synge,* § x); ll. 28-36, to John MacBride, Maud Gonne's husband.—On l. 3, p. 179, cp. Gonne, *cit. sup.*, p. 32; on ll. 20-24, *Auto.*, 369.—V. also Wade, *Letters*, 612-14; Rothenstein, *M. & M.*, II, 321; Stein,

Sewanee Rev.; Ure, 46 ff.—One apprehends Yeats's perception of an epic subject in the Easter Rising, a perception which was to grow and inform itself continuously till his death. That action, which had seemed at first a subject for ridicule, gradually assumed in his mind the qualities of a war for freedom, a war in which the conquered achieved victory six years later with the treaty of 1922. The first movement reflects accurately a mood apparently common during the Rising and immediately afterwards. The untrained Republican army, the naïveté of its commanders, gave rise to many jests among the Unionist Irish (in another mood it was "that crazy fight"), so that they were certain

> that they and I
> But lived where motley is worn.

Cp. Sean O'Casey's *The Plough and the Stars.*

"Sixteen Dead Men"; *Dial,* Nov. 1920; rptd. 49, 54, 57, 58, 63, 73, 75, 79, 80, 88, 98, 99.—Wr. 17 Dec. 1917 (Ellmann, *Iden.,* 290).—Anent the Easter "rebels" executed by the British. (Really fifteen, unless one add Casement. For list, *v.* MacManus, 703.)—L. 16: "Lord Edward" = Lord Edward Fitzgerald, on whom one may *v.* MacManus, 508-18 *passim.*—Barry O'Brien edited *The Autobiography of Wolfe Tone* (1893).

"The Rose Tree": *Dial,* Nov. 1920; *Nation* (London), 6 Nov. 1920; *49, 54, 57, 58, 63, 73, 75, 79, 80; *A Broadside,* May 1935; 88, 89, 98, 99.—Wr. 7 Apr. 1917 (Ellmann, *Iden.,* 290).—Also concerns Easter Rising; *v.* notes to preceding poem.—On Connolly, cp. *Auto.,* 450, 452; Rothenstein, *M. & M.,* II, 260-61.—*V.* also Thompson, *Hopkins Rev.,* III, 11-12.

"On a Political Prisoner": *Dial,* Nov. 1920; *Nation* (London), 13 Nov. 1920; 49, *54, 57, 58, 63, 73, 75, 79, 80, 88, 89, 98, 99.—Wr. 10-29 Jan. 1919 (Ellmann, *Iden.,* 290); Jeffares says the poem was begun the previous year (188; 323 fn. 7).—The prisoner (in Holloway Gaol for her share in the Easter Rising) is Constance Gore-Booth Markievicz (MacNeice, 130), who, like her sister Eva, was once a daring horsewoman. Cp. "Easter, 1916," "In Memory of Eva Gore-Booth . . ."; *Markievicz;* A. Bax, 98; Ure, 49-50; Lady Gregory, *Jour.,* 237-38.—Henn (96 fn. 3) glosses "blind and led by the blind" of the *Upanishads* for l. 11.—V. especially Colum, 278-81.

"The Leaders of the Crowd": *49, 54, 57, 58, 63, 75, 79, 80, 98, 99.—Jeffares (189) dates composition 1918; Ellmann (*Iden.,* 290) says 1918–19.—Supposedly referent to the "crowd" of Dublin Bohemians Constance Markievicz (*v.* preceding poem) had joined.

"Towards Break of Day": *Dial,* Nov. 1920; *Nation* (London), 13 Nov. 1920; 49, 54, 57, 58, 63, 75, 79, 80, 98, 99.—Ellmann (*Iden.,* 290) dates the poem "Dec. 1918–Jan. 1919"; Jeffares (325 fn. 69) writes: "The poem is an actual record of the dreams experienced by the poet and his wife when they were staying in the Powerscourt Arms Hotel, Enniskerry, Co. Wicklow, in January 1919." Jeffares (210) supposes the poem (which according to a reference in *A Vision* illustrates the fact that " 'When two people meditate upon the one theme, who have established a supersensual link, they will invariably . . . see . . . complementary images . . .' ") to have been written then.— Though there seems to be no logic in the allusion, the "marvellous stag" of the last stanza is presumably the proud white stag hunted and slain by Arthur in

the *Mabinogion's* "Geraint the Son of Erbin"; cp. Chrétien's *Erec et Enide*. In "Miraculous Creatures" (*The
Celtic Twilight*) Yeats refers vaguely to "the white
stag that flits in and out of the tales of Arthur." (Saul,
N & Q.)

"Demon and Beast": *Dial*, Nov. 1920; 49, 54, 57, 58, 63,
73, 75, *79, 80, 88, 98, 99.—Ellmann (*Iden.*, 290)
dates the piece 23 Nov. 1918; Jeffares (211) says it
was written during the 1918 winter at 73 St. Stephen's
Green, Dublin. Citing Mrs. Yeats's authority, Jeffares
also (337 fn. 67) gives two sources: J. O. Hannay's
The Spirit and Origin of Christian Monasticism (London: Methuen, 1903; p. 101) and *The Wisdom of the
Desert* (*Idem*, 1904; pp. 7-10); cp. Dume, 175-76. V.
Auto. (ed. London 1926, p. 387) and *Essays, 1931–
1936* (p. 39).—Ure (32) cps. the "idea" with that of
"The Grey Rock."—St. 3, "aimless joy": cp. "Tom
O'Roughley," l. 4.—The reference to "the Mareotic
sea" in the last stanza connotes Shelley (*Witch of Atlas*, St. LVIII); Ure (*Rev. of Eng. Studies*, N. S. II,
39) refers to "the anchorites who joined St. Antony by
the Mareotic Lake."—V. Mégroz, 121-22; Ure, 32-33.

"The Second Coming": *Dial*, Nov. 1920; *Nation* (London), 6 Nov. 1920; 49, *54, 57, 58, 63, 75, 79, 80, 98,
99.—Wr. Jan. 1919.—On this much-anatomized poem,
v. Yeats's *1930 Diary*, § XL, p. 55; "The Need for Au-
dacity of Thought," *Dial*, LXXX, 115 ff.; "Notes,"
Michael Robartes and the Dancer; intro. to "The Resurrection," *W. & B.;* Bk. IV, *A Vision;* "The Gyres,"
L. P. P.; and *Auto.*, 230, 238.—Cp. Blackmur, *South.
Rev.*, II; Weeks, *PMLA;* Brooks, *M. P. T.*, 173-202;
Jeffares, 203; Hone, 351; Spender, *Destructive Element* and "La crise des symboles," *France Libre;* Savage, *Adelphi;* Henn, 29, 32; Lady Gregory, *Jour.* (3

Nov. 1925); Ellmann, *Iden.*, 257 ff.; Bloom, *Univ. Kans. City Rev.*—On l. 3, one may also cp. Knights, *South. Rev.*; on possible debt to Blake in last 14 ll., Rudd, 118-19. *V.* also M. Bodkin.

ℳ "A Prayer for My Daughter": *Poetry* (Chicago), Nov. 1919; *Irish Statesman*, 8 Nov. 1919; 49, 54, 57, 58, 63, *73, 75, 79, 80, 88, 98, 99.—Anne Butler Yeats was born 26 Feb. 1919, and the June 1919 dating of the poem is lacking only in the first printing. (Jeffares, 213, says the poem was written during the summer of 1919; Hone, 338, that it "was begun a few weeks after" Anne's birth "and completed in June at Bally-lee . . ."; Ellmann, *Iden.*, 290, that it is to be dated "Feb. 26—June 1919."—On St. 3, Jeffares (326 fn. 77) glosses a line from Yeats's *Deirdre:* "But that she'd too much beauty for good luck."—St. 4, "that great Queen": Aphrodite; "a bandy-legged smith": Hephaestus.—Sts. 7 and 8 refer, of course, to Maud Gonne (as recently as 1918 in Holloway Gaol: MacNeice, 130) in their bitterness.—Last st., "the rich horn": the "horn of plenty," said to have been torn by Zeus from Amalthea, the goat that suckled him: it could reputedly provide whatever its possessor wished; "laurel tree": the favorite of Apollo, since Daphne, daughter of the Thessalian river-god Peneus, was upon prayer metamorphosed into one to escape this pursuing brother of Artemis.

"A Meditation in Time of War": *Dial*, Nov. 1920 (with the misprint "Mediation"); *Nation* (London), 13 Nov. 1920, as "Meditations . . ."; exactly titled, *49, 54, 57, 58, 63, 75, 79, 80, 98, 99.—Ellmann (*Iden.*, 290) dates the poem 9 Nov. 1914; Jeffares (*N & Q*) had earlier remarked that it "first appears in the manuscript book given to Yeats by Maud Gonne. The year of its com-

position is 1914, the month most likely November."
He finds a prose statement of its meaning in § X,
"Anima Mundi" (*Essays*, 523-24); a source in Blake's
Time, with its "a pulsation of the artery."—The 8th
printing of 99A alters "fantasy" to "phantasy."

"To Be Carved on a Stone at Thoor Ballylee": In *Michael Robartes . . .* (1921), this lacks the "Thoor" (=
"Tower"), inserted in *Later Poems*, 1922; rptd. 57, 58,
63, 65, 75, 79, 80, 98, 99.—Wr. 1918 (Ellmann, *Iden.*,
291).—L. 2, "sea-green slates": Bought, but never used
as roofing because deemed unsafe against the Atlantic
winds.—On the Norman relic, Ballylee Castle, standing in Kiltartan Barony, Co. Galway, *v.* fn. 1 to Yeats's
"Dust Hath Closed Helen's Eye," *E. P. S.*, 159; and
cp. Hone, 331; Jeffares, 327 fn. 15, and *Envoy* art.;
Moore, 282; and Wade, *Letters*, 625, 651 (for earliest
text), and 652.—The allocation of rooms in the Tower
(Wade, *idem*, 682 and 687) seems to vary in letters
written only two days apart from each other.

The Tower

"Sailing to Byzantium": First in *October Blast*, Aug. 1927;
next opens Nov. 1927 ed. of *Stories of Red Hanrahan
. . .*, where it is dedicated to the illustrator, Norah
McGuinness; next in *The Tower*, 14 Feb. 1928; then
in Pound's *The Exile* (Chicago), No. 3 (Spring 1928);
thereafter in *70, 73, 79, 80, 88, 89, 98, 99.—Yeats
(who has a brief note, *C. P.*, 453) consistently dates
this poem 1927; Ellmann (250) specifies 26 Sept.
1926; Hone agrees in 1926; Jeffares and Henn confirm
Sept. 1926.—The poem has been a happy playground
for both genuine analysts and others. Interested students would be well advised to consult (aside from
several early remarks of direct and tangential interest

by Yeats himself, e.g., in *Essays*, 367; *A Vision* [ed. London, 1937], 287; Wade, *Letters*, 730-31; and *E. P. S.*, 467) especially Bowra (209), Hone (398), Jeffares (246 and arts. in *Nineteenth Cent. and After* and *Rev. of Eng. Studies*, XXII), Henn (Ch. 12), O'Donnell (§ IV). Further comment and analysis may be experienced in Tindall (94), Ure (67-68), Stageberg (*Explicator*), Notopoulos (*Class. Jour.*), Daiches (181), Ellmann (235 ff.), MacNeice (140-41), Baker (*South. Rev.*), Bradford (*Va. Qu. Rev.*), Ussher (81), Strong (*P. R.*, 178-79), and, by the hardy, Olson (*Univ. Rev.*). Thompson even asserts (*Hopkins Rev.*, III, 13) " 'Sailing to Byzantium' might even be subtitled 'Thoughts on looking at an Irish illuminated manuscript' "!— Henn (212) places the "salmon-falls" (l. 4) in the Sligo River from Lough Gill.—St. II, l. 3 ("Soul clap its hands . . ."): Strong recalls (*P. R.*, 32) that "Blake, when his brother died, saw his soul carried up to heaven clapping its hands for joy."—St. II, l. 6: Greene (*Philol. Qu.*) finds a possible source in Johnson's *Journey to the Western Islands of Scotland.*— Miss Murphy (153, fn.) relates St. III to the "Byzantium mosaic forming a great frieze on the walls of S. Apollinare Nuovo in Ravenna. . . ."—St. IV: Dume (*Mod. Lang. Notes*) argues sensibly that the golden tree and birds probably came from Gibbon's *Decline and Fall* and the *Cambridge Medieval History.*— V. also Gwynn, notes to "Byzantium," *inf.*; Davenport art., 56-57; M. Bodkin; Campbell (on Yeats's basic concern with "the spiritual life visibly represented by the art" of Byzantium); and Hone, 392-93.

"The Tower": *Criterion*, June 1927; *New Republic*, 29 June 1927; 66, *68, 70, 79, 80, 98, 99.—Yeats has an interesting note, *C. P.*, 453-54; he told Sturge Moore

(Bridge, 114): "I like to think of that building as a permanent symbol of my work plainly visible to the passer-by."—On § I, *v.* Reynolds, 42. One recalls Hanrahan's curse on age and the aged, *E. P. S.,* 436-37, and Yeats's 7 June 1922 letter to Olivia Shakespear: Wade, *Letters,* 685.—Jeffares (217-18), recalling Milton, Shelley, and de l'Isle Adam in connection with Yeats's tower symbolism, discusses its literary sources in *English Studies,* Dec. 1947; MacNeice (144-45) emphasizes the debt to Shelley and glosses ll. 11-15 from *A Vision.* Cp. Yeats's own discussion of the tower symbolism in *Laon and Cythna* in "The Philosophy of Shelley's Poetry," *Ideas of Good and Evil.* One may also cp. Ellmann, *Iden.,* 148.—§ II: V. references, *sup.,* under "To Be Carved on a Stone. . . ." Jeffares (234) says Mrs. Yeats had read Yeats the story referred to in St. 2 from Sir Jonah Barrington's *Sketches of His Own Times* (London: Routledge, 1869). On Mary Hynes and Raftery (Sts. 3-5), cp. "'Dust Hath Closed Helen's Eye,'" *The Celtic Twilight;* on Hanrahan (Sts. 6-7), *v. Stories of Red Hanrahan,* especially "Red Hanrahan." On "Whose images . . . ," St. 9, *v.* "Anima Mundi," *Per Amica Silentia Lunae.* The "old lecher" of St. 11 is Hanrahan.—§ III, dated 1925 in *October Blast,* 1926 in *C. P.,* is according to Jeffares (237) dated 7 Oct. 1925 in MS. Hone (404) links this section to Yeats's readings in Berkeley and to his Senatorial experience. Miss Moore (318) thinks l. 26 applies only to disagreement with the "eighth tractate of the First Ennead, on the source of evil." Cp. ll. 28 ff. with "Man has created death" ("Death"); and *v.* MacNeice, 148-49, and Davenport art., 60-62. In the *New Republic* version, l. 36 reads "The final Paradise."—The 8th printing of 99A alters "stair" (l. 83) to "stairs," the period of l. 152 to a comma, and the semicolon of l. 193 to a comma.

"Meditations in Time of Civil War": *London Mercury* and *Dial*, Jan. 1923 (the *Dial* version having "Jay's" in place of "Stare's" in the subtitle of § VI); next in *The Cat and the Moon* . . . , 1924, each of these three printings having an unfortunately now-omitted stanza following the second of § II. Further rptgs: *68, 70, 73, 79, 80, 88, 98, 99.—Yeats has a note, *C. P.*, 455, where he correctly dates the finished poem 1922 (cp. publication dates and Wade, *Letters*, 689-90), though he dates it 1923 on p. 204. (Hone, 358 and fn., says the series was begun in the summer of 1921 and adds, inaccurately, that it was "finished at Ballylee two years later"; Ellmann, *Iden.*, 291, also dates its beginning 1921. *V.*, in general, Lady Gregory, *Jour.* ["III. Politics."])—§ I, st. 2, ll. 5-6: Jeffares (227) traces the source of this image to *The Revolt of Islam*. —§ II: Bowra (212-13) suggests "The tower stood differently for the aspirations of the intellect and the soul, for the self's assertiveness, for the modern nation 'dead at the top.' The staircase stands for the intricate process by which the self ascends, the sword for action, the underground streams [cp. *E. P. S.*, 405, l. 15] for the spiritual forces which make for new life." —"*Il Penseroso's* Platonist" is, of course, Milton.— Jeffares (229) relates the last lines of St. 2 to Samuel Palmer's illustration for *Il Penseroso* (*v.* "The Phases of the Moon," *sup.*).—§ III: Jeffares (*idem*) says Yeats and Junzo Sato were "fellow members of a secret society" and the "gift" was made "in Portland, Oregon, in 1920"; cp. Wade, *Letters*, 662. MacNeice (146-47, obviously in reference to the third stanza of "A Dialogue of Self and Soul") equates the sword

with war, its "dress" with love. On the last line, Ure
(66 fn. 1) glosses *A Vision*, seeing the peacock's
scream as indicative of the "loss of control in a civilization."—§ V: The "Irregular" (l. 1) is a Republican
Army man; the soldiers of the second stanza are members of the National Army. For St. 3, cp. J. B. Yeats's
observation in a 11 Jan. 1917 letter (Robinson):
"Poets and men of action in this are alike, their interest is in the concrete & with children and primitive
people it is the same."—§ VI: Yeats wrote to Olivia
Shakespear of the stares' nest in May 1922 (Wade,
Letters, 681).—§ VII: Hone (371) fancies George
Sand's influence in the second stanza; relative to the
fourth, Henn (242) refers to Yeats's 8 Nov. 1936 letter to Dorothy Wellesley, with its references to Botticelli's "Spring," Gustave Moreau's "Women and Uni-
corns," and Fragonard's "Cup of Life." On Jacques de
Molay, *v.* Thomas Wright's *Narratives of Sorcery and
Magic* (1851).—Cp. MacNeice, 152-53, and Henn's
Yale Rev. art.; also Bridge (Letters 39, 41, and 42). V.
Robinson, *T. H.*, 237 ff., for Nora Dorman's vivid
recollections.

"Nineteen Hundred and Nineteen": Originally "Thoughts
upon the Present State of the World," *Dial*, Sept. 1921;
London Mercury, Nov. 1921; and *Seven Poems and a
Fragment*, 1922. Present title since *The Tower*, 1928;
rptd. *70, 79, 80, 98, 99.—Mrs. Yeats writes that
"Nineteen Nineteen" exists in many versions between
1919 and 1922, and that the MS. of "Thoughts . . ."
dates from "early 1921" (it is dated "May 1921" in the
Dial printing); cp. Wade, *Letters*, 668, showing two
of the "Thoughts" had been written by 9 April 1921.—
Hone (352): "The poem . . . was suggested by Lady
Gregory's account of some horrors at Gort" (*V.* again

her *Jour.:* "III. Politics," and Robinson, *T. H.*, 237 ff.).
It relates (note especially St. 4 of § I) to the atrocities
of the Black-and-Tans and Auxiliaries in running
down members of the Irish Republican Army: cp.
Henn, 17; Jeffares, 221; MacNeice, 153-55.—§ II:
Loie Fuller: soubrette and dancer, famed for "Ser-
pentine" dance in U.S. and Europe; born an Illinois
farm girl; lived latterly in Paris, appearing at *Folies
Bergères; ob.* 2 Jan. 1928.—"Platonic Year": cp. *A
Vision,* 254, and notes to "Two Songs from a Play,"
inf.—§ III: "Those winds . . .": Conceivably a reference to the end of the 2,000-year Christian cycle,
foretold in *A Vision;* cp. "The Second Coming."—§ V:
Jeffares (224) glosses Blake ("Mock on, mock on
. . ."). Might there also be the accents of Pound's *The
Garret?*—§ VI: Jeffares (225) sees Symons' *Dance of
the Daughters of Herodias* here. V. Wade, *Letters,*
680, 690-91. Yeats has a note on this section, *C. P.*, 455.
It also appears from Jeffares (226, with pertinent
notes) that Robert Artisson (third line from end) was
the fourteenth-century Kilkenny incubus of Alice
Kyteler.—Cp. Parkinson's "The World of Yeats' 'Nineteen Hundred and Nineteen.'"

"The Wheel": 53, *68, 70, 73, 79, 80, 88, 98, 99.—Wr. 17
Sept. 1921, at Euston: for circumstances, *v.* Jeffares,
Nineteenth Cent. and After (available in Hall-Stein-
mann, 301-2). The poem appears pretty obviously to
be a restatement of an idea attributed by Yeats to
Leonardo da Vinci: cp. *E. P. S.*, 509 (Saul, *N & Q*).

"Youth and Age": *60, 68, 70, 79, 80, 98, 99.—Wr. 1924
(Ellmann, *Iden.*, 291).—Cp. "The Coming of Wisdom
with Time," *sup.*

"The New Faces": *53, 68, 70, 79, 80, 98, 99.—Jeffares
(163 and *Rev. of Eng. Studies,* XXIII) dates this

poem about Lady Gregory and Yeats Dec. 1912; Ellmann (*Iden.*, 291) agrees. The 8th printing of 99A
hyphenates "catalpa tree" (l. 2).

"A Prayer for My Son": 53, *68, 70, 73, 79, 80, 88, 98, 99.
—Wr. Dec. 1921 (Ellmann, *Iden.*, 291).—The son is
"William Michael," born 22 Aug. 1921, at Cuttle-
brook House, Thame, England.—In his *Packet for
Ezra Pound,* Yeats says, anent *A Vision:* "When regu-
lar communication was near its end and my work of
study and arrangement begun, I was told that hence-
forth the Frustrators would attack my health and that
of my children. . . ."

"Two Songs from a Play": Originally a part of *The Resurrection* (a play "drafted in 1925," according to Jeffares: 269), and first printed in *The Adelphi,* June
1927, where "I" and "II" are respectively entitled "The
Song of the Folding and Unfolding of the Cloth" and
"Song of the Unfolding and Folding of the Cloth";
rptd. 66, 68, 70, 73, 76 (wherein the second stanza
of "II" first appears), *79, 80, 82, 83, 88 (from which,
as in the first five printings, the last stanza is missing),
98, 99, 100.—Wr. 1926 except for last stanza, which
may possibly belong to 1931 (Ellmann, *Iden.*, 291).—
V. *Essays,* 359; *A Vision,* 278.—The debt to Shelley's
concluding chorus to *Hellas* is obvious, but has been
overstressed. In his intro. to "The Resurrection"
(*W. & B.,* 93), Yeats relates ll. 6-7 to the coming of
his "system" (*A Vision:* cp. p. 254, ed. 1937). "Magnus
Annus" (St. 1) is the "Platonic Year": one may *v.*
K. F. Smith, "Ages of the World (Greek and Roman),"
Encyclopedia of Religion and Ethics, I, 192-200. On
the second stanza, cp. *The Resurrection* proper (espe-
cially p. 111, *W. & B.*); *v.* Lady Gregory's *Jour.,* 24
May 1926, for early draft and Yeats's comment.—On

"II," *v.* Ure, 44-45, and Yeats's note anent Plotinus, *C. P.*, 454.—In general, cp. O'Donnell; Jeffares, 270 (and ll. 17-21, p. 99, *P. & C.*, and ll. 1-7, p. 520, *E. P. S.*); Tindall, 385; Brooks-Warren, 615-21; Mac-Neice, 126; Henn, 188 and 192-94. Ellmann (*Iden.*, 260-63) offers detailed analysis.

"Fragments": Title and "II" first appear in *Coll. Poems*, 1933. "I" was originally included, untitled, in the first installment of "The Words upon the Window Pane: A Commentary" in **The Dublin Magazine*, Oct.–Dec. 1931 number; thereafter it was printed in 79 (*C. P.*, 1933), 80, 81, 82, 98, 99: it is dated 1931 in *W. & B.*— "II" appears in **79, 80, 82, 98, 99.—On "I," cp. intro. to *The Words* . . . ; *Auto.*, 328; "Intro." to *Fighting the Waves;* and the comments of Hone (446) and MacNeice (33, 148).—On "II," cp. intro. to *The Resurrection.* L. 1, "that truth": Yeats's "symbolical system." On the last line, Ellmann (*Iden.*, 264) glosses an O'Shaughnessy poem. V. Jeffares' "Notes on Yeats's 'Fragments,' " the best elucidation.

"Leda and the Swan": Originally, with preliminary note, in *Dial*, June 1924; next in *The Cat and the Moon* . . . , July 1924 (though the book had been printed by 1 May); then in *To-morrow* (Dublin), Aug. 1924; rptd. **62, 68, 70, 79, 80, 90, 98, 99, 101.—As "Leda" set at beginning of Bk. III, 1925 *Vision;* of Bk. V, 1937 ed.: cp. 1956 ed.—Wr. 18 Sept. 1923 (Ellmann, *Iden.*, 291).—V. Yeats's note in Cuala *The Cat and the Moon* . . . , p. 37; and cp. Hone, 387, MacNeice, 144, Rothenstein's *Since Fifty*, 242, Drew-Sweeney, 164-66, Stein (*Sewanee Rev.*), Trowbridge (*Mod. Philol.*), Reid (*Jour. Aesthet. & Art Crit.*), Burke (*South. Rev.*), Spitzer (*Mod. Philol.*).—Jeffares (224) relates this great sonnet to "Michelangelo's painting" on its subject; cp. Henn, 243.

"On a Picture of a Black Centaur by Edmund Dulac": Originally "Suggested by a Picture of a Black Centaur," *Seven Poems and a Fragment, 1922; present title, The Tower, 1928; rptd. 70, 79, 80, 98, 99. (N.B.: In The Tower, Dulac's Christian name is spelled "Edmond," the spelling "Edmund" first appearing in 79.)—On Cecil Salkeld's claim to the dedication and his placing the composition at a Glenmalure cottage (associated with Synge's In the Shadow of the Glen) during Yeats's Sept. 1920 visit to Maud Gonne, v. Hone, 348 ff.; Henn (243) makes an illuminating resolution on Mrs. Yeats's authority: all of which may make Ransom's interpretation (South. Rev.) suspect, not to mention Ellmann's complex attempt at demonstration (Iden., 264-66).—Goldgar even suggests (West. Rev., XV, 117) that the "figure of the centaur is the figure of art itself . . . and the green parrots . . . are the intellectualization of poetry into a play of mad abstractions. . . ."—On the "seven Ephesian topers" of l. 11, cp. Donne, The Good-Morrow; for the legend of "The Seven Sleepers of Ephesus" and their 309-year slumber, cp. A. J. Wensinck, "Ashāb al-Kahf," Encyclopedia of Islam, I, 497-98. Details and versions of the ancient story vary; cp. Baring-Gould.—The "long Saturnian sleep" of l. 13 recalls, of course, the opening of Hyperion.

"Among School Children": London Mercury and Dial, Aug. 1927; in October Blast the same month; rptd. 68, 70, 79, 80, 98, *99.—Ellmann (250) dates the poem 14 June 1926.—Yeats has a note, C. P., 455-56: cp. his "Philosophy of Shelley's Poetry" (Essays).— Brooks expands on this poem (W. U., 163-75), perhaps with less illumination than ambition; one may cp. Walcutt (*Explicator*).—St. V: Cp. second st. of opening song of *At the Hawk's Well*. Jeffares (245) remarks on l. 6: he might also have glossed Donne, *A Song.*— St. VI: Yeats quoted with comment an early version in a letter to Olivia Shakespear (Wade, *Letters*, 719), where he identifies "taws" (l. 3) as a "form of birch": cp. George Douglas' "under the tawse" (i.e., "under a teacher's discipline"), *The House with the Green Shutters* (1900—London: Cape rpt., 1931; p. 129). Tindall (262) traces "golden-thighed" (l. 5) to Plutarch.—On the concluding symbols, one may argue Tindall (*idem*) or Bowra (212), who will seem preferable to many. (One wonders in passing whether the "chestnut-tree, great-rooted blossomer" reflects a memory of the "great horse-chestnut tree" in the garden at Bedford Park, mentioned in § I, *Four Years*.)—Cp. R. Chase, "Myth as Literature," *English Institute Essays, 1947* (N.Y.: Columbia Univ. Press), 18-21; Drew-Sweeney, 161-62; Ellmann, *Kenyon Rev.*, XV, 370-71; Wain.—The 8th printing of 99A, to agree with the curious Yeatsian reading in 98, alters the "histories" of l. 4 to "history," though the rhyme scheme is thus violated.

"Colonus' Praise": 68, 70, *79, 80, 98, 99.—Sung by the Chorus in *Oedipus at Colonus* after Theseus, king of Athens (and therefore of Colonus), has promised the blind Oedipus his protection. (*V. C. Plays*, 543-44.)— Ellmann (*Iden.*, 291) dates this 24 Mar. 1927, though only the first stanza, in slightly variant form, was included by Yeats in his letter of that date to Olivia Shakespear (Wade, *Letters.* 724).—"Semele's lad" (l. 8): Dionysus, son of Zeus and Semele (daughter of Cadmus).—"Who comes . . ." (St. 3, l. 1): the

Persian invader; "the Great Mother" (l. 3): Demeter, mourning for Persephone.—Poseidon (St. 4, l. 4): Should be remembered as god of both horses and the sea.

"Wisdom": 66, 68, 70, *79, 80, 98, 99.—Henn (244) thinks lines 8-12 are "based on a poorish seventeenth-century painting, formerly hung in the Dublin National Gallery, and now stored in its cellars. . . . The painter is unknown."—Cp. Stein, *Sewanee Rev.*, LVII, 613, on concluding lines.

"The Fool by the Roadside": Originally the lyric following the dialogue of "Cuchulain the Girl and the Fool" in 53, which became "The Hero, the Girl, and the Fool" in 68 and again in 98; isolated for use as poem opening Bk. IV of 62 and Bk. III of 90 (cp. 101); rptd. in isolation *79, 80, 99. Replaced in 8th printing of 99A by "The Hero, the Girl, and the Fool," as in 98.

M "Owen Aherne and His Dancers": Originally two poems with separate titles: "The Lover Speaks" (now "I") and "The Heart Replies" (now "II"), *Dial*, June 1924, and *The Cat and the Moon* . . . , July 1924; present title, *68, where, as also in 70, "Aherne" (*v.* "The Phases of the Moon," *sup.*) lacks the final -*e*, which appears in 79, 80, 98, and 99.—Disregard Hone's dating: Mrs. Yeats says that "I" was written 24 Oct. 1917 and "II" 27 Oct. 1917, both at Coleman's Hatch, Sussex. (In *Eng. Studies*, XXVI, 170 fn. 12, Jeffares says the first and second stanzas of "II" are dated "October 30, 1917" in MS.)—"The dancers are the delighted senses, the principle of desire" (Henn, 47); Aherne is, of course, Yeats.—I, l. 1, "had come unsought": Jeffares (190) says Iseult Gonne proposed to Yeats "when she was fifteen," but was then rejected "because there was too much Mars in her horoscope";

she is, of course, the "young child" of II, l. 2. Cp. Wade, *Letters*, 633-34.

"A Man Young and Old": The *contents* of this sequence appear in 66, 68, 73, 79, 80, 88, 89, 98, 99. The present title groups all but No. XI of the sequence in 68, where, as in 66, this lyric stands (without quotation marks in its title) as a separate poem; indeed, XI is isolated also in 73, 88, and 89. Exactly as now, the sequence first appears in 79 (*Coll. Poems*, 1933) and is rptd. in 80, 98, and 99.—In 66 (*October Blast*), I-IV were grouped as "The Young Countryman. I-IV": these had appeared as "Four Songs from the Young Countryman," *London Mercury*, May 1927; while present V-X were grouped as "The Old Countryman. I-VI," of which those now numbered V and IX had appeared as "Two Songs from the Old Countryman," *London Mercury*, May 1927, and those now VI, VII, VIII, and X as "More Songs from an Old Countryman," *London Mercury*, Apr. 1926.—One gathers the sequence was written at Ballylee (Wade, *Letters*, 641); Ellmann (259) designates 1926–27 as the general period and assigns (*Iden.*, 291) I to 25 May 1926 (though the apparently earliest version of the second stanza is in a 7 Dec. 1926 letter to Olivia Shakespear: Wade, *Letters*, 720), IV to 31 Jan. 1926, VII to 2 July 1926, X to 1926, and XI to 13 Mar. 1927. The original version of V is in a 6 Dec. 1926 letter to Mrs. Shakespear, illustrating the remark, "One looks back to one's youth as to [a] cup that a mad man dying of thirst left half tasted. I wonder if you feel like that." (Wade, *Letters*, 721.)—Ure (104 ff.) has excellent comment on this and the "Crazy Jane" and "Woman Young and Old" sequences.—On IV, cp. Wade, *Letters*, 840-41 (or Hone, 472), and Jeffares, 244.—VI, l. 11: cp. "The

Old Men Admiring Themselves in the Water."—IX,
l. 17, "the bed of straw": the deathbed.—IX: In *The
Dreaming of the Bones,* Donough O'Brien is remembered as one who "knew the secrets of women."—XI:
Sung by the Chorus after Oedipus' daughter, Antigone, has persuaded her blind father to grant audience to Polyneices, the elder of his vile sons, who
wants his help against the usurping younger, Eteocles;
and after Theseus has assured Oedipus "no man shall
be put over you as a master." (Oedipus, of course, re-
jects and curses his sons equally.—*V. C. Pl.,* 561.)—
In a 13 Mar. 1927 letter to Mrs. Shakespear (Wade,
Letters, 723, where an earlier version of the last two
stanzas may be seen), Yeats writes: "The last line is
very bad Grecian but very good Elizabethan." Cp. the
closing lines of the Chorus, end of *King Oedipus* (*C.
Pl.,* 517): "Call no man fortunate that is not dead./
The dead are free from pain."

"The Three Monuments": *66, 68, 70, 79, 80, 98, 99.—
Yeats had directed the moralistic Senators to consider
the private lives of Nelson, Parnell, and O'Connell
during his 11 June 1925 speech supporting the
Divorce Bill, asking sarcastically whether it was "intended to remove these monuments." (Hone, 395; a
footnote dates the poem as "presently written" thereafter.)

"All Souls' Night/*Epilogue to 'A Vision'*": Originally
"All Souls' Night," *London Mercury,* Mar. 1921, and
New Republic, 9 Mar. 1921; do., 53 and 62; "All Souls'
Night. An Epilogue to 'A Vision,'" 68 and 70; "All
Souls' Night: an Epilogue," 90, 101; as now, *Coll.
Poems,* 1933; rptd. 80, *98, 99.—Editions of *A Vi-
sion* add "Autumn" to the concluding date, *"Oxford,
1920,"* found in most printings; Ellmann (*Iden.,* 291)

suggests "Nov. 2 (?), 1920."—Sts. 3 and 7: "Horton was recently dead. Mathers died in Paris just after the war . . .": Hone (351, fn.). On William Thomas Horton (1864–1919), v. Wade, *Letters*, 260 fn. 3.— Sts. 5-6: Cp. Davenport art., 58-60. "Florence Emery" was Florence Farr Emery, of whom Oliver Elton has written ("Preface" to Hone *Letters*): ". . . under an impulse noted . . . in . . . *All Souls' Night*, [she] migrated to Ceylon to teach in a native school, and there died, in 1917." The school was Ramanathan College. Miss Farr was suffering from cancer (Moore, 239); hence the "foul years." Cp. *Auto.*, 148 ff., and pp. 16-18, *The King of the Great Clock Tower* (Cuala Press, 1934); Moore, *Hail and Farewell*.—Sts. 7-8: On "MacGregor" [Mathers], v. *Auto.*, 226 ff., 414 ff.; Wade, *Letters*, 208 fn. 3.—On ll. 5-6, last stanza, cp. Ure, 57.—Cp. also Blackmur, *South. Rev.*—The 8th printing of 99A changes the period of l. 10 to a comma (Yeats to the contrary, illogically).

The Winding Stair and Other Poems: Yeats has a note, *C. P.*, 456-57.

"In Memory of Eva Gore-Booth and Con Markiewicz": *72, 78, 79, 80, 89, 98, 99.—Wr. Oct. 1927 (Ellmann, *Iden.*, 291).—Constance Gore-Booth Markievicz (note Yeats's spelling) had been jailed as one of the Easter 1916 "rebels" by a British court-martial; v. notes on "On a Political Prisoner," *sup.*—"Lissadell" (l. 1): the Sir Henry Gore-Booth home, Sligo; for an early report by Yeats to his sister Lily, v. Wade, *Letters*, 239-40, 242-43.—". . . one a gazelle" (l. 4): Eva, Yeats's particular friend.—Ll. 26-27: Cp. "He Tells of the Perfect Beauty," *The Wind.* . . .—P. 230, l. 1, "We the great gazebo built" = ? "We provided the lofty, wide outlook."—The 8th printing of 99A groups the first 20 ll. as "I," the remaining ll. as "II."

"Death": *72, 78, 79, 80, 98, 99.—Wr. 13 Sept. 1927 (Ellmann, *Iden.*, 291).—V. C. P., 456, and cp. "Blood and the Moon."—On O'Higgins, cp. Hone, *London Mercury.*—Cp. notes on next poem.

"A Dialogue of Self and Soul": 72, *78, 79, 80, 98, 99.— Yeats (*C. P.*, 457) dates this "the spring of 1928"; Jeffares (247) suggests that, like "Death" and "Blood and the Moon," it was *begun* in July 1927; Ellmann (*Iden.*, 291) places it in the period July–Dec. 1927. It is apparently the poem referred to by Yeats in a letter of 2 or 4 Oct. 1927 as "Sword and Tower": *v.* Jeffares, 251; Wade, *Letters*, 729.—The "ancient stair" (l. 1) is that of Thoor Ballylee (cp. Hone, 331). (For an elaborate interpretation of Yeats's "spiral imagery," *v.* Daiches, 170 ff., and cp. *E. P. S.*, 293 and fn.)—In the first printing, l. 8 ran (more happily): "The pole-star and the silence of the pole."—On "Sato's ancient blade" (l. 10), cp. Miss Witt (*Explicator*, V). Yeats wrote Olivia Shakespear (Wade, *Letters*, 729): "I make my Japanese sword and its silk covering my symbol of life. . . ."—Glossing the reference to "Montashigi," p. 231, Miss Murphy writes (154, fn.), "Dr. Giles tells me nothing is known of this." In the earliest printing, Yeats specifies: "Montashigi of Osafume fashioned it."—Ure (74) relates the conclusion of § I to *A Vision.*—On last stanza, cp. *Essays*, 398 (ll. 22-23) and 399 (ll. 8-17).

"Blood and the Moon": **The Exile*, No. 3 (Spring 1928); rptd. 72, 78, 79, 80, 98, 99.—Ellmann suggests composition in Aug. 1927 (*Iden.*, 291); *v. C. P.*, 456, the undated letter to Olivia Shakespear (Wade, *Letters*, 726-27), and notes to preceding poem.—I, l. 12, "Half dead at the top": the top room of Thoor Ballylee was empty and unfurnished.—II: Cp. Henn, 44-45, and "The Seven Sages," *inf.;* "the Dean" (l. 6) is Swift, from whose epitaph *Saeva Indignatio* is taken.—III, l. 1, "the unclouded moon": a symbol of pure subjectivity in Yeats's "system."—Cp. MacNeice, 143, 147, 149 ff.

"Oil and Blood": *72, 78, 79, 80, 98, 99.—Perhaps finished at Seville, late in 1928; Ellmann (*Iden.*, 291) suggests "about Dec. 1927."—On ll. 1-3, cp. § VIII of "Vacillation."—The justification for this somewhat revolting bit seems a question.

"Veronica's Napkin": *77, 78, 79, 80, 98, 99.—Wr. late 1929 (Ellmann, *Iden.*, 291, says 1929) or early 1930? —Cp. *C. P.*, 457.—The "napkin" was the cloth which legend said St. Veronica used to wipe the face of Christ while he was carrying the Cross, and which thus reportedly received an impression of his features. —L. 1, "Berenice's Hair": Constellation Coma Berenices.—L. 2, "Tent-pole . . .": Presumably "the pole of the heavens": cp. note, 3d ed. *The Wind . . .* , p. 77.

"Symbols": Originally in *Words for Music* . . . , 14 Nov. 1932; next in *Spectator*, 2 Dec. 1932; rptd. 78, 79, 80, 89, 98, 99.—Wr. Oct. 1927 (Ellmann, *Iden.*, 291). —L. 3, "sword-blade": Junzo Sato's gift.—L. 5, "Gold-sewn silk . . .": Henn (126 fn. 1) says "the silk embroidery was from Lady Gregory's court dress." (Cp. second stanza of "A Dialogue of Self and Soul.")— Ellmann (*Iden.*, 266) sees the symbols as "wisdom, power, and love."

"Spilt Milk": *77, 78, 79, 80, 98, 99.—Wr. 8 Nov. 1930 (Ellmann, *Iden.*, 291).

"The Nineteenth Century and After": *77, 78, 79, 80, 98, 99.—Ellmann (*Iden.*, 291) dates this piece (baptized

from a well-known periodical) "Jan.–Mar. 2, 1929";
Hone (429) assigns it to the latter date, that of a
letter to Mrs. Shakespear, q.v. for original version and
comment (Wade, *Letters,* 759).

"Statistics": *77, 78, 79, 80, 98, 99.—Wr. 1931 (Ellmann,
Iden., 291).—Henn (41) says this concerns "the
hatred of the abstract," and that the "he" of l. 1 is
Spengler (of *The Decline of the West*).

"Three Movements": *77, 78, 79, 80, 98, 99.—Wr. 26
Jan. 1932 (Ellmann, *Iden.,* 291). Of obvious literary
reference. Ellmann (*Idem,* 267) quotes a 20 Jan.
1932 entry from Yeats's diary: "The Passion in Shakespeare was a great fish in the sea, but from Goethe
to the end of the Romantic movement the fish was in
the net. It will soon be dead upon the shore."

"The Seven Sages": 77, *78, 79, 80, 98, 99.—Wr. 30 Jan.
1931 (Ellmann, *Iden.,* 291).—Jeffares (266) remarks
that Yeats here "disregarded Burke's Whig outlook."
—The "Bishop of Cloyne" (l. 5) is Berkeley. "Stella"
(l. 6) is, of course, Esther Johnson, one of the women
most closely associated with Swift.—Cp. Rothenstein,
Since Fifty, 241-42; Hone, *London Mercury,* XXXIX,
494.—The 8th printing of 99A deletes "a" from l. 13.

"The Crazed Moon": 77, *78, 79, 80, 98, 99.—Hone (464)
calls this "Shelley up to date." Cp. Henn (177-78),
who says (177 fn. 4): "This was written in 1923 and
then lost." Ellmann (*Iden.,* 291) specifies Apr.

"Coole Park, 1929": Originally "Coole Park" (and dated
7 Sept. 1929) in Lady Gregory's *Coole* (Dublin:
Cuala Press, 1931); present title (minus the comma)
in *Words for Music . . . ,* 1932; rptd. 78 (*London
ed.), 79, 80, 89, 98, 99.—Mrs. Yeats says the first
version of the poem is dated 1928; Ellmann (*Iden.,*
291) dates composition "1928–Sept. 7, 1929."—Cp.

Wade, *Letters*, 769.—Coole was sold to the government, 1927; thereafter Lady Gregory rented (cp. *Jour.*, 37); eventually Coole was sold by the Forestry Department and was razed, while the Seven Woods were distributed (*v.* Jeffares, 274-75. Cp. notes to "Upon a House Shaken . . . ," *sup.*).—On Hyde (St. 2), cp. *Auto.*, ed. N.Y. 1953, 131-33; also, 266-68. "That noble blade . . .": Hyde's "Anglo-Irish dialect" (*v.* p. 1 of O'Connor's N.Y. *Times* art.). The "one that ruffled . . ." is Yeats himself: *v. Dramatis Personae* (London: Macmillan, 1936), p. 75. On Shawe-Taylor, cp. MacManus, 665-66, and *Essays*, 425 ff.; on Lane, *v.* notes to "To a Wealthy Man . . . ," *sup.* (Both men were Lady Gregory's nephews; *v.* her *Jour.*)—The 8th printing of 99A ends l. 14 with a comma.

"Coole Park and Ballylee, 1931": Originally "Coole Park and Ballylee 1932" in *Words for Music* . . . , 1932. *N.B.: V.* "The Choice," *inf.*—As now, *78, 79, 80, 89, 98, 99.—In his 3 Feb. 1932 letter to his wife (Hone, 455), Yeats says he wrote the last three lines of the second stanza the day before: "a symbol of inspiration I think"; nevertheless, Ellmann (*Iden.*, 291) dates the poem Feb. 1931.—The last line of St. 1 is a reference to Porphyry; Dume (184) suggests Thomas Taylor's *Select Works of Porphyry* (1823).—L. 4, " 'dark' " Raftery: a blind poet.—The opening reference in St. 4 is to Lady Gregory; *v.* in general her *Jour.*—Yeats rightly preferred this poem to the preceding one.

"For Anne Gregory": Originally "Anne Gregory" in *Words for Music* . . . , 14 Nov. 1932; present title, *Spectator,* 2 Dec. 1932; rptd. 78, 79, 80, 98, 99.—

Wr. Sept. 1930 (Ellmann, *Iden.*, 291).—For Lady
Gregory's granddaughter.

"Swift's Epitaph": Pub'n history same with that of preceding poem, with the *Spectator* version again to be
asterisked, except that this piece also appears *untitled*
in 81 and 82. For early drafts, *v.* Lady Gregory's *Jour.*
for 28 Jan. 1930; and cp. *1930 Diary* (p. 30): "I . . .
understand that the liberty he served was that of intellect. . . ." *V.* also "Intro." to *The Words upon the
Window-Pane.*—Except for its opening line, the piece
is practically a translation; cp. "Ubi sæva indignatio/
Ulterius cor lacerare nequit./Abi viator/Et imitare, si
poteris,/Strenuum pro virili libertatis vindicem."

"At Algeciras—A Meditation upon Death": Originally
"Meditations upon Death: I" in *A Packet for Ezra
Pound,* 1929; do., *London Mercury,* Nov. 1930, and
New Republic, 14 Jan. 1931; as "A Meditation Written during Sickness at Algeciras," *Words for Music
. . . ,* 1932; present title, *78: 1933 *Winding Stair;*
rptd. 79, 80, 98, 99. Cp., *inf.,* "Mohini Chatterjee."—
Dating remains a question: In his 9 Mar. 1929 letter
to Lady Gregory, Yeats says this and "Mohini Chatterjee" were written between then and 6 Feb.; the
poem is dated 4 Feb. 1929 in the *Packet,* but Hone
(429) states that this was the date of rewriting; *C. P.*
makes the date Nov. 1928; Ellmann (*Iden.*, 291) says
23 Jan. 1929.—L. 11, "Newton's metaphor": In S.
Brodetsky's *Sir Isaac Newton* (London, 1927; p. 153),
the following quotation is ascribed to Newton: "I do
not know what I may appear to the world; but to
myself I seem to have been only like a boy playing
on the sea-shore, and diverting myself in now and
then finding a smoother pebble or a prettier shell than

ordinary, whilst the great ocean of truth lay all undiscovered before me."

"The Choice": Originally the penultimate stanza of "Coole Park and Ballylee 1932" in *Words for Music* . . . , 1932; as entity, in 78, 79, 80, 98, 99. (Properly printed without stanzaic division.)—Cp. *Auto.*, 392, 11. 16-17; Davenport art., 57-58.

"Mohini Chatterjee": Originally "II" of "Meditations upon Death," with the publishing history given, *sup.*, for "At Algeciras . . ."; became "Mohini Chatterji" in *Words for Music* . . . , 1932; present spelling since 78; rptd. 79, 80, 98, 99.—Dated 9 Feb. 1929 in the *Packet:* perhaps the date of revision, though Hone (429) accepts it as the date of composition; C. P. gives merely 1928; Ellmann (*Iden.*, 292) says "Jan. 23-Feb. 9, 1929." V. notes to "At Algeciras," *sup.*—Cp. *Auto.*, 113-14; Hone, 50-51; Gurd, 32-33; MacNeice, 150; Ellmann, 43.—Professor Witt (*Explicator,* IV) ties this to the discarded "Kanva on Himself" of the *Oisin* (1889); cp. Jeffares, 32-33, and Yeats's own note on Mohini Chatterjee in *Coll. Works*, 1908 (Vol. 8, p. 279): this note, "The Pathway," was never reprinted. —For a very early effort to incorporate "the idea of reincarnation," *v.* Ellmann, *Iden.*, 44-45.—Cp. Gibbon.

"Byzantium": 77, *78, 79, 80, 98, 99.—Misdated in *Words for Music* . . . ; dated 1930 in C. P. Hone (442) says it was "sketched out" during recuperation from Malta fever at Portofino Vetta, above the Gulf of Genoa, in the spring of 1930; and Henn (207 fn. 2) records that the MS. is dated Sept. 1930.—One may consult, but must perhaps reject, Ellmann (270-71; also *Kenyon Rev.*, XV, 360-63); and question both Baker (*South. Rev.*) and Adams (*Accent*).—V. *1930 Diary* (§ III, 2-3, dated 30 Apr.) and *A Vision*, 279; and cp. Daiches

(181 ff.), Henn (Ch. 12 and 235), MacNeice (141-42), Stauffer (*N. P.*, 173-75), Jeffares (260-61, 334 fn. 25a; *Rev. of Eng. Studies*, XXII), Ure (68-69, for ties with *A Vision*), Ussher (82), Moore, 348. One may also cp. Knight (311), Rudd (173-74), and Brooks, who professes an interpretation (*South. Rev.*, IV), though as Richards (20) remarks, "since the Superhuman . . . is speaking, if we cannot 'understand' it, there will be no help for us from less authorities." Gwynn offers (*Philol. Qu.*) a close examination; cp. also Dume (*Mod. Lang. Notes*), Bridge (Letters 135, 138, and 140), and the "Letters to the Editor" in *LTLS* by Auty, R. Murphy, G. Murphy, Christopherson, Watkins, and Dobrée.—Miss Murphy writes (153, fn.): "Mr. Yeats tells me 'I certainly got the idea of the dolphins carrying souls to Paradise from a book on Roman sculpture.' "—Cp. the two articles by Masson.

"The Mother of God": 77, *78, 79, 80, 98, 99.—Wr. 3 Sept. 1931 (Ellmann, *Iden.*, 292; Jeffares, 271, says merely Sept.).—Yeats has an illuminating note (*C. P.*, 456) on the image in ll. 1-2, which Henn (234) relates to "an Annunciation, presumably Crivelli's." Cp. "A Nativity," *inf.*, and *v.* Allt, *Sewanee Rev.*, LX, 647-48.

"Vacillation": Originally in *Words for Music* . . . , 1932, where the sequence is organized into seven sections, numbered and named as indicated below; the sequence first appears in its present state in *78 (1933 *Winding Stair*) and was rptd. in 79, 80, 98, and 99. (§ VIII appeared alone in 89.)

Words for Music ...	1933 Winding Stair
I. What Is Joy	I
II. The Burning Tree	II and III
III. Happiness	IV

Words for Music . . .	*1933 Winding Stair*
IV. Conscience	V
V. Conquerors	VI
VI. A Dialogue	VII
VII. Von Hügel	VIII

Presumably finished (and entitled "Wisdom") in Jan. 1932 (Jeffares, 272), and dated 1932 in *C. P.* In a 15 Dec. 1931 letter, Yeats tells Olivia Shakespear he has begun the poem standing first; Ellmann (*Iden.*, 292) dates "I" Dec. 1931. What are now IV and V Ellmann also assigns to 1931: the first to Nov. Ellmann also dates VI Jan.-5 Mar. 1932; VII, 3-4 Jan. 1932 (*v.* Wade, *Letters*, 789-90: a 3 Jan. 1932 letter to Olivia Shakespear dates VII for that day and gives, with comment, an early version); VIII, 3 Jan. 1932.— Well analyzed by Stauffer (88-91).—On I and the debt to Blake, *v.* Quinn (*Va. Qu. Rev.*, espec. "II"); also Henn, 149-50.—On II cp. MacNeice (144), who calls it a "metaphysical wedding of opposites," which the original draft (Ellmann, *Iden.*, 272) suggests were "ignorance and knowledge"; Ure, 75: Yeats (cp. Stauffer, 157 fn. 30) quotes from the *Mabinogion* ("They saw a tall tree . . .": p. 86, Guest trans., London: Temple Classics, 1902); Bronowski (243) thinks in this image "the ideal and the living are set against one another and yet held together." Henn (245) says the Attis reference owes to a passage in *The Orations of Julian*, V; but cp. Ellmann, *Iden.*, 171-72 and 273. V. also Frazer, Vol. 5.—On III, l. 3, cp. the misquotation from Ben Jonson's *Poetaster* in § XIV, "Anima Mundi" (*Essays*, 528): "So rammed with life. . . ." On the second stanza, cp. George Russell's remark to Sean O'Faoláin: "I really tried to write poetry as if I were on the slopes of death myself and was testing my thought by that consciousness. . . ." (Eglinton, 179.)— IV: Ure (72) points a parallel in *Per Amica* . . . : *v. Essays*, 533.—VI: L. 3, "lord of Chou": ? Chóu-kung, Duke of Chóu (12th cent.). On the opening lines of the last stanza, cp. the close of "Two Songs from a Play."—VII: On "Isaiah's coal," *v.* Isaiah 6:6-7. It will be recalled that "fire" (l. 4) is the fourth element and one of Yeats's "primary tinctures." On the last line of this section, see the story told by Jeffares (273) and the variant retailed by O'Connor (Ch. XV), as well as Day Lewis' poem *Few Things Can More Inflame. V.* also Davenport art., 58.—VIII: On ll. 3-4, *v.* Henn, 160 fn. 2, and Jeffares, 272-73, and cp. "Oil and Blood" (St. Teresa: 1515–82); on ll. 5-7, *v.* Bjersby, 109; on l. 11, *v.* Judges 14:5-18, and Stauffer's gloss (90-91). Menon (70) declares that Yeats dismisses von Hügel "because he rejected the theory of reincarnation." (Baron Friedrich von Hügel was the Roman Catholic author of *The Mystical Element of Religion:* London, 2d ed., 1927.) Cp. *W. & B.*, 96, and Wilder, 196 ff.

ʍ "Quarrel in Old Age": 77, *78, 79, 80, 98, 99.—Jeffares (271), dating its composition Nov. 1931, calls it "a recording of some quarrel with Maud Gonne, probably over the treatment of women prisoners or Mary MacSwiney's hunger strike."—"Targeted" (last l.): Yeats confirmed Maurice Wollmann's interpretation of this word as "protected as with a target, a round shield" (Hone, 472). On the simile, same l., cp. *Auto.*, 152.

"The Results of Thought": 77, *78, 79, 80, 98, 99.—Wr. 18-28 Aug. 1931 (Ellmann, *Iden.*, 292). The 8th printing of 99A restores another Yeatsian mispunctuation by printing a comma after l. 13, and changes "Time's" (l. 15) to "time's."

"Gratitude to the Unknown Instructors": Originally in *77, with "Powers" in place of "Instructors," which was substituted in 78; rptd. 79, 80, 98, 99.—The "instructors" are the "spirits" Yeats claimed as his helpers on *A Vision*.

"Remorse for Intemperate Speech": First in *Words for Music* . . . , 14 Nov. 1932; next in *Spectator*, 18 Nov. 1932; rptd. 78, 79, 80, 98, 99.—Wr. 28 Aug. 1931 (Ellmann, *Iden.*, 292).—On the third stanza, cp. ll. 4-7, p. 113, *P. & C.*

M "Stream and Sun at Glendalough": 77, *78, 79, 80, 98, 99. —Wr. 23 June 1932 (Ellmann, *Iden.*, 292).—On the opening l. of the second stanza, Henn (285) glosses the mid-lines of the last stanza of "A Dialogue of Self and Soul."—Glendalough is in Wicklow; here, at Laragh Castle, Francis and Iseult Gonne Stuart had their chicken farm. There are three mountains and a lake; and O'Connor (55) says, "A more beautiful and desolate spot it would be hard to conceive of." Cp. Rothenstein, *M. & M.*, II, 373; Gogarty, 183. The lake was in Finn's time called Lough Ethnea, after the hydra said to have lived there until destroyed by St. Kevin (*v.* O'Grady, 68-69).

"Words for Music Perhaps": Title sequence of 1932 Cuala volume, in which the lyrics are unnumbered, and some not in the present order, though titles are as now. What is now "VI" was inserted in the 1933 *Winding Stair* printing. V. Hone (455) on the "old woman" whom Yeats may have had in mind as something of a model for Crazy Jane (cp. the "ruined" female of that name in a piece by M. G. Lewis: *v.* E. Tomkin's anthology, *Poems on Various Subjects:*

London, 1804); cp. Wade, *Letters,* 785-86. Yeats had originally called his heroine "Cracked Mary," probably after a once-known creature of the roads: *v.* Ellmann, *Iden.,* 275.—Cp. Jeffares, 333 fn. 114, on the matter of a character prototype.—On the debt to Plotinus in this sequence, *v.* Daiches, 187-88; on the sequence in general, *v.* MacNeice (Ch. VIII), Ure (104 ff.), and Ussher (83-84). Houghton has (*Mod. Philol.*) also considered the sequence.—The series was begun after Yeats's 1929 attack of Malta fever; a 2 Mar. letter to Mrs. Shakespear (Hone, 430) indicates he originally planned "Twelve Poems for Music," "not so much that they may be sung as that I may define their kind of emotion to myself. I want them to be all emotion and all impersonal . . . all praise of joyous life. . . ." Hone (455) also says that some were written at Coole during the winter of 1931–32 and records (429 and fn.) an unpublished one, "Cracked Mary's Vision," since printed by Ellmann (*Iden.,* 101-2). (Gogarty, 241, 255, mentions and excerpts another, "Crazy Jane and the King.")—According to Yeats's 9 Mar. 1929 letter to Lady Gregory, five of the poems had been written between that date and 6 Feb. On 13 Sept. 1929, the poet wrote Olivia Shakespear that over half the "thirty poems for music" were finished. Unhappily, the poet's practices too often leave the student pondering an early remark to Katharine Tynan (Wade, *Letters,* 54): ". . . dates are the firstborn of Satan, mainly." Incidentally, Yeats wrote to Mrs. Shakespear anent the Crazy Jane lyrics and "the little group of love poems that follow": "Sexual abstinence fed their fire—I was ill and yet full of desire" (Wade, *Letters,* 814).

I / "Crazy Jane and the Bishop": *London Mercury,* Nov.

1930, and *The New Republic* (as "Cracked Mary and
. . ."), 12 Nov. 1930; rptd. 77, *78, 79, 80, 98, 99.—
Wr. 2 Mar. 1929 (Ellmann, *Iden.*, 292).—Cp. Hough-
ton, *cit. sup.* Ellmann (*Idem*, 274-75) recalls that
"Jack the Journeyman" first is named in a song in *The
Pot of Broth.*

II / "Crazy Jane Reproved": *London Merc.*, Nov. 1930;
New Republic (as "Cracked Mary . . ."), 12 Nov.
1930; 77, *78, 79, 80, 98, 99.—Wr. 27 Mar. 1929
(Hone, 429).—On "joints of Heaven" (l. 11), cp.
Henn, 68 and 68 fn. 2; Ellmann, *Iden.*, 276.

III / "Crazy Jane on the Day of Judgment": 77, 78, 79,
*80, 98, 99.—Wr. Oct. 1930 (Ellmann, *Iden.*, 292).—
St. 1: Rothenstein (*Since Fifty*, 242) quotes Yeats as
saying that "the tragedy of sexual intercourse is the
perpetual virginity of the souls," an assertion which
seems not to have interfered with the poet's evident
endorsement of such "tragedy."

IV / "Crazy Jane and Jack the Journeyman": Printings as
for III, though 98 should be asterisked.—Wr. Nov.
1931 (Jeffares, 271). Cp. Wade, *Letters*, 785.—On
concluding two ll. of second st., Miss Moore glosses
"The Gates of Pluto," original ed. of *A Vision.*

V / "Crazy Jane on God": Printings as for III, though 78
should be asterisked.—Wr. 18 July 1931 (Ellmann,
Iden., 292; cp. Jeffares, 270).—V. "Preface" to *The
Words upon the Window-Pane* (1931) and the play
proper (espec. pp. 42-43, *W. & B.*); on the third st.,
"Anima Mundi," *Per Amica* . . . , *A Vision* (Bk. III),
and *Purgatory.* Cp. also Houghton (*cit. sup.*) and
Ellmann, *Iden.*, 276-77.—In O'Casey's *Juno and the
Paycock*, II, Bentham says, "Scientists . . . say that
sensational actions . . . demand great energy, and that
that energy lingers in the place where the action oc-

curs. People may live in the place and see nothing, when some . . . person sees the whole affair."—The 8th printing of 99A alters the semicolon of l. 5 to a comma; the colon of l. 23 to a semicolon. (A colon would be logical in each case.)

VI / "Crazy Jane Talks with the Bishop": *78, 79, 80, 98, 99: *v.* general note on sequence, *sup.*—Wr. Nov. 1931 (Jeffares, 271).—Cp. Henn, 41; Houghton, *cit. sup.;* Jeffares, 272; Ellmann, *Iden.*, 278.—W. R. Johnson's "Crazy Jane and Henry More," *Furioso*, III, 50-53, is of course a spoof.

VII / "Crazy Jane Grown Old Looks at the Dancers": Originally "Crazy Jane and the Dancers," *London Merc.*, Nov. 1930; "Cracked Mary and . . . ," *New Republic*, 12 Nov. 1930; present title, 77; rptd. *78, 79, 80, 98, 99.—Wr. 2 Mar. 1929 (Ellmann, *Iden.*, 292: discount Hone's dating, 429): at least, described as dream-rooted by Yeats in a letter under that date to Mrs. Shakespear (Wade, *Letters*, 758; Jeffares, 255). —St. 3, l. 4: "Cared not a thraneen . . ." is equivalent to slangy American "cared not a hoot" (cp. O'Casey, *The Shadow of a Gunman*, II: "Nobody cares a traneen . . ."; and Synge's Pegeen Mike, *The Playboy* . . . , II: "I wouldn't give a thraneen for a lad hadn't a mighty spirit in him. . . .").

VIII / "Girl's Song": *New Republic*, 22 Oct. 1930; book inclusions as for VII.—Wr. 29 Mar. 1929 (Hone, 429).

IX / "Young Man's Song": *New Republic*, 22 Oct. 1930, where the third stanza is inexplicably transferred to XIV ("His Bargain")! Book inclusions as for VII, though 77 should be asterisked.—Wr. "1929 (after March 29)" (Ellmann, *Iden.*, 292).—Cp. "A Woman Young and Old," "II."

X / "Her Anxiety": *New Republic*, 22 Oct. 1930; book

inclusions as for VII.—Wr. "1929 (after April 17)"
(Ellmann, *Iden.*, 292).

XI / "His Confidence": *New Republic*, 22 Oct. 1930;
book inclusions as for VII, with 78 asterisked.—Wr.
"1929 (after March 29)" (Ellmann, *Iden.*, 292).—Ll.
2-4: i.e., developed crow's-feet?

XII / "Love's Loneliness": *New Republic*, 22 Oct. 1930;
London Merc., Nov. 1930; book inclusions as for VII.
—Wr. 12 Apr. 1929 (Ellmann, *Iden.*, 292).

XIII / "Her Dream": *New Republic*, 22 Oct. 1930; *London Merc.*, Nov. 1930; book inclusions as for VII.—
Wr. "1929 (after March 29)" (Ellmann, *Iden.*, 292).
—The 8th printing of 99A alters the colon (l. 4) to a
semicolon.

XIV / "His Bargain": *New Republic*, 22 Oct. 1930 (*v.*
"IX," *sup.*); *London Merc.*, Nov. 1930; book inclusions as for VII, with 78 asterisked.—Wr. "1929 (after
March 29)" (Ellmann, *Iden.*, 292; cp. also 279).—Ll.
1-2: Apparently a reference to the Platonic Years following each other in unending circuit. Cp. second
speech, 86. On the "spindle" as an emblem of the soul,
v. Jeffares, *Rev. of Eng. Studies*, XXII, 51. On the conclusion of the poem, cp. *The Cutting of an Agate* and
its ascription to Hafiz: "I made a bargain with that
brown hair from the beginning of time. . . ."; also Mrs.
Radford's lines, "The love within my heart for thee /
Before the world was had its birth," quoted by Yeats
in a letter to Katharine Tynan (Wade, *Letters*, 171).
V., further, Dume, 141; Stauffer, 41, 148.

XV / "Three Things": *New Republic*, 2 Oct. 1929; next
in 74 (No. 18 of Faber and Faber's *Ariel Poems*, 9 Oct.
1929); rptd. 77, *78, 79, 80, 89, 98, 99.—Wr. 14-24
Feb. 1929 (Hone, 429).—In a 2 Mar. 1929 letter to
Mrs. Shakespear (Hone, 430), Yeats calls this the best

of "Twelve Poems for Music." Cp. *The Player Queen* (*P. P. V.*, 403-4).—The 8th printing of 99A alters the semicolon of l. 14 to a comma.

XVI / "Lullaby": First in *The New Keepsake* (London: Cobden-Sanderson, 1931), pp. 21-22; rptd. 77, *78, 79, 80, 89, 98, 99.—Hone (429) dates this 20 Mar., Ellmann (*Iden.*, 292) 27 Mar., 1929.—For original version, *v.* 29 Mar. 1929 letter to Mrs. Shakespear (Wade, *Letters*, 760-61).—Eventually, perhaps Yeats's favorite (Jeffares, 257).—One may cp. Saul, *S. Y. O. I.*, 29.

XVII / "After Long Silence": *77, 78, 79, 80, 89, 98, 99.— Ellmann (*Iden.*, 292) assigns composition to Nov. 1929, though the final version may belong to the next month; certainly the poem was included, untitled, in a 16 Dec. 1929 letter to Mrs. Shakespear, having presumably been developed, from a prose draft of (?) the month before, soon after Yeats's return to Rapallo. *V.* Wade, *Letters*, 772.—On this lyric, one may consult Mercier (*Irish Writing*, No. 6), Millett (166-68, for two opposed student readings), Matthiessen (*South. Rev.*), and Brooks-Warren (224-30).

XVIII / "Mad as the Mist and Snow": *77, 78, 79, 80, 98, 99.—Wr. 12 Feb. 1929 (Hone, 429).

XIX / "Those Dancing Days Are Gone": Originally "A Song for Music," *London Merc.*, Nov. 1930, and *New Republic*, 12 Nov. 1930; present title, 77; rptd. 78, 79, 80, 98, 99.—Wr. 8 Mar. 1929 (Hone, 429).—*V. C. P.*, 456.

XX / " 'I Am of Ireland' ": 77, *78, 79, 80, 98, 99.—Wr. Aug. 1929 (Ellmann, *Iden.*, 292).—On genesis, at Frank O'Connor's home, *v.* Ellmann, *Idem*, 280.—Cp. *C. P.*, 456, though Henn (286, and cp. 287) says the Middle English original was familiar from Seymour's *Anglo-Irish Literature, 1200–1582*. *V.* Wells, 493, and

Margot R. Adamson's *Treasury of Middle English Verse* (1930), p. 56.—One may perhaps be more entertained than informed by the comments in Houghton (*cit. sup.*), Matthiessen (*cit. sup.*), and Gregory (*South. Rev.*). Thompson (*Hopkins Rev.*, III, 13) sees the characters as Yeats and "Cathleen ni Houlihan." Miss Sickels proposes further exuberant interpretation.—In the 8th printing of 99A, Yeats's illogical comma appears at the end of ll. 17 and 30.—The phrase "and time runs on" appears in one of the First Merchant's speeches in a now-discarded segment of Sc. III, *The Countess Cathleen* (cp. 1912 ed.).

XXI / "The Dancer at Cruachan and Cro-Patrick": 77, where the present "Cro-Patrick" (cp. *The Countess Cathleen*, Sc. II), with Lough Derg one of the two great traditional Irish centers of Christian pilgrimage, is written "Croagh Patrick"; as now, *78; rptd. 79, 80, 98, 99.—Wr. Aug. 1931 (Jeffares, 271; Ellmann, *Iden.*, 292).—The "I" of l. 1 is said, on the attributed authority of Mrs. Yeats, to be St. Cellach (Jeffares, 335 fn. 52).

XXII / "Tom the Lunatic": *77, 78, 79, 80, 98, 99.—Ellmann (*Iden.*, 292) dates this 27 July 1931; Jeffares (270) assigns it to June.—On l. 7, cp. the lyric at the beginning of the introduction to "Stories of Michael Robartes and His Friends . . . ," 1937 *Vision,* and notes to "V," *sup.*

XXIII / "Tom at Cruachan": Originally "Old Tom at Cruachan" in 77; present title, *78; rptd. 79, 80, 98, 99. —Wr. 29 July 1931 (Ellmann, *Iden.*, 292; cp. Jeffares, 270).

XXIV / "Old Tom Again": Printings as for XXIII, though 79 should be asterisked.—Wr. Oct. 1931: "'a reply to the dancer's song' as he described it to Mrs. Shake-spear" (Jeffares, 271).—Cp. Henn, 283.

XXV / "The Delphic Oracle upon Plotinus": Printings as for XXIII, with 78 asterisked.—Wr. 19 Aug. 1931 (Ell-mann, *Iden.*, 292, and cp. 281).—Cp. Henn, 133; Moore, 319-20; Pearce, *N & Q;* Tindall, 262 and 261 fn. 23. The oracle's song quoted by Porphyry calls Minos and Rhadamanthus "great brethren of the golden race of mighty Zeus," mentions Plato, and speaks of "stately Pythagoras and all else that form the Choir of Immortal Love" (MacKenna, 23); it also (*Idem*, 22) refers to "the bitter waves of this blood-drenched life." There should be a break between lines 5 and 6.

"A Woman Young and Old": 72, 78, 79, 80, 98, 99.—Ex-cept for minor changes in punctuation and capitaliza-tion, the first was the final form in each poem of this sequence except VIII and XI, in the second (78) printing of which small changes appear. (In the first printing of IV, "Saint," l. 10, is abbreviated to "St."; and certain breaks are missing from VII in 78A.)— One gathers from Wade (*Letters,* 641) that the se-quence was written at Ballylee, but this must be a matter of uncertainty in the case of some of its items until, if ever, dating of composition can become exact. On this latter question there is sharp disagreement. Jeffares (246) says the sequence "was completed in Sept. [1926]": cp. Yeats's 5 and 24 Sept. 1926 letters to Olivia Shakespear (Wade, *Letters,* 718-19, and *v.* 727); Hone (398) also dates the writing 1926; Ell-mann's assignments are given with the individual titles. (*N.B.:* These investigators have presumably all been given direct access to Yeats's papers.)

I / "Father and Child": Cp. Hone, 400; Jeffares, 245; Wade, *cit. sup.*

II / "Before the World Was Made": Dated Feb. 1928 by Ellmann (*Iden.*, 292): *v.* also his art., *Kenyon Rev.* (XV, 368).—Cp. "Young Man's Song" and "His Bargain."

III / "A First Confession": Dated June 1927 by Ellmann (*Iden.*, 292); *v.* Wade, *Letters*, 725-26, for earlier version in 23 June 1927 letter to Mrs. Shakespear.— St. 3, "the Zodiac": a boundary of thought?—the Wheel of the Principles in *A Vision?*—Cp. "the one disastrous zodiac" of "The Two Kings"?

IV / "Her Triumph": Dated Nov. 1929 by Ellmann (*Iden.*, 293).—Last l.: Henn (236 fn. 3) cps. the cockerel of "Solomon and the Witch." Cp. Saul, *S. Y. O. I.*, 27.

V / "Consolation": Dated June 1927 by Ellmann (*Iden.*, 293); *v.* Wade, *Letters*, 725-26, for earlier version in 23 June 1927 letter to Mrs. Shakespear.—Henn (63 fn. 1) remarks Sophocles here and compares the close of Donne's *A Valediction: Forbidding Mourning* with the last two lines.

VI / "Chosen": Entitled "The Choice" in the first printing only.—Ellmann (260) dates this 1927.—*V. C. P.*, 456; and, on last four lines, Henn, 188.

VII / "Parting": Dated Aug. 1926 by Ellmann (*Iden.*, 293).—Hone (464) glosses *Romeo and Juliet.* Might Walther von der Vogelweide's *Song at Daybreak,* Swinburne's *In the Orchard,* and Pound's *Alba Innominata* and *Langue D'OC* (§IV) be also in the background?

VIII / "Her Vision in the Wood": Ellmann dates this 1926 (*Iden.*, 293).—*V.* Ure (107-8) for a convincing interpretation.—The "wine-dark" (l. 2) is from Homer,

perhaps by way of Mangan.—Henn (63) notes "the
Adonis image," ll. 3-4; and the end of the second stanza
refers to the boar that slew Adonis. Cp. Ellmann,
Iden., 172-73.—Of ll. 3-4, St. 3, Henn writes (246):
"I can find no corresponding picture in Mantegna."

IX / "A Last Confession": Dated June 1926 by Ellmann
(*Iden.*, 293).

X / "Meeting": Like "I," not specifically dated.

XI / "From the 'Antigone'": "From 'The Antigone'" in
the first printing.—Dated 1927–28 by Ellmann (*Iden.*,
293).—It will be remembered that "Brother and
brother" (l. 10) connotes Polyneices and Eteocles,
Antigone's contending brothers; and (final ll.) that
when Antigone, in violation of orders, buried her dead
brother Polyneices, her maternal uncle, King Creon of
Thebes, had her confined in an underground cavern,
where she committed suicide, as did her lover,
Hæmon, Creon's son.—Cp. Ussher, 83-84.—In the 8th
printing of 99A, "Gods" (l. 6) is not capitalized.

From *A Full Moon in March*

"Parnell's Funeral": Though Ellmann (*Identity*, 293)
dates composition Apr. 1933, the third stanza was first
published, untitled, in "Introduction to 'Fighting the
Waves,'" *Dublin Magazine*, Apr.–June, 1932; do., 82.
"I" as an entity first appeared as "A Parnellite at Parnell's Funeral" and "II" as "Forty Years Later" in
Spectator, 19 Oct. 1934; then "A Parnellite . . ." appeared in *K. G. C. T.*, 14 Dec. 1934, "Forty . . ." being
included *untitled* in the "Commentary on 'A Parnellite . . .'" (84, 85). Complete piece as now, under
present title, first in *86: A Full Moon . . . , 1935;
rptd. 98, 99.—Cp. "To a Shade" and "September 1913."
—I, l. 1: On p. 29 of *K. G. C. T.*, Yeats says "[Daniel]

O'Connell, the great comedian" was replaced by "the tragedian Parnell"; on p. 27, he suggests that the star of l. 4 may in falling "symbolise an accepted sacrifice." L. 7: Perhaps refers to the star-archer seen on some Cretan coins: for this and other speculation, *v.* Henn, 156 fn. 2, and cp. Bk. V, § VI, *The Trembling of the Veil,* with relative "Notes"; p. 27, *K. G. C. T.;* and § XI, "Anima Hominis" (*Essays,* 503).—St. 2, l. 4: In an Aug. 1896 letter to William Sharp (Wade, *Letters,* 266), Yeats says: "I invoked one night the spirits of the moon and saw between sleep and waking a beautiful woman firing an arrow among the stars."—St. 3: Cp. "Intro." to *Fighting the Waves* (*W. & B.*). Robert Emmet, Lord Edward Fitzgerald, and Wolfe Tone met death as "rebels" at the hands of the English, whereas Parnell was broken by his own people, whom he had served: a victim of irrational emotion for which Yeats admits (St. 4) he must, in a sense, share blame. The "lie" of St. 4 is the typically Irish romantic conception (cp. the opening of "Beautiful Lofty Things"). L. 2, p. 276, recalls to Henn (46 fn. 1) "Rosalind's Irish rats in *As You Like It*" (III, ii, 170-71, in ref. to Irish efforts to kill rats by uttering spells in rhyme).—II: On eating men's hearts to acquire their qualities, *v.* Frazer, Vol. 8, 148 ff.—In the pref. to *K. G. C. T.*, Yeats remarks: "In 'At Parnell's Funeral' I rhymed passages from a lecture I had given in America. . . ." One may cp. his early "Mourn—and then Onward" (*United Ireland,* 10 Oct. 1891), rptd. in Ellmann (100), *q. v.*—On Parnell, *v. Auto.,* 440, l. 4 ff.; one may cp. T. P. O'Connor's *Memoirs of an Old Parliamentarian,* J. Haslip's *Parnell. A Biography* (London, 1936).—The opening seven-line stanza of I was seldom used by Yeats (who, incidentally, had a weakness for eight-line lyrics), and never elsewhere by him with this particular rhyme scheme.

"Three Songs to the Same Tune": *Spectator*, 23 Feb. 1934 (with a long explanatory note by Yeats); *Poetry* (Chicago), Dec. 1934; 84, 85, 86, 98, 99. Italics appear only in printings under last three issues. "I" assumes substantially final form in *Poetry;* "II," in 84; "III," in 86. The third was also printed, with italics as now, as "The Soldier Takes Pride," in *A Broadside*, No. 12 (New Series), Dec. 1935.—Wr. 30 Nov. 1933–27 Feb. 1934 (Ellmann, *Iden.*, 293: a 30 Nov. letter to Olivia Shakespear says the first of these is in course of composition).—A result of Yeats's temporary interest in the fascistic O'Duffy "blue shirt" movement. For "commentary," *v. K. G. C. T.*, 34 ff.; but cp. Wade, *Letters*, 812-15.—I, ll. 15-16, p. 277: Cp. eighteenth-century popular ballad, "The Night before Larry Was Stretched": "He kicked, too—but that was all pride."—II: "O'Donnell": Hugh; "both O'Neills": probably Henry and Art; "Emmet": Robert. —V. "Three Marching Songs," *inf.*

"Alternative Song . . .": From the original (prose) version of *K. G. C. T.* (84); rptd. 85, *86, 93, 98, 99, 100: untitled in 84 and 85.—St. 2: Cuchulain: V. "Cuchulain's Fight with the Sea," *sup.;* Niamh: *v.* ". . . Oisin," *inf.;* "lad and lass": Naoise and Deirdre in the Red Branch fortress the night before death: *v. Deirdre* and Saul.—St. 3: "Aleel, his Countess": *v. Countess Cathleen;* "Hanrahan": *v.* "The Tower," *sup.* Ll. 5-6, p. 280, apparently refer to the young ruler in "The Wisdom of the King," *The Secret Rose.*

"Two Songs Rewritten for the Tune's Sake": First published in *A Full Moon . . .* , 1935; rptd. 98, 99.—"I" was considerably changed in phrasing after the first printing; "II" was not altered.—I: *"Oro, oro!"* (Originally "Aro, aro,"), cp. "Hurroo!"—II, St. 2, "dreepy," cp. Scot. *dree:* to suffer, or endure.—Cp. also various eds. of *The Pot of Broth* and *The Player Queen*, beginning with *P. P. V.*, ed. 1922: 54a, 54b, 87a, 100.

"A Prayer for Old Age": Originally "Old Age," *Spectator*, 2 Nov. 1934; untitled, in "Preface" to *K. G. C. T.*, 14 Dec. 1934; do., 85; present title, 86: *A Full Moon* . . . , 1935; rptd. 98, 99.—St. 1: Cp. *Essays*, 291: "We only believe in those thoughts which have been conceived not in the brain but in the whole body"; *v.* also, *idem*, 360, ll. 22-27.

"Church and State": Originally "A Vain Hope," *Spectator*, 23 Nov. 1934, and as untitled conclusion to "Commentary on the Three Songs," *Poetry* (Chicago), Dec. 1934; then, again untitled, in "Postscript" (dated Aug. 1934 and following "Commentary on the 'Three Songs'"), *K. G. C. T.*, 14 Dec. 1934 (and cp. 85); present title, 86: *A Full Moon* . . . , 1935; rptd. 98, 99.

"Supernatural Songs": All but III, IV, VII, and VIII (which are printed only in 86, 98, and 99) had been published in *London Mercury* and *Poetry* (Chicago), Dec. 1934, as well as in 84 (14 Dec. 1934) and 85, before the complete sequence was assembled in *86: *A Full Moon* . . . , 1935, and rptd. in 98 and 99.— Miss Moore says (358) the sequence was begun in 1934. Except for punctuation, most of these poems were essentially unchanged after initial publication. Ure studies the first four in "Yeats's Supernatural Songs," *Rev. of Eng. Studies*, N.S., Vol. II, No. 25.

I / "Ribh at the Tomb of Baile and Aillinn": Wr. 24 July 1934 (Ellmann, *Iden.*, 293).—Analyzed by Henn, 292-99; l. 8: cp. Saul, 59-60. *V.* "Baile and Aillinn," *inf.;* and with the end of the first paragraph of this poem, cp. ll. 7-12, p. 201, *P. & C.* ("A People's Theatre.") All printings except first seven of 99A have a break between ll. 9 and 10.

II / "Ribh Denounces Patrick": Prior to its **Full Moon . . .* version, II was entitled "Ribh Prefers an Older Theology"; originally it began: "Abstractions of the Greek Philosophy have crazed the man, / Recall his Trinity. A father, mother, child. . . ."—Wr. July 1934 (Ellmann, *Iden.,* 293).—According to a letter Yeats wrote to Olivia Shakespear on 24 July 1934 (Wade, *Letters,* 824), the "point" of II "is that we beget and bear because of the incompleteness of our love." Yet who can blame Frank O'Connor for saying, on hearing Yeats's reading, that he " 'didn't understand a word of it' " (Ellmann, *Iden.,* 282)? L. 6, "the Great Smaragdine Tablet said": Of Hermetic association ("What is below is like that which is above . . ."): *v.* Mme. Blavatsky's *Isis Unveiled,* or cp. Moore, 103-4.

III / "Ribh in Ecstasy": L. 1, "you": Probably Maud Gonne again; cp. "Words."

IV / "There": Ellmann (*Iden.,* 152) considers "There" to designate Yeats's symbolic sphere (*A Vision*).

V / "Ribh Considers Christian Love Insufficient": Wr. ? 1934 (Ellmann, *Iden.,* 293).—St. 1: Cp. "Crazy Jane Grown Old Looks at the Dancers": "They had all that had their hate."—One may cp. Ellmann, *Iden.,* 283.

VI / "He and She": Wr. "before Aug. 25, 1934" (Ellmann, *Iden.,* 293).—Yeats (*v.* Wade, *Letters,* 828) told Mrs. Shakespear this poem was "on the soul," here "she," answering to lunar changes (*A Vision*); cp. Ellmann, *Iden.,* 283.—N.B. The word *sacred,* in l. 3, is a misprint in numerous impressions of 99 for *scared,* though corrected in the 8th printing of 99A; Yeats originally wrote "crazed" (Wade, *ibid.*).

VII / "What Magic Drum?" Wr. 1934?—Cp. Ellmann, *Iden.,* 283.

VIII / "Whence Had They Come?"—Line 2: Read "their sexual joy," as in the 8th printing of 99A.

IX / "The Four Ages of Man": Dated by Ellmann 24 July–6 Aug. 1934; in his 7 Aug. letter to Mrs. Shakespear (Wade, *Letters,* 826), Yeats says it was written the day before. Here also the poet gave an interpretation, saying that the four ages "are the four ages of individual man, but they are also the four ages of civilization. . . . First age, *earth,* vegetative functions. Second age, *water,* blood, sex. Third age, *air,* breath, intellect. Fourth age, *fire,* soul, etc. In the first two the moon comes to the full—resurrection of Christ and Dionysus. Man becomes rational, no longer driven from below or above."—Cp. *A Vision* and "The Four Contests of the Antithetical within Itself." (But it may be pleasanter and quite rational to take the poem as it most obviously is!)

X/ "Conjunctions": Ellmann (*Iden.,* 293) dates this "a few days before Aug. 25, 1934"; in his 25 Aug. letter to Mrs. Shakespear (Wade, *Letters,* 827-28), Yeats says "some days." Here, too, the poet explains: "I was told . . . that my two children would be Mars conjunctive Venus, Saturn conjunctive Jupiter respectively; and so they were—Anne the Mars-Venus personality. Then I was told that they would develop so that I could study in them the alternating dispensations, the Christian or objective, then the Antithetical or subjective. The Christian is the Mars-Venus—it is democratic. The Jupiter-Saturn civilization is born free among the most cultivated, out of tradition, out of rule. . . . George said . . . Michael is always thinking about life Anne always thinks of death. Then I remembered that the children were the two dispensations. . . ."

XI / "A Needle's Eye."

XII / "Meru": One of Yeats's relatively few sonnets. On p. 44 of *K. G. C. T.*, the poet speaks of "Bagwan Shri Hansa's pilgrimage to Mount Kaílás, the legendary Meru": *v.* the full "commentary" (44-45) of which this is a part. Hone (468) says Yeats wrote the poem "after reading *The Holy Mountain*" (trans. Shri Purohit Swami, with intro. by Yeats; 1934); O'Connor (N.Y. *Times Book Rev.*, 31 May 1953; p. 16) sees it as dealing "with the end of Western European civilization."—*V.* in general Ussher, 83-84; Ellmann, *Kenyon Rev.*, XV, 373.

Last Poems

". . . I am still of opinion that only two topics can be of the least interest to a serious and studious mind —sex and the dead": Yeats to Olivia Shakespear (Wade, *Letters*, 730).

"The Gyres": *94, 97, 98, 99.—Jeffares (*Huntington Lib. Qu.*) suggests the poem was written between July 1936 and Jan. 1937; Miss Koch (96) opines 1935 to be the "probable date" of composition with the same self-confidence with which she identifies (99) "Old Rocky Face" (l. 1) as the poet himself, addressed by the antithetical self: a reversal of Blackmur's notion (*South. Rev.*, VII, 420) that "Rocky Face" was Yeats's "antithetical self." But Rocky Face has endured several novel identifications: Miss Moore takes him to be Blake's Urizen (420); Ellmann (*Iden.*, 154) calls him "the Delphic Oracle." Nevertheless, and whether or not Yeats injected something of himself into this recluse, Jeffares (289) seems on firmer ground in recognizing the cavern-dwelling Jew of Shelley's *Hellas* (cp. *Auto.*, 212 ff.): and Henn (cp. 302-6) notes that the initial draft of the poem had "Old Cavern Face."—Stauffer (Chap. 2) finds the central idea of the piece in Dryden's *Secular Masque.* Cp. also Ure, 45.—On "What matter?" (St. 3, l. 2) cp. "All things fall . . ." from the next poem; in both instances, *Essays*, 398-99. (The 8th printing of 99A corrects the "come" of l. 15 to "comes.")

"Lapis Lazuli": *London Mercury*, Mar. 1938; *New Republic*, 13 Apr. 1938; *New Poems*, 18 May 1938; 97, 98, 99.—Finished 25 July 1936: *v.* Wellesley, 91; Henn, 306-7.—L. 3: Cp. Seanchan, in *The King's Threshold:* "In ruin, poetry calls out in joy," etc.— L. 7: The seventh line of "The Boyne Water" (*Historical Songs of Ireland,* Percy Soc'y Pubns., Vol. I, ed. T. C. Croker: London, 1840; p. 60) runs: "But King William threw his bomb-balls in." Jeffares (*Mod. Lang. Notes*) derives "bomb-balls" from "The Battle of the Boyne," a ballad in *Irish Minstrelsy* (1888), ed. by H. H. Sparling; and remarks that the piece of lapis lazuli described in St. 4 suggests the "great piece carved by some Chinese sculptor" described in a letter to Dorothy Wellesley (8). (See Henn's amusing observation, "Intro.," xv.)—On "Lear and Hamlet are gay" (St. 2), cp. Ure, 74-75; Henn, 204 fn. 2.—On St. 3, cp. "Two Songs from a Play, I"; *A Vision*, 206; and *Essays*, 359. One may also cp. Ellmann, *Iden.*, 93 and 185-87.

"Imitated from the Japanese": *94, 97, 98, 99.—From Wellesley (128) one gathers this was fashioned 31

Dec. 1936 "out of a prose translation of a Japanese Hokku in praise of Spring."

"Sweet Dancer": *London Mercury*, Apr. 1938; *New Poems*, 18 May 1938; 97, 98, 99.—In original form, in 8 Jan. 1937 letter to Dorothy Wellesley, who said in her 27 Jan. reply that she did not like the poem.— On the "black cloud" of St. 1, cp. Blake's *Los the Terrible* (ll. 15-16) and *William Bond* (St. 4).

"The Three Bushes": *London Mercury*, Jan. 1937; Cuala *Broadsides*, N.S. No. 3: Mar. 1937; *94, 97, 98, 99. (The typographical setting of the subtitle varies insignificantly in the first and third printings.)—For original version, *v.* July 1936 letter, Wellesley (83 ff.). —Stauffer (113 and 163 fn. 5) attempts to tie this to the juvenile "Anashuya and Vijaya."—The 8th printing of 99A deletes the quotation marks after "man" in l. 6 and "chastity?" in l. 20; it also changes the period of l. 23 to a comma.

"The Lady's First Song": *94, 97, 98, 99.—Original version in 20 Nov. 1936 letter to Dorothy Wellesley, *q. v.*

"The Lady's Second Song," "The Lady's Third Song," "The Lover's Song," "The Chambermaid's First Song," and "The Chambermaid's Second Song": 94, 97, 98, 99; the first is badly punctuated in 94, and the fourth in 94 and 97.—The first and second of these five were revised, with regrouping of lines, from the two parts of "The Lady to Her Chambermaid" sent Dorothy Wellesley in a July 1936 letter: *v.* Wellesley, 85-87. Yeats thought them and "The Three Bushes" of his "best"!—On St. 2 of "The Lady's Second Song" and on "The Lady's Third Song," cp. certain ideas of Yeats's father: Hone *Letters*, No. 81, "A Last Confession," and "Ribh Denounces Patrick."—The first draft of "The Lover's Song" was sent as written 9

Nov. 1936 to Dorothy Wellesley (*v.* 112).—The last
two of the group are revised from "The Chambermaid's Prayer before Dawn" and "The Chambermaid's
Song after His Death," included in a 15 Nov. 1936
letter to Dorothy Wellesley and altered in later letters.
The "Chambermaid's" "worm" comparisons remind
one, trivially enough, that Oona (*Countess Cathleen,*
Sc. II) recalls the countess as a baby "helpless as a
worm," and that the same phrase recurs in Robartes'
third speech in "The Phases of the Moon."

"An Acre of Grass": *London Mercury, Apr. 1938; *Atlantic Monthly,* do.; *New Poems,* 18 May 1938; 97, 98,
99.—On Sts. 3 and 4, cp. MacNeice, 177-78.

"What Then?"—*The Erasmian (Dublin), Apr. 1937; 94,
97, 98, 99.—Jeffares (302 fn. 3) corrects Hone (482)
on this and tries (295), on perhaps very tenuous
grounds, to relate the refrain to Nietzsche's *The
Dawn of Day.* Cp. Ure, 59.—The "small old house"
of St. 3 is Yeats's place at Riversdale.

M "Beautiful Lofty Things": 94, *97, 98, 99.—On l. 2, *v.*
Hone, 230-32, and Hone *Letters,* No. 152.—L. 8: Jeffares (292) counts "eightieth" an error for "seven-
tieth," but may be himself mistaken; cp. also his comment on p. 351 of his *Rev. of Eng. Studies,* XXIII,
art. (In her *Jour.* Lady Gregory calls 15 Mar. 1930 the
date of her "78th" birthday, thus setting 1852 as her
birth-year.)—On "Maud Gonne at Howth" (l. 10),
v. Hone, 92; on O'Leary, *v.* notes to "September 1913,"
sup.; on O'Grady, *v. Auto.,* 271 ff.

"A Crazed Girl": Originally "At Barcelona," as prefatory
contribution, preceding "Intro." by Yeats, to Margot
Ruddock's *The Lemon Tree (London: Dent, 1937),
vii; present title, *New Poems,* 1938; 97, 98, 99.—For
the story involved, *v.* Hone, 477-78; Moore, 360-61;

and Yeats's 22 May 1936 letter to Olivia Shakespear (Wade, *Letters*, 856).—On punctuation, *v.* Freyer, *LTLS;* on Margot Ruddock's acting in *The Player Queen*, Rothenstein, *Since Fifty*, 246.

"To Dorothy Wellesley": Originally "To a Friend," *London Mercury*, Mar. 1938; do., *Nation* (N.Y.), 12 Mar. 1938, and *New Poems*, 1938; present title, *L. P. P.*, 1940; 98, 99.—Wr. 1 Aug. 1936 (Ellmann, *Iden.*, 293).—For earliest version, *v.* Wellesley, 93.—The "Great Dane" was Dorothy Wellesley's "Brutus," who died in Oct. 1937. On the line in parentheses, *v.* Wellesley, 58, fn.—Query on last two lines: Lacking Greek, was Yeats likely to insist on the strictly literal meaning of *Eumenides?*—or does the clause somehow tie in with his concept of tragedy as joy to the fatally overwhelmed?—On Dorothy Wellesley and her home, *v.* Rothenstein, *Since Fifty*, 249 ff.

"The Curse of Cromwell": Cuala *Broadsides*, N.S. No. 8: Aug. 1937; 94, *97, 98, 99.—Cp. Yeats's 8 and 28 Jan. 1937 letters to Dorothy Wellesley, and *v.* Wade, *Letters*, 886.—On "beaten into the clay" (l. 3), *v.* notes to "Under Ben Bulben," § V.—Jeffares (289) finds the first four lines of St. 2 "based on *A Vision*." St. 3, l. 2: Re the Spartan lad who concealed a fox beneath his tunic and stoically ignored the vicious clawing and biting (Plutarch, *Life of Lycurgus*).—On last stanza, cp. notes on "Crazy Jane on God," *sup.*

"Roger Casement": *Irish Press*, 2 Feb. 1937; *rev. version, with letter (rptd. Wade, *Letters*, 882-83), *idem*, 13 Feb.; 94, 97, 98, 99.—Apparently wr. 1936 (*v.* Hone, 480); Ellmann (*Iden.*, 293) says Nov. 1936.—V. Wellesley, 138 and 141; Alfred Noyes, *Two Worlds for Memory* (Philadelphia: Lippincott, 1953); Hone *Letters*, 195 fn.; Rothenstein, *M. & M.*, II, 170-71;

Griffin, 116-30; Colum, Chap. 16, § 1, and Chaps. 19 and 21.

"The Ghost of Roger Casement": *94, 97, 98, 99.—Perhaps wr. 1936 (*v.* Hone, 480); Ellmann (*Iden.,* 293) claims Jan. 1937.—Jeffares (*Nineteenth Cent. and After*) glosses Gray's *Elegy* . . . on the last stanza; in his book (336 fn. 42) he also cites the evidence of *On the Boiler.*—Cp. Thompson, *Hopkins Rev.,* III, 14-15; and *v.* notes to preceding poem.

"The O'Rahilly": *94, 97, 98, 99.—Cp. Jeffares, 337 fn. 45A, with his reference to A. Bax (100); Henn, 311 fn. 1; MacManus, 703; Strong, 26; and the poems ("Sixteen Dead Men," "The Rose Tree," etc.) relating to the Easter Rising.

"Come Gather Round Me, Parnellites": Cuala *Broadsides,* N.S. [3d] No. 1: Jan. 1937; *Essays, 1931 to 1936,* 14 Dec. 1937; 94, *97, 98, 99. The comma is missing from the title and the first line in the first three printings; the first two printings had in l. 27, more musically, "husband who had" instead of "husband that had."—In *Essays* . . . , dated Aug. 1936; in original form, enclosed in 8 Sept. 1936 letter to Dorothy Wellesley from Riversdale, entitled "Come Stand About Me, Parnellites" and said to have been written at the request of old Henry Harrison, a Parnellite.—Cp. notes to "Parnell's Funeral" and "Parnell."

"The Wild Old Wicked Man": *London Mercury,* Apr. 1938; *Atlantic Monthly,* do.; *New Poems,* 18 May 1938; *97, 98, 99.—Jeffares (288) finds "a certain autobiographical flavor" and says (336 fn. 44) this was "written to Lady Elizabeth Pelham." One may cp. the partial analysis in the last two pages of Wasserman's review of Koch.—L. 5, "on the straw": in bed.—Sts. 1, 3, and 7, "the old man in the skies": God (in Sc. II of *The Player Queen* called "the Old Man in the Sky").—St. 5, "warty lads": sexually potent, in Irish peasant belief, as Yeats explained to Dorothy Wellesley.

"The Great Day": *London Mercury,* Mar. 1938 (as first in group of four "Fragments" including also the poems of the next entry, *inf.*); *New Poems,* 18 May 1938; *97, 98, 99.—In a 28 Jan. 1937 letter to Dorothy Wellesley, Yeats says this and the next two lyrics (all subsequently revised) "give the essence of my politics."

"Parnell," "What Was Lost," and "The Spur": Publishing history identical with that of preceding poem. The concluding reference in the second is evidently to a tombstone. The last piece is revised from a version in a 9 Dec. 1936 letter to Dorothy Wellesley.—On Parnell, *v.* notes to "Parnell's Funeral," *sup.* Rothenstein (*Since Fifty,* 230) refers to Yeats's quotation.

"A Drunken Man's Praise of Sobriety": 94, *97, 98, 99.

"The Pilgrim": Cuala *Broadsides,* N.S. No. 10: Oct. 1937; 94, *97, 98, 99. (First two printings had no italics.)— Henn (311) calls this "a return to the thought that the holy places of Ireland might effect a union of the two religions."

"Colonel Martin": Cuala *Broadsides,* N.S. No. 12: Dec. 1937; 94, *97, 98, 99. In the first printing only, the refrain was "Lullabulloo, buloo, buloo, lullabullo, bullo."—On 10 Aug. 1937 Yeats wrote Edith Shackleton Heald that he had "just finished" this (Wade, *Letters,* 896-97). In his 13 Aug. letter to Dorothy Wellesley (158), he called it "among the best things, almost the strangest thing I have written. It is meant to be sung with a chorus of concertina and whistle."— Cp. Ellmann, *Iden.,* 205-6, on source (though the

poem is misdated on the first of the pages in reference); Jeffares (288) says the poem was "founded on
a Ballina legend."

"A Model for the Laureate": 94, *97, 98, 99.—Jeffares
remarks (288): "King Edward's abdication provoked
this." The original version, "A Marriage Ode," was
sent in a 26 July 1937 letter to Dorothy Wellesley,
q. v., 156.

"The Old Stone Cross": *London Mercury*, Mar. 1938;
Nation (N.Y.), 12 Mar. 1938; *New Poems*, 18 May
1938; 97, 98, 99.—Wr. June 1937 (Ellmann, *Iden.*,
294).

"The Spirit Medium": 94, *97, 98, 99.—L. 4: Cp. conclusion of "The Cold Heaven."—L. 6: Cp. "perne in
a gyre," "Sailing to Byzantium."

"Those Images": *London Mercury*, Mar. 1938; *New
Republic*, 13 Apr. 1938; *New Poems*, 18 May 1938;
97, 98, 99.—Ellmann dates composition "before Aug.
13, 1937" (*Iden.*, 294); but apparently "before Aug.
10" would be even closer (v. Wade, *Letters*, 896).—
Miss Witt feels that this contains "Yeats's concept of
relative values and . . . the theory of symbols he had
fully stated almost forty years earlier. . . ." (*PMLA*,
LXIV, 55.)—On Sts. 3-4, cp. Henn, 38.—St. 4, "the
five": presumably the five senses.

"The Municipal Gallery Revisited": Originally (with
hyphen in "Revisited") in *A Speech and Two Poems*,
1937; do., *94; as now, *L. P. P.*, 1940; 98, 99.—A 5
September 1937 letter to Dorothy Wellesley (159)
says Yeats has "just finished this . . . perhaps the
best poem I have written for some years, unless the
'Curse of Cromwell' is." On the same date he told
Edith Shackleton Heald (Wade, *Letters*, 898) he had
worked "about ten days" on the poem.—*A Speech . . .*

was sent as a pamphlet to James A. Farrell and his "Testimonial Committee" in 1937.—Cp. Henn, 344, 128.—I: On O'Higgins, cp. "Death" and "Blood and the Moon."—II: "Tricolour": usually, the French national flag; here presumably the Irish national flag, referred to by O'Casey (*Cock-a-Doodle Dandy*) as "the Irish Tricolour."—III: On Hugh Lane, *v.* notes on "To a Wealthy Man . . ."; Hazel Lavery: Chicagoborn second wife of Sir John, distinguished Belfastborn painter; she died in 1935. (L. Robinson, *Curtain Up*, 205 ff.; & Gregory, *Jour.*)—V: Cp. Yeats's note, *C. P.*, 457, and Craig, *LTLS.*—VII: Cp. notes on "In Memory of Major Robert Gregory."

"Are You Content?" *London Mercury*, Apr. 1938; *Atlantic Monthly*, Apr. 1938; 94, 97, 98, 99.—Cp. prefatory poem of *Responsibilities.*—On St. 2, cp. notes on "Under Ben Bulben," § VI; *v.* Hone on Yeats's ancestry and relatives.—On "By an old hunter . . ." (last stanza), cp. "An old hunter . . . ," p. xxvii of Yeats's introduction and p. 133 of Hone and Rossi's *Berkeley* (1931): Yeats also used the extract from *Pauline* in his preface to Lady Gregory's *G. F. M.*

"Three Songs to the One Burden": *Spectator*, 26 May 1939; *Last Poems and Two Plays*, 10 July 1939; *97, 98, 99.—I, ll. 5-6: Cp. philosophy of Old Man in *Purgatory;* on concluding lines, cp. "States are justified . . . by . . . the best born of the best" (§ IV, "Intro.," *Fighting the Waves: W. & B.*), and the quotation from *The Anatomy of Melancholy* in *On the Boiler* (15): ". . . it were happy for human kind, if only such parents as are sound of body and mind should be suffered to marry." On Manannan, son of the sea-god Ler, one may cp. Saul. On Crazy Jane, *v.* notes on "Words for Music Perhaps" and "Crazy Jane

on the Mountain."—II, "Henry Middleton" (l. 1):
Yeats's eccentric cousin; cp. Hone, 23. The "small
demesne" of l. 2 is "Elsinore," The Rosses, by repute
smuggler-haunted.—III: On Pearse and Connolly, *v.*
notes on the poems of the Easter Rising ("Sixteen
Dead Men," etc.); cp. *The Death of Cuchulain.* On
the last stanza, cp. the anonymous "Proclamation of
the Irish Republic" (17 Apr. 1916), rptd. in Mercier
and Greene, pp. 245-46.

"In Tara's Halls": 95, *97, 98, 99.—The mythological
references in this poem have to date escaped identification. (Tara was, of course, traditionally the seat of
the High King.)

"The Statues": *London Mercury,* Mar. 1939; *Nation*
(N.Y.), 15 Apr. 1939; *Last Poems and Two Plays,* 10
July 1939; 97, 98, 99.—Dated 9 Apr. 1938.—Yeats
wrote Dorothy Wellesley (181) on 10 June 1938 of
finishing this, adding, "You were its suggestion."—Cp.
"The Phases of the Moon," p. 162 (*C. P.*), ll. 14 ff.—
On ll. 4-6, cp. *Auto.,* 448, anent Maud Gonne.—On
St. 3, cp. *The Death of Cuchulain. V.* Henn, 308.—
On 28 June 1938 Yeats wrote to Edith Shackleton
Heald (Wade, *Letters,* 911): "In reading the third
stanza remember the influence on modern sculpture
and on the great seated Buddha of the sculptors who
followed Alexander. Cuchulain is in the last stanza because Pearse and some of his followers had a cult of
him. The Government has put a statue of Cuchulain
in the rebuilt post office to commemorate this."—V.
MacNeice, 175, for a gloss from *On the Boiler;* Ure
(*Rev. of Eng. Studies*), for interpretation and associ-
ative reference. Ure explains the opening statement
by remarking that Pythagoras " 'planned it' in the
sense that the whole manifestation of artistic creation

which made the 'statues' possible was prepared for by Pythagoras' doctrine of numbers. . . ." He also points out that the last stanza "affirms that the Irish, in a movement of history which brings about the return of the Pythagorean philosophy, must and will adopt a like artistic principle." One may cp. Ellmann, *Iden.*, 188-90.—In *On the Boiler* (37), Yeats remarks: "There are moments when I am certain that art must once again accept those Greek proportions." (This is one of the poems at the interpretation of which Miss Koch struggles most strenuously.)

"News for the Delphic Oracle": *London Mercury,* Mar. 1939; *New Republic,* 22 Mar. 1939; 95, *97, 98, 99.— For what seems a semistrained interpretation, *v.* Ellmann, *Iden.*, 284-85.— I, ll. 5-6: Niamh and Oisin: *v.* notes to ". . . Oisin." Ll. 7-8: cp. "The Delphic Oracle upon Plotinus."—For the opening image of II, cp. "Byzantium" ("Astraddle on the dolphin's mire and blood"); Henn (235) points to "the Ostia Mosaic" and a plaster cast in Victoria and Albert Museum. Henn also finds III a description of Poussin's "The Marriage of Peleus and Thetis" (one of the Lane pictures).—The misspelling "Pelius" (l. 26) in the first three printings perhaps betrays Yeats's pronunciation.

"Three Marching Songs": Rewritten (after Yeats's disillusionment by the "Blue-shirts": Hone, 467) from "Three Songs to the Same Tune" (*q. v.*) and published in *Last Poems and Two Plays,* 1939; rptd. *97 with the fn. "Rewritten December 1938," despite which Ellmann (*Iden.*, 294) dates composition the same as for the original "Three Songs . . ."; without fn., 98, 99.—Freyer, *LTLS,* is concerned with punctuation. The 8th printing of 99A corrects the "Oh" of III, l. 16, to "On."

M "Long-Legged Fly": *London Mercury,* Mar. 1939; *Nation* (N.Y.), 15 Apr. 1939; *95, 97, 98, 99. *N.B.:* 99A misprints "Her" as "His" in l. 20 prior to the eighth impression.—Ellmann (*Iden.,* 294) dates composition Nov. 1937. An 11 Apr. 1938 letter to Dorothy Wellesley has a version of this. Marlowe and, as Henn (60) suggests, a memory of Iseult Gonne dancing on a Normandy beach may both have been in Yeats's mind when he wrote the second stanza.—Cp. Drew-Sweeney, 153.

*A Bronze Head": *London Mercury,* Mar. 1939; *New Republic,* 22 Mar. 1939; 95, *97, 98, 99.—The head is that of the bronze-painted plaster bust of Maud Gonne by Laurence Campbell, in the Dublin Municipal Gallery (Hone, 504).—"McTaggart" (J. M. E. McTaggart, 1866–1925), of St. 2, was the philosopher-author of *Studies in Hegelian Cosmology* (1901), which Miss Koch (81) recalls "Yeats had read in 1928" (cp. Hone, 394), and of *The Nature of Existence* (2 vols.; 1921–27).—For an additional, unpublished stanza, with at least one good line, *v.* Jeffares, 294.—St. 3, ll. 2-4: Ure (21) cps. first musician's song, *At the Hawk's Well* ("How many centuries spent"); cp. also "The Phases of the Moon," p. 162 (*C. P.*), ll. 14 ff.

"A Stick of Incense": *95, 97, 98, 99.—? Cp. *On the Boiler,* 27: "Yet we must hold to what we have that the next civilization may be born, not from a virgin's womb, nor a tomb without a body, but of our own rich experience."

"John Kinsella's Lament for Mrs. Mary Moore": *London Mercury,* Dec. 1938; *New Republic,* 15 Feb. 1939; 95, *97, 98, 99.—Earlier version sent in letter to Dorothy Wellesley, 29 July 1938; but Yeats was meditating the

piece eight days before that: cp. Wade, *Letters,* 912.
—L. 21: "put a skin": made lively; embellished.

"Hound Voice": *London Mercury,* Dec. 1938; *Nation*
(N.Y.), 10 Dec. 1938; *95, 97, 98, 99.—MacNeice
(176) cps. "The Fisherman," "At Galway Races," and
the Robert Gregory memorials. Cp. also "Under Ben
Bulben," § V.—The 8th printing supplies the period
at the end of l. 9 missing in earlier impressions of 99A.

"High Talk": *London Mercury,* Dec. 1938; *Nation* (N. Y.),
10 Dec. 1938; *95, 97, 98, 99.—Here, says Bowra
(215), Yeats "makes fun of those who have great pre-
tensions and seems to place himself in their company."
—L. 9, "Malachi Stilt-Jack": Whether or not "metaphor" (l. 11), the association seems personal, arbi-
trary, and unclear. The historical Malachi (5th cent.
B.C.) was one of the minor Hebrew prophets (*v.* last
book of Old Testament).

"The Apparitions": *London Mercury,* Dec. 1938; *New
Republic,* 15 Feb. 1939 (with the misprints of St. 1
corrected in the 28 June issue); 95, 97, 98, 99.—Burke
(*South. Rev.*) makes what seems a curiously solemn
attempt to interpret this and link it with *A Vision,* "A
Coat," and "Sailing to Byzantium."—Of the refrain,
Henn (140) says there were only seven "apparitions"
and adds: " 'The Apparitions' are a series of death-
dreams that occurred after his illness in Majorca, and
were of special significance in relation to Lady Gregory's death, and to his own."

"A Nativity": *London Mercury,* Dec. 1938; *New Republic,* 15 Feb. 1939; 95, 97, 98, 99.—V. Henn, 39, 234,
247.—On first couplet, cp. "The Mother of God," *sup.*
—Henn (247) says Mrs. Yeats thinks Yeats put Delacroix (the French Romantic painter who died in 1863:
for a passing comment, *v.* Lewis, 56; cp. Palmer, *Lon-*

don Merc.) in the second couplet merely because he "liked the rotundity of Delacroix's name." On the same authority, Henn identifies the Irving of l. 8 as the actor, Henry, once met by Yeats, at the same time recalling Cloudsley's suggestion of Edward Irving, the preacher-editor of Blake.—Talma (l. 10) is presumably the eighteenth-century French actor.

"Why Should Not Old Men Be Mad?" Originally included, untitled, in "The Name," *On the Boiler,* 1939; separately, as now, *L. P. P.,* 1940; 98, 99.—Jeffares (202) identifies the "girl" (ll. 5-6) as Mrs. Francis (Iseult Gonne) Stuart, and (244) re-emphasizes Yeats's disapproval of this marriage; however, cp. the 25 July 1932 letter to Olivia Shakespear (Wade, *Letters,* 799-800). Ll. 7-8 presumably refer to Maud Gonne.

"The Statesman's Holiday": Originally included, untitled, in "Other Matters," *On the Boiler,* 1939, where Yeats writes in prelude: "In my savage [*sic!*] youth I was accustomed to say that no man should be permitted to open his mouth in Parliament until he had sung or written his Utopia . . . and I still think that artists of all kinds should once again praise or represent great or happy people. Here in Monte Carlo [? fall, 1938], where I am writing, somebody talked of a man with a monkey and some sort of stringed instrument, and it has pleased me to imagine him a great politician. I will make him sing to the sort of tune that goes well with my early sentimental poems." Poem as now, *L. P. P.,* 1940; 98, 99.—According to Ellmann (*Iden.,* 294), wr. Apr. 1938; but note query, above. Presumably the Oscar of l. 5 is "Oscar [Tschirky] of the Waldorf" (N.Y.).—St. 2, "the man that made the motors": ? Henry Ford.—Cp. Bowra, 216, on the refrain.

"Crazy Jane on the Mountain": Originally included, untitled, in "Ireland after the Revolution," *On the Boiler*, 1939; as now, *L. P. P.*, 1940; 98, 99.—Ll. 7-10 are thought to refer to George V of England and the Bolshevik-manhandled Russian royal family.—On the dainty subject of Emer's bladder, *v.* the fn. observation in *On the Boiler*, 24, or MacNeice, 74-75.—On 13 July 1938 Yeats wrote to Dorothy Wellesley, "I am writing a new 'Crazy Jane' poem—a wild affair."—V. notes to "Words for Music Perhaps."

M. "The Circus Animals' Desertion": *London Mercury* and *Atlantic Monthly*, Jan. 1939; 95, *97, 98, 99.—Cp. Henn, 345.—II, St. 1, Oisin: *v.* notes to ". . . Oisin." The "my dear" of st. 2 is Maud Gonne. The reference at the opening of st. 3 is to *On Baile's Strand*.—On III one may cp. MacNeice, 127 fn. 1, if one has Freudian sympathies. Crazy Jane is presumably "that raving slut" referred to.—Cp. § VII of Fraser.

"Politics": *London Mercury* and *Atlantic Monthly*, Jan. 1939; 95, *97, 98, 99.—Cp. Hone, 502, and Yeats's 24 May and 10 June 1938 letters to Dorothy Wellesley (for comment and early versions, the second called "The Theme").

"The Man and the Echo": Originally without initial article, *London Mercury* and *Atlantic Monthly*, Jan. 1939; as now, *Last Poems and Two Plays*, 1939; *97, 98, 99.—Original version, labeled "July 1938. (Copied at Penns.)," in Wellesley, 198-99.—L. 1: "The 'cleft that's christened Alt' is near Sligo, and has magical associations . . .": hence Yeats associated it with the Delphic chasm (Henn, 7-8; *v.* also 43-44).—L. 11: *Cathleen ni Houlihan;* cp. p. 16, *P. & C.:* "We wish to grow peaceful crops, but we must dig our furrows with the sword" ("Samhain: 1901"). Cp. Robinson,

T. H., 218: "... *Kathleen ni Houlihan* and *The Rising of the Moon* have made more rebels in Ireland than a thousand political speeches or a hundred reasoned books."—Ll. 13-14, "that woman's reeling brain": ? Margot Ruddock's: cp. "A Crazed Girl."—Ll. 15-16: ? Reference to the fate of Coole: cp. "Upon a House Shaken ...," "Coole Park, 1929," and "Coole Park and Ballylee, 1931."—*N. B.:* Only the *Atlantic Monthly* printing has what one suspects to be the proper reading of l. 42: "Its joy or night seems but a dream."

"Cuchulain Comforted": 95, *97, 98, 99.—Dorothy Wellesley (212) says Yeats read "the prose theme" of this at Cap Martin; Henn (321 fn. 5) gives Mrs. Yeats as authority for saying that "The prose draft, the result of a dream, was dictated at 3 a.m. on 7 Jan. 1939." The poem is dated 13 Jan. 1939 (*C. P.*); nevertheless, a letter written by Yeats prior to 27 Dec. 1938 (Wade, *Letters,* 921) speaks of his writing (or having written?) this poem as an outgrowth of his just-finished *Death of Cuchulain.*—In *The Death of Cuchulain,* the *mórrigu* (old Irish war-goddess, often shapen like a crow) refers to the "six mortal wounds" of the hero (and cp. l. 1); however, Henn (309) calls this Yeats's "prophetic poem on his own entrance to the Kingdom of the Dead."—If the poem has any significant point or concealed symbol, it fails to become clear (despite Miss Moore, who, 438, sees St. 6's " 'all we do / All must together do' " as "community," "love," wherein Cuchulain is "comforted"!).—On the segment just quoted, Mrs. Bjersby glosses *A Vision* (London, 1937), p. 234. —Last line: The speech of lovers in Tir-nan-oge (*Tír-na-nÓg:* Land of the Young) is said in *K. G. C. T.* (verse version, First Attendant's opening speech) to

be "the speech of birds."—The *terza rima* is, of course,
unusual in Yeats.

"The Black Tower": 95, *97, 98, 99.—Dated 21 Jan. 1939
except in 99E, where 23 Jan. is given.—Yeats's last-
written poem (Wellesley, 213). Henn (322) says it
"celebrates the warrior Eoghan Bel buried near
Maeve's cairn on the summit of Knocknarea," having
earlier explained (1) that "After the Battle of Sligo in
A.D. 537 Eoghan Bel 'was buried standing, his red
javelin in his hand, as if bidding defiance to his enemies.'" Cp. O'Rahilly, 396-98. Such burial was not
exceptional among the old Irish, as an effort at halting
an enemy: cp. O'Curry, I (Intro.), cccxix ff., and
Joyce, II, 539 ff.—Jeffares (337 fn. 74), citing Mrs.
Yeats's authority, says the poem was written "on the
subject of political propaganda." Miss Moore (439-40)
offers a fantastically strained "interpretation"; cp. also
Ellmann (*Iden.*, 209).—Ll. 18 and 28: All printings
except the first seven of 99A have (more illogically, it
would seem) "But wind comes up . . ." instead of "But
winds come up. . . ."

"Under Ben Bulben": Pub. in both the *Irish Times* and
the *Irish Independent*, 3 Feb. 1939; § VI was also published separately, on the same date, in the *Irish Press*.
The complete poem next appeared in *Last Poems and
Two Plays*, 1939; rptd. *97, 98, 99.—Dated 4 Sept.
1938 (on which date Yeats—in a letter to Edith Shackleton Heald: Wade, *Letters*, 915—made it clear that
one version had by then been written). Hone (508)
dates the prose draft of this Aug. 1938; Dorothy Wellesley (203, fn.) says Yeats gave her "a first draft" of
the poem "at Penns in the Rocks in September," and
that the original title was "His Convictions."—Ben
Bulben (*Benn Boilbin*) is a hill traditionally associated

with the *Fianna* (*v.* Saul).—I, l. 11: Original printing, 99 has the misprint "When" for "Where."—II, ll. 1-2: Cp. No. XV of Henley's "Rhymes and Rhythms," *Poems* (N. Y.: Scribner's, 1898), Frost's "The Wind and the Rain," *A Witness Tree* (N. Y.: Holt, 1942), and Yeats's own "Death." L. 6: Only the first 7 printings of 99A have (grammatically proper) "rifle knock" instead of "rifle knocks."—III, l. 2: Mitchel's *Jail Journal* has "Give us war in our time, O Lord!" Cp. McHugh, 29 and 38.—IV: Cp. MacNeice, 176, and "The Statues"; Henn, 197. On the concluding ll. of the section, *v.* Witt, *Mod. Philol.*—V, ll. 11-12: Cp. Frank O'Connor's translation *Kilcash* ("The earls, the lady, the people / Beaten into the clay").—VI: On Drumcliff, *v. E. P. S.*, 247; the "ancestor" (l. 3) was the Reverend John Yeats, the poet's great-grandfather: *v. Auto.*, 22-23. On the famous concluding epitaph, *v.* Yeats's 15 Aug. 1938 letter to Dorothy Wellesley and its contradiction (since confirmed by Mrs. Yeats) by Hone (507 fn.), as well as O'Connor's bemused comment (257), the latter incidentally justified by a confession in one of Yeats's letters to Professor Grierson in T. R. Henn's possession.—Cp. Higgins in *The Arrow,* Summer 1939; Henn, 318-22; and Bradford, *Va. Qu. Rev.*, XXV, 212-14.

"NARRATIVE AND DRAMATIC"

"The Wanderings of Oisin": Title piece of 1889 volume, much revised thereafter; originally "The Wanderings of Oisin and How a Demon Trapped Him," in 3 "parts": "The Island of the Living," "The Island of Victories," and "The Island of Forgetfulness." Rptd., with clipped title, 9, 12, 14, 18, 21, 23, 24(1), 30, 32, 33 (Bk. III only), 45, 47, 51, 52, 55, 56, 61, 64, 69, 73,

*79, 80, 88, 98, 99. N.B.: "Oisin" is spelled "Usheen" in
9, 30, 32, 33, 45, 47, 51, 52, 55, 56, 61, 64, 69, 73, and
88.—Composition frequently misdated: as McHugh
(160, n. 12) has demonstrated, the MS of the first
printed version was completed in the autumn of 1887.
—Yeats has a note, C. P., 457; v. also his E. P. S., 527,
and *Estrangement,* § LIII.—The most careful study
of sources is by Alspach (*PMLA*). V. also Yeats's letter to the editor of the *Spectator,* 3 Aug. 1889; Hoare;
Chap. III, Gurd (allowing for some faulty assump-
tions of influence and sources, as well as some error
in mythological reference); Tynan, *M. Y.,* espec. p. 47;
Reid, 28-39; Menon, 10-11; Hone, 64, but corrected
from McHugh, 67-68 (and v. also 84); Archer, 534-41;
Jeffares, 47; and Wade, *Letters,* 132. Ellmann's attempt (Chap. IV) at biographical parallelism seems
decidedly strained; Seiden's sexual interpretation (*Accent*) is, to the writer, nauseating. (Incidentally, as a
study based by claim on the 1889 edition, Seiden's commentary suggests, 181, the anachronistic in its pontifical
"On the conscious level, it [*Oisin*] is an expression of the
artist's sense of impotence in the midst of our highly in-
dustrialized, and somewhat sterile, twentieth century.")
—"Oisin" = "The little fawn": son of Finn, chief of
the *Fianna,* by Saeve, his wife out of the *síde;* great
poet-warrior, in Scotland known as "Ossian." V. James
Stephens' "Oisin's Mother," *Irish Fairy Tales.*—Bk. I:
Shelley's moon, "wandering companionless," will be
recognized in l. 12.—Caoilte (Cailte Mac Ronain:
Finn's favorite among the warriors of the *Fianna*) and
Conan (Conan Mail: a loud-mouthed, cowardly brag-
gart: cp. the Yeats-Moore *Diarmuid and Grania*), l.
13, figure largely in the tales of the Fenian Cycle.—
Bran and Sceolan (l. 15) were Finn's chief hounds
and his own cousins (v. Reinhard and Hull, *Specu-*

lum), his maternal aunt, Uirne, having while pregnant suffered transformation through the *druidecht* of Imcad's jealous queen; Lomair was one of their three famous whelps, the others being Brod and Lomlu.— L. 16, "Firbolg" (*Fir Bolg*): "Men of the Bags," or "Men of the god Bolg" (O'Rahilly, 52-53), one of the fabled bodies of prehistoric invaders of Ireland; possibly the *Pretani*, called *Cruithin* by the later Irish, a short, dark-complexioned, black-haired people of the Bronze Age? Cp. the *Leabhar Gabhála* ("Book of Invasions"), ed. by Macalister and MacNeill, Dublin, 1916; and Hyde, *Lit. Hist. of Ireland*, 281.—On Maeve's grave, Knocknarea, Sligo (ll. 17-18), *v*. notes to "The Black Tower" and "Red Hanrahan's Song about Ireland" and cp. *The Countess Cathleen*, Sc. II, ll. 15-16; *Auto.*, 329-30; and Hone, 16.—The metal "findrinny" (*findruine*; l. 21) was an alloy, perhaps white bronze. —On ll. 22-23, cp. Jeffares, 100.—The "pearl-pale" (l. 28) recurs in "He Gives His Beloved Certain Rhymes." —Oscar (352, l. 11) was Oisin's son: cp. Gurd, 41; Menon, 10; or Jeffares, 45, on association with Ferguson's *Aideen's Grave*.—L. 13, Gabhra: Site of battle marking the virtual annihilation of the *Fianna* (A.D. 284; *v*. Saul): modern Garristown, Co. Dublin.—Aengus (*v*. notes to "Under the Moon") and Edain ("Étain," originally the wife of Midir, later of Eochaid; l. 17: *v*. notes to "The Two Kings") belong historically to the Irish Mythological Cycle; Miss Gurd (55, and cp. Yeats, *Monthly Rev.*, July 1902) remarks that Aengus' "kisses were changed to birds and flew always about his head."—Niamh "means brightness or beauty," as Yeats says in "The Philosophy of Shelley's Poetry."— "Danaan" (353, l. 2): *Tuatha Dé Danann* ("Tribes of the Goddess Dana"), a magical legendary race who supposedly conquered the *Fir Bolg*, only to be them-

selves driven underground about two centuries later
by the Milesians. They became the *síde*, or elf-folk.
Three of their queens (Eire, Fódhla, and Banba) have
given names to Ireland.—L. 10, "brazen bell": iron,
of oblong shape (Gurd, 53).—Of the phantoms described on p. 355, Yeats spoke in his note on "He
Mourns . . . ," *C. P.,* 448-49, and again wrote in the
attendants' dialogue at the opening of the verse version of *K. G. C. T.,* as well as (with faulty memory)
in the "Intro." to *The Resurrection.*—P. 355, ll. 5-7:
Fiona Macleod (*No. Amer. Rev.,* CLXXV, 477) notes
the Gaelic symbolizing of Love by a white fawn; of
Death, by a white hound.—L. 22: Almhuin (modern
"Allen") was Finn's hall.—P. 356, l. 33: Miss Gurd
(63) glosses Keats (*Endymion,* St. 10): "By thy love's
milky brow."—P. 358, l. 27: Miss Gurd (56) finds the
simile adapted from a Yeats "quotation from a friend."
—On the osprey (359, l. 20) cp. Alspach, 861, and
also *Tristan and Iseult* (Belloc trans. of Bedier's recon-
struction, Portland: Mosher, 1922; p. 112—by way of
illustrating a medieval association).—P. 360, ll. 20-24:
Cp. *E. P. S.,* 232, ll. 12-14.—P. 362, ll. 3-4: Miss Gurd
(62) glosses the *Voyages* of Bran and Brendan.—Miss
Hoare (114) feels that Bk. II "obviously derives from
the Glaucus episode in *Endymion*"; Krans (69) sees
Hyperion in the description of the hall at the head of
p. 364; Miss Gurd (59) thinks the "great fortress . . .
may have been suggested by Shelley's *Temple of the
Spirit*" (*Revolt of Islam,* Sts. 49-53); and one also recalls "the chasm-like portals open to the sea, / And
steps that met the breaker" of "the enchanted towers
of Carbonek" in Tennyson's *Holy Grail.*—P. 365, ll.
3-6: The eagles recall to Miss Gurd (62) an ancient
eagle of the *Mabinogion;* l. 13, "the Seven Hazel
Trees": Miss Gurd (55) believes these "the same as

the nine hazels of wisdom of the Tuatha de Danaan,"
growing undersea.—Heber (p. 365, l. 24): *Eber,* a
son of Milesius (*Miledh Easpáin,* an epithet for
Golamh), supposedly ruler of southern Ireland (*Ériu*)
after the Milesian conquest.—"Ogham" (*ogam;* p. 366,
l. 24): a kind of alphabetic engraving, once thought
very ancient, but now generally regarded as an adaptation from the Latin alphabet, postdating the Christian-
ization by St. Patrick (*Patricius Magonus Sucatus*).
"Manannan" is the sea god, son of Ler.—On Bk. III,
cp. Yeats's comment to Katharine Tynan (*M. Y.,* 47:
and *v.* McHugh, 67), slightly garbled by Hone (64).
—On the sleeping heroes, p. 371, cp. Alspach (862-
63) and consider Kennedy's "The Enchantment of
Gearoidh Iarla" and A. Nutt's *Studies on the Legend
of the Holy Grail* (London: Folklore Soc'y, 1888).
Alspach also remarks (863-65) on the bell-branch
(foot of p. 372).—P. 374: L. 6, "the name of the
demon": Really Culann, the smith, one of the "dark"
Celtic divinities, who made Conchobar's sword, spear,
and shield on the Isle of Man (*v.* Rhys, 638).—L. 15,
Blanid: wife of Curoi, king of Munster, illicitly in love
with Cuchulainn (*v.* Spence; Rolleston, 228-29; Rhys,
473-78, *s. v.* "Bláthnat"). MacNessa ("Son of Ness")
is Conchobar, king of Uladh (eastern Ulster); Fergus
is Conchobar's stepfather, forced to attend a feast
given at Conchobar's order by Barach, by way of re-
moving him as protector of Deirdre and the sons of
Usna on their return from exile; Balor is the Fomorian
king of the poisonous single eye (on Yeats's "Balor . . .
car-borne," Alspach, *PMLA,* 865 fn. 78, glosses Mac-
pherson's "car-borne Cormac," etc., from the *Ossian*),
which was originally "death-pouring" rather than
"death-making"; Grania is the fiancée who jilted Finn
and forced Diarmuid into elopement. "Balor . . . Borne

in his heavy car," Barach, and other of these figures will also be found in *The Countess Cathleen,* Sc. V. One may cp. Saul on the mythological figures. For charming retellings of Fenian tales, *v.* James Stephens' *Irish Fairy Tales* and Ella Young's *The Tangle-Coated Horse.*—P. 378, l. 3: "Bera of ships": modern Dunboy. —The 8th printing of 99A makes the following changes: § I: A break between ll. 114-15, 145-46, and 363-64; deletion of the commas ending ll. 405 and 406. §III: Change of semicolon to colon, l. 19; change in spelling "Blanid" to "Blanaid," l. 89; deletion of the first comma, l. 109; insertion of hyphen in "saddle-bow," l. 147; substitution of "because" for "before," l. 169.—Cp. Darrell Figgis' *The Return of the Hero.*

"The Old Age of Queen Maeve": *Fortnightly Review,* Apr. 1903; *The Gael* (N. Y.), June 1903; second item, *In the Seven Woods,* Aug. 1903; 17, 20, 21, 24(1), 25, 33, 50, 54, 57, 58, 63, 75, *79 (in which the italicized opening stanza first appears), 80, 98, 99.—In course of composition when Yeats wrote Robert Bridges on 20 July 1901, and apparently "just finished" when he wrote Sturge Moore on 11 Aug.: cp. Bridge, 2.—Continues, though with very indifferent success, to further the intention stated by Yeats in 1901: "I hope to get our heroic age into verse. . . ." It is hardly suggestive of the tradition surviving in *Aislinge Œnguso* ("The Dream of Œngus"), MS Egerton 1782, transcribed by Müller in *Rev. Celt.,* III, 344, where it is faultily translated (347). Cp. also Thurneysen, *Zeit. für Celt. Phil.,* XII, 400.—There is a translation by Miss Hoare (166 ff.), who remarks (119) that Yeats "has abstracted from the story the fact that Maeve (with Ailill) helps Angus to obtain Caer, and makes this the basis for an excursion into the fantastic." On Medb ("Maeve") in folk tradition, cp. "And Fair, Fierce

Women," *The Celtic Twilight.*—Cruachan (l. 11) was Medb's seat in Connacht.—The reference at the foot of p. 385, like the apostrophe in the lower portion of p. 388, concerns Maud Gonne.—P. 386, ll. 5-7: ? Cp. Yeats's quotation from Hyde (*Auto.*, ed. N. Y. 1938, 376): "I was myself one time a poor barnacle goose. . . ."—The "great war" (386, l. 26) is the *Táin Bó Cuálnge,* Medb's "cattle-raid of Cooley" involving invasion of Uladh (Ulster).—*Nessa's* (387, l. 3) is a combination of the Irish with the English genitive: bad grammar for "Ness's" (Ness was Conchobar's mother: *v.* notes on "Fergus and the Druid"). "Magh Ai" (387, l. 9: *Magh Aoi: Machaire Chonnacht*) is a plain in Co. Roscommon.—On the Maines (387, l. 24), *v.* notes on "The Hour before Dawn." "Bual's hill" (following l.): Caer's father's name was really Etal Anbual (and more than half a dozen earlier printings of the poem read ". . . digging into Anbual's hill").— P. 388, l. 5: "the painted house": the old Irish commonly used whitewash on their houses.—The 8th printing of 99A ends l. 30 with a comma and deletes the comma from l. 80.

"Baile and Aillinn": *Monthly Review,* July 1902 (where Yeats prints a fn. to the title referring the reader to Lady Gregory's *Cuchulain of Muirthemne,* and gives certain explanations and identifications); third item, *In the Seven Woods,* 1903; 17, 20, 21, 24(1), 25, 33, 35, 50, 54, 57, 58, 63, 73, 75, *79, 80, 88, 98, 99.— Though highly praised by Yeats's father, rightly labeled "rather insipid" by MacNeice (99).—Original story (*v.* Hoare, 116-18): *Scél Baili Binnbérlaig* (cp. *Rev. Celt.,* XIII, 220), though Alspach (*Amer. Folklore,* LIX) finds the immediate source in Kennedy. V. Hyde (7 ff.) for a translation of this "Story of Baile mac Buain, the Sweet Spoken," discovered by O'Curry

(*Manuscript Materials,* 472) as Trinity College MS. H. 3. 18; cp. Saul.—There are two other sixteenth-century recensions: cp. Dillon, *C. K.,* 27, or *E. I. L.,* 85-86. —Yeats's preliminary "Argument" appears to be a falsification of the part originally played, not by Aengus, but by a lying specter.—"Uladh": Ulster.—"Lugaidh" (l. 7): Lewy Farriga.—Ll. 14-15 refer to the *Táin Bó Cuálnge.*—L. 18, "Emain": capital of Uladh. —L. 21, "Muirthemne": in Co. Louth.—L. 23, "there": the planned meeting-place, *Ros na Ríg* ("Rosnaree"), on the Boyne; l. 25, "there": the place now called Dundalk.—P. 395, l. 9, "the Hound of Uladh": Cuchulain (the "Hound of Culann"); l. 12, "the harper's daughter and her friend": Felimid's daughter, Deirdre, and her lover, Naoise (*v.* notes to "Under the Moon"). —P. 396, l. 22, "the Great Plain": In Yeats's fn. to the title, *Monthly Rev.,* "the Land of the Dead and of the Happy." The same fn. says, anent ll. 4-6, p. 397: "Midhir was a king of the Sidhe, or people of faery, and Etain his wife, when driven away by a jealous woman, took refuge once upon a time with Aengus in a house of glass, and there I have imagined her weaving harpstrings out of Aengus' hair. I have brought the harpstrings into 'The Shadowy Waters,' where I interpret the myth in my own way." We are also reminded that "The birds that flutter over the head of Aengus are four birds that he made out of his kisses. . . ." (Cp. notes on ". . . Oisin.") *V.* James Stephens' *In the Land of Youth* and Yeats's own *The Two Kings.*—P. 397: On the fabled ancient Celtic cities of Gorias, Findrias (Finias), Falias, and Murias, *v.* Keating and Rolleston (105); from these cities, respectively, the Dé Dananns were said to have brought the sword and spear of Lugh, the *Lia Fail* ["Stone of Destiny": supposedly carried to Scotland by fifth-century Irish invaders and

later taken to England (by Edward I) as the "Stone
of Scone"], and the Dagda's cauldron.—P. 398, l. 4:
cp. "The Song of Wandering Aengus"; l. 6: cp. "In
the Seven Woods"; l. 8, "glass boat": Miss Gurd (79)
glosses J. Bonwick, *Irish Druids and Old Irish Religion* (London, 1894), 293; l. 22, "that long fighting
. . .": the duel between Cuchulain and Fer Diad
("The Man of Smoke") in the *Táin Bó Cuálnge.*—
The "Beloved" of the concluding apostrophe is Maud
Gonne.—The 8th printing of 99A substitutes semicolon for comma, l. 106, and makes a break between
ll. 176 and 177.

"The Shadowy Waters": *North American Review,* May
1900; 13, 20, 22, 24(2), 25, 28, 29, 54, 57, 58, 63, 75,
*79, 80, 98, 99.—Finished Dec. 1899: *v.* Wade, *Letters,* 332.—Yeats has a note, *C. P.,* 458, in which the
first date should properly be 1900; there was no 1902
edition. The version in *C. P.* is revised from that of
Poems, 1899–1905 (London: Bullen, and Dublin:
Maunsel, 1906), which, except for essential plot, is by
comparison with that of 1900 practically a new, as also
a longer, work. The subtitle first appears in 1933 *C. P.*
—In one of the now-omitted early directions, incidentally, Yeats gives Dectora "dull red" hair.—*N.B.: C.
Plays* uses the version introduced at the Abbey on 8
Dec. 1906. This was first published by Bullen: London, 1907, though Yeats dates publication 1911 in *C.
Plays.* The acting version is touched in the prose passages with Lady Gregory's "Kiltartan" lingo.

This work was planned when Yeats was a young art
student with Æ: cp. Hone, 175, and Æ's *Song and Its
Fountains,* 11; also *Reveries over Childhood and
Youth.* The dedication was first published as "Introduction to a Dramatic Poem," *The Speaker,* 1 Dec.
1900, and reprinted untitled in the first edition of the

work, as also thereafter in *20, 22, 24(2), 25, 28, 29, 54, 57, 58, 63, 65, 75, 79, 80, 98, 99.—In the compound names of the Coole woods, "Kyle" < *coill:* a wood; "Pairc" is Ir. *páirc* (a park, or field) unaltered except for omission of accent. For the rest, "Shan-walla" < ? *sean-bhalla:* old wall; "na" = of; "no" (*gno*) < *gcná:* nuts; "dortha" < *dorcha:* dark; "lee" < ? *lighe:* grave; "carraig" (*carraige*) = headland, cliff, rock; "tarav" < *tairbh:* bull; "Inchy" < ? *inis* (island): perhaps "water meadow" is indicated.

On the second preliminary poem, "The Harp of Aengus" (present in every printing of the work, and taking final form in 13), *v.* Yeats, "The Legendary and Mythological Foundation of the Plays," *P. P. V.,* 426, and "A Voice," *The Celtic Twilight;* but cp. the notes on "Baile and Aillinn," *sup.* On the "tower of glass" (here and p. 407), *v.* Rhys, 145-46.

"New" critics might sanely consider Yeats's remark in *The Arrow,* No. 2 (24 Nov. 1906), before indulging themselves: "If the audience will understand it as a fairy-tale and not look too anxiously for a meaning, all will be well." Nevertheless, by the time he has finished his examination, Ellmann (*Iden.,* Chap. IV, § IV) has discovered so many symbols in this work that he sounds almost apologetic about his perceptiveness. Miscellaneous comment is available in Reid, 108 ff.; Guthrie, *Sewanee Rev.;* Macleod, *No. Amer. Rev.,* CLXXV, 479 ff.; Ellis-Fermor, 102-3; Goldgar, *Revue de Litt. Comparée;* Killen, *Comp. Lit. Studies.* —On Forgael's last speech on p. 408, *v.* Yeats's letter to Florence Farr (C. Bax, 43); on the bird cries, p. 423, *v. Auto.,* 90-91.—The "ancient worm" of Dectora's final speech recalls "the old worm of the world" which in *The Countess Cathleen* (Sc. I) appears to represent Change and the misery it entails.—"Iollan," p. 419:

Named for the Ulsterman who was Finn's uncle by
marriage (*Birth of Bran*)?—or for Iollan, son of Fergus Mac Roy?—The 8th printing of 99A makes the
following alterations: l. 193, "shown" > "known"; l. 315,
"of the wind" > "of wind"; l. 400, comma > period;
l. 456, semicolon > comma; l. 460, "And you" > "And
if you"; l. 522, "O, I" > "O I"; l. 616, "And knitting
mesh" > "And knitted mesh."

"The Two Kings": *Poetry* (Chicago) and *British Review*,
Oct. 1913; 38, 40, 54, 57, 58, 63, 75, 79, 80, *98, 99.—
Wr. Oct. 1912 (Ellmann, *Iden.*, 294); dated 1914 by
Yeats, obviously for earliest book-publication.—Cp.
J. B. Yeats, in Hone, 289; other handlings of the story
by James Stephens, *In the Land of Youth,* and Fiona
Macleod, *The Immortal Hour.*—Original story (one
version in the *Yellow Book of Lecan*) fragmentarily
preserved in "Tochmarc Étaíne" ("The Wooing of
Étain") in the *Book of the Dun Cow* (*Leabhar na
h-Uidhre:* Royal Irish Academy MS. 23, E. 25.): cp.
Windisch, *Irische Texte*, I, 117 ff.; Saul; and A. H.
Leahy, *Heroic Romances of Ireland,* I and II (London, 1905–6). Questionably full translation by Leahy;
translation by Miss Hoare (151 ff.; *v.* also 124-27);
summary in Meyer-Nutt, II, 47 ff. V. also Dillon,
E. I. L., 54 ff., and Mackimmie. (Mrs. Mackimmie
gives bibliographical history, variorum text, and criticism.)—"King Eochaid": Eochaid Airem, High King
(wherefore seated at Tara): cp. Best, Chap. XIV.—
The "stag" is a Yeats invention (l. 6); in Miss Hoare's
words (124) it "symbolises Étain's lover" (Midir).—
The "cry" (p. 432, l. 5) is "mournful" (l. 6) because
Yeats changes the old story and makes Midir's loss of
Étain permanent.—"Ardan" (p. 433, l. 8) in the original Irish was *Ailill Anguba.*—"Loughlan" (p. 434,
l. 4): Norse; what the writer considers the misprint

"mound's" (l. 20) is corrected to "wound's" (cp. *Poetry*, Oct. 1913) in the Second Printing of 99A, but "mound's" returns in the 1956 printing.—The man (p. 435) appealing to Étain is, of course, Midir, of the *síde*. (In the original Irish, Étain has three trysts with a man supposedly Ailill, who reveals his true identity as Midir on the third meeting and asks her return to Faery. Her agreement, conditional on Eochaid's permission, is secured.)—Étain's repulsion of Midir (p. 436) for the sake of mere human love violates the original story, the beginning and end of which Yeats disregards; cp. Alexander Smith: "Of Death and the Fear of Dying," *Dreamthorp*.

"The Gift of Harun Al-Rashid": *English Life and the Illustrated Review*, Jan. 1924, as "The Gift of Haroun El Rashid"; *The Dial*, June 1924, with preliminary note and the name given as "Harun-al-Rashid"; 60, 62 (as the opening item of Bk. II, under the title "Desert Geometry Or The Gift Of Harun Al-Raschid"), *68, 70, 79, 80, 98, 99.—Dated 1923 by Yeats, presumably for year of composition.

The "gift" is, of course, a bride for Kusta-ben-Luka. V. Yeats's long explanatory note (rightly labeled "flippant" by Jeffares: 329 fn. 64A) on pp. 38 ff. of 60.— In another note (*idem*, 41), Yeats explains that the Abbasid Caliph's banners (l. 6) were black in "mourning for those who had fallen in battle at the establishment of the Dynasty. . . ."—L. 8, "war's music": Flecker has "War's star-smiting music" (*The Burial in England*).—The latter part of the piece concerns Mrs. Yeats and the claimed origin of *A Vision*: cp. *A Packet for Ezra Pound*. On the "midnight things" (p. 444, l. 12), cp., again, 60, p. 41.—The 8th printing of 99A ends l. 50 with a comma instead of a period.

DIVISIONAL INDEX

TITLE INDEX